CENTRE FOR EDUCATIONAL RESE

New School Management Approaches

OECD

ORGANISATION FOR ECONOMIC CO-OPERATION AND DEVELOPMENT

ORGANISATION FOR ECONOMIC CO-OPERATION AND DEVELOPMENT

Pursuant to Article 1 of the Convention signed in Paris on 14th December 1960, and which came into force on 30th September 1961, the Organisation for Economic Co-operation and Development (OECD) shall promote policies designed:
- to achieve the highest sustainable economic growth and employment and a rising standard of living in Member countries, while maintaining financial stability, and thus to contribute to the development of the world economy;
- to contribute to sound economic expansion in Member as well as non-member countries in the process of economic development; and
- to contribute to the expansion of world trade on a multilateral, non-discriminatory basis in accordance with international obligations.

The original Member countries of the OECD are Austria, Belgium, Canada, Denmark, France, Germany, Greece, Iceland, Ireland, Italy, Luxembourg, the Netherlands, Norway, Portugal, Spain, Sweden, Switzerland, Turkey, the United Kingdom and the United States. The following countries became Members subsequently through accession at the dates indicated hereafter: Japan (28th April 1964), Finland (28th January 1969), Australia (7th June 1971), New Zealand (29th May 1973), Mexico (18th May 1994), the Czech Republic (21st December 1995), Hungary (7th May 1996), Poland (22nd November 1996), Korea (12th December 1996) and the Slovak Republic (14th December 2000). The Commission of the European Communities takes part in the work of the OECD (Article 13 of the OECD Convention).

The Centre for Educational Research and Innovation was created in June 1968 by the Council of the Organisation for Economic Co-operation and Development and all Member countries of the OECD are participants.

The main objectives of the Centre are as follows:
- *analyse and develop research, innovation and key indicators in current and emerging education and learning issues, and their links to other sectors of policy;*
- *explore forward-looking coherent approaches to education and learning in the context of national and international cultural, social and economic change; and*
- *facilitate practical co-operation among Member countries and, where relevant, with non-member countries, in order to seek solutions and exchange views of educational problems of common interest.*

The Centre functions within the Organisation for Economic Co-operation and Development in accordance with the decisions of the Council of the Organisation, under the authority of the Secretary-General. It is supervised by a Governing Board composed of one national expert in its field of competence from each of the countries participating in its programme of work.

Publié en français sous le titre :
Gestion des établissements : de nouvelles approches

Foreword

This nine-country study on innovative initiatives in school management is the latest publication in the *What Works in Innovation in Education series* produced by the OECD's Centre for Educational Research and Innovation (CERI).

Since 1993, the series has carried out yearly analysis of education issues and pointed to some of the most important innovations that are taking place in education systems within OECD countries.

The objective of this project is to produce empirically based and highly accessible studies over a relatively short period of time, usually one year. Previous studies have examined such topics as school choice, career guidance, professional development of teachers, ways of tackling social exclusion through adult learning and student motivation for lifelong learning.

This year's report focuses on new school management approaches at the primary and secondary school levels within the broad educational system contexts. It involved nine countries – Flanders (Belgium), Greece, Hungary, Mexico, Japan, the Netherlands, Sweden, England (the United Kingdom) and the United States.

The report is based upon background reports prepared by experts appointed by each participating country and visits to the nine countries by the OCED Secretariat and/or consultants to the study.

Part I of this report provides a synthesis of the main developments and issues concerning school management that emerges from the country studies. Part II consists of nine country chapters that contain background information on national policy approaches as well as descriptions of the innovative work being undertaken in the cases visited.

Under the overall responsibility of the CERI Secretariat, Dr. Dale Shuttleworth, lead consultant (Training Renewal Foundation, Toronto, Canada) worked on earlier drafts while Mr. Donald Hirsch (Independent consultant, UK) and Mr. John Walshe (the Irish Independent, Dublin, Ireland) prepared the report. Within the Secretariat, the responsible official was Motoyo Kamiya who also contributed to the drafting. Other officials within the Secretariat made contributions at various stages of this study.

The report is published on the responsibility of the Secretary-General.

Table of Contents

Acknowledgements.. 9

Part I
SYNTHESIS OF THE MAIN ISSUES AND TRENDS

Introduction.. 13

Chapter 1 **Challenges for School Management**... 17
    Challenges for Schools: Educational Change and the Rise and Fall of Taylorism 18
    Challenges for Public Management.. 19
    Challenges for Knowledge Management.. 21
    Bibliography 22

Chapter 2 **A Snapshot of Responses** 23
    School-based Management 23
    Accountability through Inspection and Student Assessment................... 24
    School Autonomy from Within 25
    New Forms of Governance and Partnership 26
    New Forms of Staff Assessment and In-service Training.......................... 27
    New Forms of Learning... 28
    Bibliography 29

Chapter 3 **New Approaches in School Management**................................. 31
    Developing School Leaders.. 32
    Managing People and Resources within a School.................................... 36
    Managing Relations with the Centre 41
    Managing Relationships outside the School.. 42
    Bibliography 45

Chapter 4 **Emerging Issues, the Process of Change and New Directions
           for the Learning School** 47
    New Roles... 47
    New Leaders 48
    New Tensions.. 50
    The Process of Change 51
    New Directions for Learning at School 53
    Lessons Learned 54
    Bibliography 56

Part II
COUNTRY CASE STUDIES

Belgium (Flanders) 59
    Country context 60
    Challenges Facing School Management 61
    Main Policy Approaches 61
    Framework 62
    Case Studies 66
    Innovation and Effectiveness 71
    Bibliography 75

Greece 77
    Country context 78
    Challenges Facing School Management 79
    Main Policy Approaches 79
    Framework 81
    Case Studies 83
    Innovation and Effectiveness 91
    Bibliography 93

Hungary 95
    Country context 96
    Challenges Facing School Management 97
    Main Policy Approaches 98
    Framework 99
    Case Studies 101
    Innovation and Effectiveness 107
    Bibliography 111

Japan 113
    Country context 114
    Challenges Facing School Management 115
    Main Policy Approaches 116
    Framework 118
    Case Studies 121
    Innovation and Effectiveness 127
    Bibliography 129

Mexico 131
    Country context 132
    Challenges Facing School Management 133
    Main Policy Approaches and Framework 133
    Case Studies 136
    Innovation and Effectiveness 144
    Bibliography 147

Netherlands 149
    Country context.. 150
    Challenges Facing School Management.. 151
    Main Policy Approaches 152
    Framework 155
    Case Studies.. 157
    Innovation and Effectiveness.. 161
    Bibliography 166

Sweden 169
    Country context.. 170
    Challenges Facing School Management.. 171
    Main Policy Approaches 172
    Framework 174
    Case Studies.. 175
    Innovation and Effectiveness.. 182
    Bibliography 184

United Kingdom (England) 185
    Country context.. 186
    Challenges Facing School Management.. 187
    Main Policy Approaches 189
    Framework 193
    Case Studies.. 193
    Innovation and Effectiveness.. 200
    Bibliography 202

United States 205
    Country context.. 206
    Challenges Facing School Management.. 207
    Main Policy Approaches 208
    Framework 211
    Case Studies.. 212
    Innovation and Effectiveness.. 223
    Bibliography 225

Acknowledgements

We appreciate the work and support of country experts: Prof. Roland Vandenberghe (Flanders, Belgium), Dr. Manolis Koutouzis (Greece), Dr. János Setényi (Hungary), Dr. Naoko Ota and Dr. Hidenori Fujita (Japan), Ms. Marcela Ramírez (Mexico), Dr. J. van der Pluijm and Prof. Dr. P. Sleegers (Netherlands), Dr. Hans-Ake Scherp (Sweden), Prof. Mel West (United Kingdom) and Dr. Carolyn J. Kelley (United States). We are also grateful for contributions made by consultants: Mr. Olivier Bertrand, Mr. Ray Kennedy, Prof. Jean-Michel Saussois and Prof. Michael Williams.

This study has been made possible by the financial assistance, through voluntary contributions, of the Department of Education (Ministry of the Flemish Community) of Belgium; the Ministry of Education of Greece; the Ministry of Education of Hungary; the Ministry of Education, Science, Sports and Culture of Japan; the Ministry of Education of Mexico; the Ministry of Education, Culture and Science of the Netherlands; the National Agency for Education (*Skolverket*) of Sweden; the Department of Education and Employment in the United Kingdom; and the Department of Education of the United States.

Part I

SYNTHESIS OF THE MAIN ISSUES AND TRENDS

Introduction

Wanted: *Experienced manager; someone who can influence client groups of all ages, boost staff morale, hold spending under budget, juggle union contracts, referee arguments, defuse violence, schmooze politicians, grasp new legislation and spell it out for others, who can be discreet yet speak out when needed and who, in any spare time, can charm the larger community into donating items for which there is no longer any budget.*

Warning: *The hours are long, job security is weak and you will bear the brunt of public reaction to every change to hit the school system.*

(Mock job advertisement, Toronto Star)

Schools everywhere are being asked to do more than ever before. They face a complex world and a seemingly endless set of pressures. Those who manage schools must take responsibility for an arduous task. The above job description captures the sense of crisis and despair that can easily affect educational managers in such a demanding new social, political and economic age. Yet throughout OECD Member countries, school systems and individual schools are experimenting with new approaches to management that seek to run schools in ways that are right for the 21st century.

This study looks at how such innovation is working, in nine countries – Flanders (Belgium), Greece, Hungary, Japan, Mexico, the Netherlands, Sweden, England (the United Kingdom) and the United States – and in 29 individual projects. Some of them are national projects, such as the Hungarian and Mexican cases studies, yet some other projects are at the local or school levels. Most of the projects examined in this report are targeted at relatively large urban schools and school systems, except one specifically situated in a rural setting. Of 31 schools under 29 projects visited, 12 were primary schools, 4 lower secondary schools and 15 were upper secondary schools.

Nobody has discovered a perfect way of dealing with all the demands of school management, yet many schools have transformed management for the better, as the report shows. It is evident that transformation, rather than changes at the margin, is what is needed. The experiences of innovation in school management in nine countries are described in Part II. Part One explores trends at a more general level, with reference to what is happening across the countries studied.

The management of school education takes place at many different levels, from national government down to individual schools. This report focuses on the management of the school within a broad education framework. Definitions may vary from country to country, but for the purposes of this report, the terms school managers and school leaders are used inter-changeably. The focus is mainly on the role of school principals or, in some cases, on teachers and other stake-holders who are charged with the responsibility of organising and running schools.

Part One starts off, in Chapters 1 and 2, by setting the context for new approaches to school management. Chapter 1 gives an overview of the challenges being faced by school management at the beginning of the 21st century. It looks first at the evolving history of schools and their management. It argues that school managers have become the lynchpins of historical transformation from a Tayloristic factory model of industry and of education, into a new and more flexible world of learning organisations. At the same time, they are having to adapt to a new style of public management, based more around performance, outcomes and responsiveness to clients than in the past. And in changing in these directions, school managers are also having to manage knowledge itself in new ways, in order to spread a true understanding of what educational improvement entails.

Chapter 2 gives a snapshot of the responses that are emerging within OECD countries, drawing on previous studies of various aspects of educational reform. Some of the changes introduced address the management of schools directly, whilst others deal more with the content of education, yet they also impact on how schools are run.

Chapter 3 then gives a round-up of the trends which, in this context, have emerged from the study. It looks at four aspects of new approaches to school management. First, at the managers themselves – at their competencies and at how they are prepared for their role. Second, at relationships within the school: the ways in which management is organised and in which human, physical and intellectual resources are managed. Third, at "vertical" relationships between the school and others – that is, with different tiers of government or administration. Finally, at "horizontal" relationships – with partners in the community.

Chapter 4 identifies emerging issues more generally and draws some lessons learned from innovative examples. It encourages, among others, policy makers to think carefully about creating an atmosphere in which managers have the space and the encouragement to innovate.

Part II consists of nine country chapters, prepared with the assistance of country experts and consultant field visits. Each chapter looks at the context of the country, the main approaches being taken at present and some case studies.

Chapter 1

Challenges for School Management

School management is essentially a twentieth century invention. In the days of the one-room schoolhouse, the teacher ran the school. Even in somewhat larger establishments, a practising teacher with added supervisory skills (in plant operations, discipline and record keeping) could be in charge of the building, other teachers and students. With the advent of large multi-classroom institutions in industrial cities and consolidated rural areas, more systematic management was needed. This created a trend towards a full-time professional manager responsible for financial, instructional, human resources and facilities leadership. But in many cases this manager became not so much the leader of the school as an institution, so much as an administrator in a wider schools' system, run by the central bureaucracies set up to deliver universal public education.

Towards the end of the twentieth century, school governance and the role of the manager started again to change profoundly. Central authorities, with control of legislation, funding and curriculum and programme standards, were increasingly downloading some of these responsibilities to local municipalities or individual schools.

This change is putting school managers centre-stage – at a time when the nature and purposes of schooling itself are being re-assessed. As the cases in this study clearly illustrate, new approaches to school management are not simply concerned with how better to deliver a stable set of educational processes. They must be viewed as part of a wider movement for school reform. As schools are asked to change, they need to consider what forms of management can best support the transformations that they seek.

Such transformations pose a triple challenge for school managers. First, they must manage educational change at a time when the character and mission of schools is being redefined. Second, they must be part of a new understanding about public management which is moving way from a bureaucratic and institution-led approach towards a performance-driven public sector that is more aware of the service it delivers to its users. Third, they are having to find new, effective ways of managing knowledge, in organisations that need themselves to learn continuously.

Challenges for Schools: Educational Change and the Rise and Fall of Taylorism

The development of schooling during the past 150 years has to be viewed in relation to economic and social trends.

The emergence of schooling as an essential public service in the second half of the 19th century followed from the accelerated need for literacy, numeracy and scientific skills as a result of the industrial revolution and growing urbanisation. As more parents were drawn on to production lines, schools also became agents of socialisation, morality and citizenship.

Moreover the organisation and content of schooling in many ways reflected industrial development. Just as factories were organised as branches of a larger enterprise conforming to predetermined common standards, so public education came to follow a supervisory style with anticipated outcomes and the principal in the role of branch manager. The adoption of Taylor's principles of scientific production to raise productivity in the first decades of the 20th century required workers to read and comprehend manuals and do basic calculations. Schools met this challenge very successfully, raising literacy levels from single digits to between the 80th and 90th percentiles of the population over a relatively short period.

A further essential function of schools in this model was to sort individuals to suit the needs of the increasingly specialised labour market. A system of meritocracy evolved to decide which students should receive advanced education and training to assume managerial and leadership positions, and which should be relegated to toil on the factory floor. It was a system that operated under the premise that 10% would lead and 90% would follow. This process of educational sorting and meritocracy was seen by governments of the day as a just way to reward intelligence and avoid corruption or discrimination.

The late 20th century, however, saw a revolutionary break from the cultural, social and economic environment that had followed from the industrial revolution. The need is no longer for scientifically managed mass production and cohorts of disciplined workers to perform it, but for flexible, learning organisations and workers. Everybody needs the general skills to make day-to-day decisions – there is no longer a mass of wholly routine jobs. An education system designed for a different time is struggling to cope with this radically transforming post-industrial age. In the analysis of many, it has lagged behind. An extreme articulation of this gap is given by Professor Howard Gardner of Harvard University:

> "... it would not be an exaggeration to maintain that schools have not changed in a hundred years. There are new topics (such as ecology), new tools (personal computers, VCRs) and at least some new practices – universal kindergarten,

special education for those with learning problems, efforts to mainstream' students who have physical or emotional problems. Still, apart from a few relatively superficial changes, human beings miraculously transported from 1900 would recognise much of what goes on in today's classrooms – the prevalent lecturing, the emphasis on drill, the decontextualised materials and activities ranging from basal readers to weekly spelling tests. With the possible exception of the Church, few institutions have changed as little in fundamental ways as those charged with the formal education of the next generation" (Gardner, 1999).

Today's social and economic environment argues for a new model of learning based on foundations such as:

- Mastery of basic skills.

- Ability to work with others.

- Being able to deal with constant distractions.

- Working at different levels across different disciplines.

- Improving verbal skills.

- Problem-solving and decision-making (Abbott and Ryan, 2000).

While schools and their managers face a big task in re-orienting the *content* of education in this direction, they need simultaneously to think about the way they operate. In a post-Tayloristic world they need themselves to learn continuously: to adapt to changing conditions rather than follow pre-set procedures largely ordered from above. Yet this does not mean they have become free to develop their own model of education: while decentralising and deregulating, many governments have simultaneously become more demanding on schools in terms of achieving measured outcomes – enforced through testing or inspection regimes. This tightening up of requirements derives partly from an erosion of confidence in schools to deliver desired outcomes without greater political accountability.

It is the intersection of these three demands for change by schools – to update their content, to become learning organisations and to deliver measurable outcomes – that creates the intense and potentially conflicting pressures described in the job advertisement in the introduction.

Challenges for Public Management

A recent study prepared for the OECD's Public Management Service (PUMA) describes four key objectives for performance and financial management to improve resource planning and allocation in public services:

- Setting objectives and allocations for government actions (*e.g.* based on input, outputs, and/or outcomes; historical incrementalism or strategic prioritisation).

- Establishing the types of authorities for carrying out those actions (*e.g.* centralised, decentralised, devolved, contractual, legal).

- Determining what information is needed to know if actions are executed properly (*e.g.* measurement, information and reporting needs).

- Rewards and sanctions for performance (*e.g.*, incentive systems, accountability framework) (OECD/PUMA, 1999).

The study differentiates between performance and financial responsibilities. Performance management involves: setting goals and objectives with the responsibility to implement them; measuring and reporting on performance; making informed decisions based on outcomes; and sharing information externally as required. Financial management, on the other hand, concerns: the operation of systems for budget-making and implementation; the maintenance of an accounting system, recording decisions, transactions and audits.

While the management of resources has long been an essential component of the administration of public services, the history of its application in the school setting remains inconsistent. The role of the principal (or headteacher) has evolved from the practising teacher, with added technical and administrative duties, to the full-time manager and developer of human, financial and physical resources.

Many (especially from within education) would argue that it is risky to apply principles of management, or of public management, too directly to the unique context of schools. Yet the main threads of the reform of public management are certainly valid with regards to education, and are starting to be applied there. In particular, the objectives described above represent an attempt by the public sector to become more precise and accountable for what it delivers, and to put power into the hands of those most able to achieve required objectives.

School systems have tried to do these things in a number of different ways. For example, through:

- Localising delivery while centralising mandated standards. As discussed in Chapter 2 below, an apparent contradiction can arise between putting more decisions in the hands of local managers and tightly constraining their behaviour, for example through centralised control of curriculum and assessment. The conflict is not inevitable, providing central prescription is kept at an appropriate level of generality, and genuinely concentrates on defining outcomes rather than interfering excessively in processes.

- Encouraging communities to rebuild schools from the "bottom up". Policies reordering responsibilities do not in themselves create renewal of public institutions – that has to come from within. Community-based educational renewal mobilises a broad range of human and educational partners including school leaders, teachers, parents, students, employers and other citizens, to improve the quality of human and educational services.

- Providing some services on contract rather than directly by governmental authorities. The private operation of state-funded schools is nothing new – in a number of countries, religious or culturally-based groups have long operated institutions funded by central government. But in some countries, notably the United Kingdom and the United States, contracting of educational services has become part of a movement to create a clearer division between those who specify services and those who deliver them. From the point of view of educational management, however, it is not necessarily the status of the school, but rather the tightness with which it is regulated from the outside, that has the greatest impact. The principal of a Dutch "private" (denominational) school, for example, in many respects has less financial independence than the head of a school run by an English local education authority. Within each country, introducing greater detachment from the central administration for some or all schools has certainly signalled an intention to allow the school to shape its own mission. But the degree to which it is left to do so may depend on a range of other influences – including the readiness of managers themselves to take up the challenge.

Challenges for Knowledge Management

Education should, in principle, provide the fuel for the knowledge-powered economy. At the same time, educators need themselves to become effective at harnessing knowledge in their own service. As a recent CERI report has elaborated, rising demands on educators can only be met by "smarter use of knowledge in changed organisational cultures" (OECD, 2000). This should entail a new way of thinking about the creation, transmission and use of educational know-how – based on the principle of *knowledge management*. Rather than basing educational knowledge purely on university generated research, schools need to build up and manage their own distinctive body of intellectual capital, adapted to their distinctive aims.

The need for better knowledge management in schools arises from the centrality of know-how derived directly from classroom practice, combined with the weakness of mechanisms for disseminating this know-how within or beyond the school. Teachers are transmitters of knowledge but are increasingly expected to be knowledge "facilitators" for their students, so that they can create their own learning agenda. They are also knowledge producers, constantly conducting their own informal classroom experiments. But how do they share the results? To do so, they need time, strong networks and an ethos that encourages them strongly to do so. An important job of school managers is to ensure that these factors are present in order to generate ideas for improvement within the school. So managers in schools must not only think of themselves as managers of people and physical/ financial resources, but also as managers of knowledge. This is not a side issue, but a central feature of managing change in modern organisations. In many areas of private industry, such a notion of knowledge management is already well established.

Bibliography

ABBOTT, J. and RYAN, T. (2000),
   The Unfinished Revolution (draft manuscript), 21st Century Learning Initiativen, VA.
GARDNER, H. (1999),
   The Disciplined Mind, Simon and Schuster, New York.
OECD (2000),
   Knowledge Management in the Learning Society, Paris.
OECD/PUMA (1999),
   "Performance Management and Financial Management – How to Integrate Them", Paris.

Chapter 2

A Snapshot of Responses

Educational reform has been a powerful theme in many OECD countries over the past two decades. How has it affected the management of schools? A range of OECD studies published over the past decade has reviewed various aspects of the reform agenda (see OECD, 1994, 1995, 1999). But this chapter helps set the context for a study of new management approaches, by giving a simplified characterisation of some of the main strands of recent change in education. Some of these changes, such as school-based management, directly address the way in which schools are run. Others, such as the introduction of more experiential forms of learning, have more of an indirect effect.

School-based Management

Most countries in this study have been giving a greater amount of decision-making power to schools. Principals, teachers, parents and other community members are gaining more authority over budget, personnel and curriculum. The scope of such decision-making varies greatly from one country to another. Successful school-based management depends on a combination of the scope of powers and incentives given to schools and the ability of school managers and others to grasp the opportunity. A range of technical, interpersonal and managerial skills, combined with a grasp of information regarding school performance, needs to be deployed. These requirements extend greatly the attributes needed by school managers compared to the past.

Decentralised delivery of education does not prevent key decisions about entitlements and target outcomes from being set at a more central or political level. But there is a prevailing view that leaders of delivery organisations are best placed to develop organisations that are effective at achieving the desired results. So, for example:

- School reforms in *England* since 1988 (see the chapter on the United Kingdom) have delegated organisational decision-making to the school level and divided curricular decision-making between central government (content) and schools (pedagogy). Parents have been encouraged to choose schools on the basis of their examination results. School funding, in turn, is dependent upon per pupil grants, meaning they must improve their recruitment strategies to survive.

- In the *Netherlands*, school directors (principals) are responsible for the quality of their schools. They are free to spend the part of the budget known as the *lump sum*. But if building repairs are necessary, and there are no financial reserves, funds must be taken from other budgetary reserves such as the salary account (which amounts to 80% of total expenditures). The school director also has responsibility for all personnel matters including hiring and firing, staff appraisals, and union negotiations (see the chapter on the Netherlands and Karstanje, 1999).

It is not as easy as it sounds to introduce decentralisation successfully. The highly political issues surrounding delivery of public education create an inevitable tussle between different levels about where decisions belong. Moreover, the leader of a local school mandated to deliver good public education is not in the same position as a commercial leader whose mission is to enhance profitability or shareholder value. The former has potentially less scope to shape a distinctive strategy, because outcomes are less clearly defined, and central authorities are more inclined to specify particular aspects of the process, or to specify intermediate outcomes (*e.g.* students who do well on tests, rather than students with a range of wider competencies) that pre-empt more adventurous educational strategies.

In particular, while some decisions about budgets, personnel and day-to-day decisions are passed down to the school, the central (or state) government may continue to control the content of what is taught through a *national curriculum* enforced by external standardised testing. The programme of the school and the performance of principals and teachers may also be regularly scrutinised through personnel assessment or inspectoral visits by central authorities or their delegates.

Accountability through Inspection and Student Assessment

In practice, in many countries this tension has manifested itself most clearly through the trend towards more *assessment* as a means of enforcing greater *accountability* of schools for their results. In particular in the United Kingdom and North America, but also increasingly in Nordic countries and in other countries, reform movements have been characterised by closer inspection of schools and testing of students as a means of ensuring that schools are performing their mandated mission. The danger is that this recreates a "Tayloristic", industrial-type model of each "plant" using recognised processes to conform to uniform standards, rather than enabling school managers creatively to define their mission. Centrally-defined output criteria and local innovation in finding ways of meeting them are not *necessarily* contradictory; what matters is the degree to which specification of standards becomes so detailed and interventionist that a *culture* of control rather than autonomy develops.

Central inspection is a further parameter within which local school managers must work. Its mission is "to guarantee the quality of education provided by schools and to guarantee the quality of the system to all pupils" (Portuguese Inspectorate of Education, 1998). School inspection is not new, but potentially takes on a new role in a system of decentralised delivery but central mandating of standards – as an external form of quality control against which managers and their performance are judged.

The form of inspection varies by country. For example, in the Netherlands, the Inspectorate in Primary Education conducts formal visits to produce a *quality card* for each school. The results are published in league tables in national newspapers (see the chapter on the Netherlands). In England, every school is inspected on a regular cycle by the Office for Standards in Education (OFSTED). Specially trained teams of external inspectors utilise procedures set out in a *Framework of Inspection* to review the quality of teaching and learning in each subject, as well as overall school management (see the chapter on the United Kingdom). The system in Flanders combines school self-evaluation with a complementary external assessment by the inspectorate. Teams of three to four inspectors visit schools for one week while undertaking a comprehensive analysis of the coherence between national curricular objectives and the school work plan (see the chapter on Flanders). Greece has opted for only school self-evaluation due to its traditional rejection of external school inspection (see the chapter on Greece).

School Autonomy from Within

Research on decentralisation shows that, *in itself*, it is not enough to transform the way a school is run. The Consortium for Policy Research in Education conducted an in-depth study of 27 schools in three US school districts, one Canadian and one Australian state, that had been involved in school-based management (SBM) for at least four years. Slightly more than half of the schools studied could be characterised as *actively restructuring*, in that reform efforts had produced changes in curriculum and instruction. The other half was going through the motions of SBM but little change had occurred. The study concluded that four key sources are essential if SBM is to contribute to an improvement in local school performance: power; information; knowledge and skills; and performance-based rewards. It found that "the decentralisation of power is most likely to lead to performance improvement if accompanied by organisational changes that enhance the information, knowledge and skills of local participants, and that align the reward system with clearly articulated desired outcomes" (Wohlstetter and Mohrman, 1994).

25

Policies reordering responsibilities do not in themselves create renewal of public institutions – that has to come from within. Gardner believes educational renewal begins with *self-renewal* (Gardner, 1963). In living a renewing life people are apt to:

- Recognise and break out of ruts or patterns.
- Reflect on and carry out an ongoing process of self-inquiry.
- See education as a lifelong process.
- Embrace failure as one of the best of all learning experiences.
- Be capable of mutually respectful, just and caring relationships with others (Gardner, 1963).

Renewal is about collaboration, and its leaders need to acquire five critical skills to improve the educational environment:

- To establish a shared mission.
- To work as change agents.
- To collaborate with colleagues.
- To think inclusively about all constituents.
- To perceive and make explicit the connections between theory and practice (Smith, 1999).

Governments may help create conditions in which this kind of renewal takes place, but it is only the actions and imagination of school managers and those they work with that can genuinely create the change that is needed. This needs to come in partnership with communities.

Community-based educational renewal mobilises a broad range of human and educational partners including school leaders, teachers, parents, students, employers and other citizens, to improve the quality of human and educational services. The need for community involvement is recognised as an essential component in school improvement. Whether as part of the shared decision-making school-based governance model or as a source of volunteer assistance or funding support, the community is an essential partner in the school management process across the nine nations. The case studies show that community-driven school renewal is anything but new, but the erosion of faith in public education within communities makes this approach more essential than ever before.

New Forms of Governance and Partnership

Decentralisation requires in most cases a process of shared decision-making to guide school management. In many cases parents, teachers and members of the community are being brought formally or informally into the school decision-making process (see for example the chapter on Flanders). Parents' and teachers' unions are also encouraged to participate in management of schools. This again profoundly affects the managers' role: in such circumstances, their influence needs to be felt through *leadership* of a wide coalition rather than through autocratic direction.

Over the past decade, schools have been opening up to the outside, forming partnerships both with business (OECD, 1991) and with parents (OECD, 1997) and communities. It has everywhere come to be accepted that it is not possible any more to run a school as a closed organisation. But this opening up greatly expands the task of school management. School leaders must become coalition builders as much as managers of the "internal" running of schools themselves.

Today's students may actively question a number of aspects of their school: curricular content; teacher performance; behavioural and dress codes; and freedom of expression. In some cases they are being given some role in determining how schools are run. In Sweden, teamwork is encouraged among students and between students and teachers. Students have an increasing role in decision-making in the belief that they should take on responsibility for their own learning. Each class, at both the primary and secondary level, participates in a weekly *class council* where day-to-day routines are discussed. At the upper secondary level, students participate in policy and budgetary decisions (see the chapter on Sweden).

New Forms of Staff Assessment and In-service Training

Among the ways in which the management of school staff are open to change, some countries are rethinking how teaching staff should be assessed. The prevailing tendency has been for a professional ethos with little or no direct control or evaluation of performance from school managers. But as principals become more directly responsible for the performance of their schools, this is open to change. They are often expected to hire, evaluate and dismiss staff. Performance appraisals may increasingly be used, although in most cases teachers are resistant and managers hesitant. The United Kingdom's introduction of a performance management system backed by performance-linked pay (see the chapter on the United Kingdom) illustrates both the determination of a government to change management practice in this direction and the resistance within the system to such reform.

In-service training is fundamental to the transformation of school systems, since it requires serving teachers to do things in new ways. In recent years, teacher development has in many countries become more closely related to organisational change rather than just individual objectives such as career progression (OECD, 1998). Indeed, staff development (INSET) can be central to the way principals manage schools, in at least two respects: first, as instructional leaders, principals may be expected to co-ordinate the professional progression of their staff; second,

27

they need to manage the learning community as a whole, using development as part of school change.

New Forms of Learning

The growing importance of information and communication technologies (ICT) has had a profound impact on family, school, recreation and working life. Part of the school manager's task is to manage knowledge about how best to harness these technologies in schools. This may require considerable inter-school co-operation, rather than trying to be an expert in everything "in-house".

Nor is learning itself any more restricted to what goes on within the school's walls. Experiential learning is conducted, wholly or in part, through practical, community-based, on-site experience. Examples of such activities include: co-operative education; internships; experience-based career education; work study; work experience and job shadowing (Shuttleworth, 1993). One such example was to be found in a primary school in the Netherlands, which incorporates student-centred projects combining both concrete and abstract learning. The community becomes the classroom to integrate social studies, mathematics, science and language into a multi-disciplinary theme (see the chapter on the Netherlands). Such approaches affect the way managers must organise learning.

****

Each of these trends has a different degree of importance, and may take a different form, in each country or local context. The country and case studies described in Part Two take a wide variety of forms, reflecting these different contexts. Yet there are also powerful common strands. The following chapter identifies both the parallels and the contrasts in the variety of new approaches to management that are presented in this study.

Bibliography

BROWN, L. (2000),
"Crisis in the Classroom", *Toronto Star*, May 14.

GARDNER, J. (1963),
Self-renewal: The Individual and the Innovative Society, Harper and Row, New York.

KARSTANJE (1999),
"Development in School Management from a European Perspective", in Bolam, R. and Fons van Wieringen (eds.), *Research in Educational Management in Europe*, Waxmann Munster, New York.

OECD (1991),
Schools and Business: A New Partnership, Paris.

OECD (1994),
School: A Matter of Choice, Paris.

OECD (1995),
Schools under Scrutiny, Paris.

OECD (1997),
Parents as Partners in Schooling, Paris.

OECD (1998),
Staying Ahead, In-service Training and Teacher Professional Development, Paris.

OECD (1999),
Innovating Schools, Paris.

PORTUGUESE INSPECTORATE OF EDUCATION (1998),
"Report on School Management Workshops", Nov. 25-27.

SHUTTLEWORTH, D.E. (1993),
Enterprise Learning in Action, Routledge, London.

SMITH, W.F. (1999),
Leadership for Educational Renewal, Phi Delta Kappan, April.

WOHLSLETTER, P. and MOHRMAN, S.A. (1994),
School-based Management: Promise and Process, CPRE Finance Briefs, February 5.

Chapter 3

New Approaches in School Management

Schools need to be managed in new ways. Chapters 1 and 2 above set out why. In the past 20 years countries have been rethinking the mission of their schools, the role of public managers and the characteristics of learning organisations. Transformational change is not straightforward. It cannot simply be ordered by policy-makers. A range of conditions is needed to change from within the way in which organisations are managed. This study has not sought a perfect model, but has looked for inspiration at a range of examples of innovation that address the way schools are managed.

It is difficult to categorise these examples neatly: the context of each school and project is unique. But four broad aspects of how schools are managed are illustrated in Figure 1. First, there is the issue of the competencies needed by

Figure 1. **Four aspects of school management**

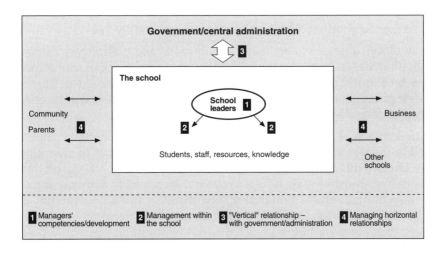

school leaders themselves, and how they are developed. Second, leaders need to find appropriate ways of managing the resources within their schools. Third, their relationship to administrative and governmental bodies outside the school needs to be resolved. And last but not least, modern school management must entail the management of many relationships beyond the school. This categorisation is used below to summarise some interesting approaches that emerge from the countries in this study.

Developing School Leaders

What Kinds of Skills are Needed: The Roles School Leaders Play

The school improvement movement of the past 20 years has put great emphasis on the role of leaders. The "quality of leadership of the principal" has been found repeatedly to play a crucial role in improvement initiatives (OECD, 1989, Schools and Quality). But this should not be interpreted as simply meaning that the principal should be made more powerful. Goodlad stated that "the role of the principal was strategic, as much in impeding, as in facilitating change". Fullan, in his 1981 review of American and Canadian research, also concluded "that the positive or negative role of the principal has a critical influence on teachers' receptiveness to new ideas" (OECD, 1989).

Modern principals need to be able to take on a wide variety of roles. The breadth of their function varies from one country to another, but is likely to include:

- Managing teaching staff and their in-service needs.
- Fostering good relations with surrounding communities.
- Defining the distinctive ethos of the school.
- Promoting good teaching and leading educational change.

In addition, a range of administrative, financial and disciplinary responsibilities falls ultimately to school managers (although the amount can vary according to how much control is taken by central and other layers of authorities). But the ability to delegate such functions, especially on a day-to-day basis, can be one of the most crucial competencies for a busy school leader.

A description of responsibilities, however, does not define the competencies needed to manage *effectively* in a modern school. For example, in managing staff, very different skills are needed to run a collegiate system of shared decision-making and responsibility than for a pyramidal hierarchy of authoritarian control. Where educational reform demands standardisation and accountability, a traditional control orientation for school managers may in some cases be reinforced. A more appropriate style in the post-industrial information age would be for the principal to be a developer of the *learning organisation*. Such organisations "… continually expand their capacity to create results they truly desire, where new and expansive patterns of thinking are nurtured, where collective aspiration is set free and where people are continually learning how to learn together" (Senge, 1990). The school is seen as a *community of learners* where all participants – principals, teachers, parents and students – engage in learning and teaching (Barth, 1990).

The Netherlands has one of the more comprehensive appreciations for management styles, congruent to today's complex educational milieu:

- *Instructional leader*: serves as a role model, co-ordinating the educational pro-gramme, encouraging professional development, monitoring pupil and aca-demic performance and maintaining an orderly, and peaceful learning environment.

- *Transformational leader*: promotes school improvement and renewal through professional co-operation, professional development and effective problem-solving.

- *Integrative leader*: combines a personnel, educational and financial management vision which encompasses the school's mission of continuous improvement.

- *Co-operative leadership* – leadership is viewed as a shared responsibility of the whole school and is undertaken by professional staff who are qualified to assume managerial responsibilities such as instruction, teacher co-opera-tion, vision development, facilities management, professional develop-ment, encouragement and recognition, standardisation of procedures and monitoring of change (see the chapter on the Netherlands).

Strategies for School Leader Development

Given the complex set of competencies needed to adapt to these multiple roles, the in-service and pre-service training of school leaders is of primary impor-tance to the nine nations participating in this report. Three dimensions of such training are important: its *content*, its *delivery mode* and its *timing/coverage*.

The *content* depends heavily on how the role of school leader is conceived. At one level, there is a need for people who have been trained as teachers to pre-pare to take up various administrative responsibilities. If, for example, they will be responsible for resource management, some basic business skills will be needed. But a more adventurous approach is to prepare school leaders to become trans-formational managers of learning organisations.

The country chapters below describe a number of innovative programmes aim-ing to prepare leaders who will make a real difference to their schools. For example:

- The Fontys University for Professional Education and the Catholic Training Institute in the Netherlands emphasise the school manager's role as a strategic leader, a human resources manager, a quality performer and a reflective practitioner.

- The Vlerick School of Management at the University of Ghent, Belgium, has a new in-service programme for school teams aiming to stimulate creative, critical, problem-solving skills through a "school-based management contest", based on Master of Business Administration (MBA) exercises. This focuses on solving real problems in one's own environment rather than being abstract.

- Japan is trying to shift the traditional role from that of "school administrator" to "school manager". This change must be seen in the context of a system in which the main function of heads has been with regards to teaching, but now considerable emphasis is being placed on a managerial approach to matters such as staff development, external relations and financial control.

- In a partnership between the Pinellas County School District in Florida and a teacher union, a "Quality Academy" has been established to improve classroom, school, department and district level performance. The *Quality Challenge* is an integrated management system with a core set of values to guide the cultural transformation of the school, classroom and team.

Such programmes need to relate to the particular stage that a country has reached in educational reform. In some other countries, the present emphasis is on engineering whole-school change. Management development models from the business world have been proving highly relevant in such circumstances. As school leaders try to understand organisational change as a process, there is much to be drawn from the experience of other organisations.

A wide variety of *delivery modes* is used in leader development – ranging from university-based courses to team exercises on the school site, with scope for use of distance learning modes. Another variable is whether delivery is through course work or through some other method such as school-based apprenticeship/mentoring, which encourages team-work and personal fulfilment.

The examples in this report show that imaginative methods can be used to ensure that leader development is useful and relevant for the work of principals and other managers. For example:

- In some countries, *special centres* have been set up to address the needs of educational management. In the Netherlands, five universities have come together to create the Netherlands School for Educational Management, offering a part-time course for secondary school leaders. A similar management training school in Hungary is an example of bilateral colllaboration between the Netherlands and Hungary. In the United Kingdom, eleven Assessment Centres and a similar number of Development Centres provide an assessment of development needs and individually tailored courses for those seeking appointment as head teachers.

- University faculties across the United States provide a vast array of leadership training programmes for individuals, generally as graduate school masters courses. But the examples of separate institutes in Cincinnati and Seattle described in the country chapter illustrate a growing emphasis on delivering team-based training and support directly on-site at the local school.

- Leadership development can be strengthened by the involvement of a wide range of partners. In Mexico, Sweden and the US, teacher unions are very actively involved in a variety of workplace issues, including staff development. The case study in rural Wisconsin describes a joint venture between New Paradigm Partners and Mount Senario College, offering collaborative leadership development for principals, teachers, parents, students and other citizens involved in school improvement and community development.

Finally, the *timing and coverage* of leader development can also vary. Typically, the targeted participants are those just about to take on leadership positions. But there can be great value in a wider coverage, to include either those who are already in post or people who play a significant part in school change processes even though they are not part of the senior management team. Broadly, three models of development can be identified from countries' experience though they are by no means mutually exclusive:

- *Training that qualifies teachers to take on leadership roles.* In the United Kingdom nationally agreed standards together with pre-service development for head teachers will become mandatory for the first time, following the introduction of a National Professional Qualification for Headship in 1997. Establishing a "pre-service" qualification for principals or senior managers sends a clear message that managing a school is not simply a matter of being a teacher and adding on some extra responsibilities. It has taken a long time to recognise this. Where it is recognised, those entering senior school management are being forced to think about what is needed to lead a large organisation, and are starting to draw on general management know-how from beyond the education world. For example, candidates for the position of principal in Antwerp must complete a two-year part-time course emphasising human resources management and the process of change required to create a learning organisation.

- *In-service development opportunities for serving school leaders.* The Netherlands School for Educational Management course referred to above and in the country chapter is a good example. Like other forms of in-service professional development, such schemes often work best when well-integrated with the work already being carried out by those in post. The Dutch example encourages participants from different regions to work together to gain insight into good

35

practice. Even in a country such as Greece, where there has never been any formal training for principals, opportunities are emerging for serving leaders to undergo development through distance learning modules

Note that it is impossible to draw a sharp distinction between in-service and preparatory development for school managers. In larger schools, senior staff already with managerial responsibilities may need further development prior to becoming a principal. And principals of smaller schools can benefit from training that enables them to move successfully to larger ones where their responsibilities will be greater.

- *Development addressing school management that is not restricted to senior managers or those close to being appointed to such posts.* In Sweden, for example, there is a view that management training should be an activity for all members of the school staff, as well as being part of initial teacher training. In a society where democratic ideas are deeply ingrained, it is believed that, just as teachers encourage students to manage their own studies, they have to work as part of a team and understand how teamwork is essential to the running and management of a school.

- Further school-oriented development activities engage other stakeholders in the mission of change. The Vlerick School of Management course in Belgium, referred to above, illustrates how such engagement can be developed: the programme required teams of administrators, teachers and parents to take part in simulation games in which they had to solve problems related to a school's management. Mexico's School Management in Elementary Education Research and Innovation Project engages principals, teachers and parents in developing their process of self-evaluation to improve educational outcomes. In Hungary, principles of total quality management are being introduced in schools as well as in the municipalities and other school "maintainers" through various quality assurance programmes, including most recently the Comenius Programme, described in the country chapter. So at best, development can not only prepare appointed managers to manage, but also widen the range of people who understand and get involved in the management of change within a school. This is in line with a view that managing the modern organisation must be a collaborative rather than a hierarchical process.

Managing People and Resources within a School

As discussed in Chapter 2, the model of the principal as an all-powerful commander of school life does not fit the requirements of modern education. The principal needs to play a crucial role, not through control but through leadership.

This requires the effective management of people, resources and knowledge around a commonly shared mission.

Principals must, among other things, be able to:

- Manage real change where necessary.
- Hold together an effective staff team.
- Manage the deployment of physical resources.
- Manage knowledge and ideas.
- Prioritise his or her time in order not to get distracted from these essential tasks.

Some of the biggest challenges for school managers are most visible in cases where radical and *fundamental change* is needed. The case studies report, for example, on the transformation of Parham School in Cincinatti, USA, on Botvidsgymnasiet in Stockholm, Sweden, and on Frances Combe School in Watford, United Kingdom. Each faced difficult circumstances and each has been improved by a visionary leader. However, these leaders have taken very different styles, according to what are perceived as the needs in particular circumstances. In Parham School, this involved creating a tougher and more disciplined learning environment; in Botvidsgymnasiet, where draconian solutions had failed, it involved removing barriers between staff and pupils; Frances Combe School emphasises greater personal understanding of disadvantaged pupils. What is common, however, to all these cases is that school leaders project a common set of values and hence a consistent approach throughout the school. This requires a strong personality and sense of direction which brings a potentially disparate set of teachers willingly together around a common approach.

While such leadership of change is often most apparent in schools with severe difficulties, similar principles apply to the transformation of schools more generally. Deacon's School in Peterborough, United Kingdom, for example, has overcome organisational inertia and resistance from traditional school culture to become a "beacon" of change, through the introduction of new practices based on performance management. It has succeeded in doing so because change has been skilfully and effectively presented and implemented by the head teacher and senior staff, and because the whole staff feel a sense of "ownership" of the new systems. The attempts under Hungary's Comenius 2000 programme will similarly need to engage staff across each school in a fundamental change of style, based on total quality management.

The example of Deacon's School also illustrates new approaches to holding together a *staff team*. It has succeeded in introducing a new appraisal system and principles of performance management in a co-operative rather than conflictual manner. In a number of cases in this study, the principle of team working has transformed management styles. In Sweden, the working of teachers in teams is an important component of change, as illustrated in Elinburg School in Helsinborg and Skare school in Karlstad. Here, the reformation of teachers into work teams has constituted a radical change in the way in which education is delivered. Moreover, teachers can play an important role not just in following but also in initiating change. This comes across strongly in two schools in Flanders: the Institute for Paramedical Professions in Ghent, and Middenschool H. Hart in Bree. In the latter in particular, the management style and the work of the school are based on an "Educational Project" developed by the staff, in co-operation with the parents and students. The potential for initiative to be taken at this level should not cause school leaders to neglect their role of taking the lead where it is needed. But such experiences reinforce the message that changes in school work best where everybody involved feels a sense of "ownership".

But the successful staff practices described in this report should not hide the fact that relations between school management and staff have often been problematic in recent years. The biggest cause is the growing pressure to hold staff to account for their performance. When this appears to be presented in a "controlling" context, it meets opposition from teachers and their unions. This is no more so than when matters of pay are involved.

The Foundation for Catholic Education in Maastricht, the Netherlands is but one advocate in a growing movement to provide salary differentiation on the basis of merit. Through consultation with professional unions, criteria have been established for a system of premium pay and temporary extra increments for teachers demonstrating exceptional performance. Principals are trained in assessment procedures to identify personnel to receive merit pay. A large number of states and school districts in the United States provide salary bonuses or other incentives for teachers who earn National Board for Professional Teaching Standards certification. Merit pay has been almost universally unpopular with teacher unions, however. Its introduction by the UK Department for Education and Employment has been one of the most strongly resisted changes in over a decade of educational reform.

Human resources are clearly the most important assets of a school, which need nurturing. Handling human resources cannot be separated from other components of management such as dealing with physical and financial resources where there are also very rapid changes taking place. In Greece, for instance, a project that focuses on the improvement of school premises is impacting on teacher and student morale and other changes in schools. It has been estimated, for example, that in the United States, spending on computers and software now outstrips spending on books and written materials (OECD, 1999, pp. 49-50). Educational budgets need to adapt across school systems, but in addition a big pressure has been exerted on schools themselves to keep up (often through fundraising) with rapid changes in resourcing needs. At the same time, school managers in many countries have been given new responsibilities in managing financial resources. In countries where such roles are least familiar, their adoption figures prominently in new approaches to school management.

More generally, as competition grows for a limited supply of public funds, schools and school authorities are reaching out for alternative sources of financial and in-kind support. Special government project funding, philanthropic donations and commercial partnerships are prompting school leaders to acquire new skills of "grantsmanship" and proposal writing. One such approach would be the creation of an arm's length educational foundation or non-profit charitable organisation to seek alternative sources of funding and material support for school innovation and programme enrichment (see chapter on the United States).

Perhaps the biggest challenge in the management of schools today is not managing people and physical resources, but *managing knowledge and ideas*. To bring about genuine change and improvement is not simply a matter of implementing formulaic solutions based on studies (such as this one) of "what works". As discussed at the end of Chapter 2, knowledge emanates from multiple sources, and needs to be managed effectively within schools if it is to be well utilised. This means both harnessing knowledge from within a school and drawing it in from outside. To the extent that knowledge must be managed beyond as well as within the boundaries of the school, Figure 1 is imperfect. But this topic is being considered under Category 2 in the figure, since the prime objective relates to internal school processes, even though the tools to do so must be drawn from further afield.

Knowledge management within a school can be roughly equated with school-oriented development. Schools and their staff need to develop their understanding of school improvement as a process. They are constantly doing so subconsciously, as each teacher learns from experience, and to the extent that this learning is shared with others, for example through staffroom discussions. But knowledge systems can potentially become more powerful if they are managed consciously. An excellent example of this can be seen in Sharnbrook School in Bedfordshire, United Kingdom. Here, six "research groups" look at different aspects of the curriculum, in order to move towards improved teaching and learning methods. This programme is linked with an academic institution, the University of Cambridge, which helps the school build *internal* capacity to improve education. Sharnbrook is a still rare example of a school which has consciously become its own laboratory of learning.

39

What is easier to see, yet has been all too rare in the past, is collaboration among different schools to share their knowledge. Some examples that stand out from this study's cases are:

- In the Netherlands, the Foundation of Catholic Education has created a network of knowledge management in Maastricht, through the Hendric von Veldeke Foundation. This central management organisation creates a single structure to run 12 schools with 4 000 pupils and 250 staff. A key objective is to create a "learning organisation" in which good performance and professional renewal are systematically encouraged. The creation of a wide organisation of this type helps bring together quality circles and specialised training opportunities, and helps to develop educational management skills in an environment that could not be replicated within a single small school. (Note that the principle of school choice in the Netherlands has historically created a tension between the advantages and limitations of small schools – see OECD, 1994, *School: A Matter of Choice*, pp. 67-68 and OECD, 1991, *Reviews of National Policies for Education: Netherlands*, p. 75 – which potentially can be addressed through such over-arching structures.)

But exchange of knowledge most often does not always require an overseeing management structure; rather a method for voluntary collaboration. Thus:

- In Hungary, participants on training courses for school-based programmes/ curricula created an association of self-developing schools, an Internet-based network, which became a vehicle for spreading reform.

- In rural Wisconsin, USA, a dynamic community education director has brought together fifteen school leaders committed to educational improvement. The resulting non-profit consortium has helped put new dynamism into a depressed rural region, encouraging entrepreneurship and innovation among its leaders.

- Deacon School, Peterborough, United Kingdom, is an example of a "Beacon School" with a mission to spread good practice to others. Its cited areas of expertise are the use of Advanced Skills Teachers and its appraisal system. Advanced Skills Teachers have recently been accredited by the government to spread knowledge among as well as within schools. The attempt also to disseminate expertise in the use of teacher appraisals demonstrates that not just curriculum and teaching knowledge, but also management knowledge, can usefully be exchanged beyond the boundaries of the individual school.

Finally, one of the biggest difficulties of any school leader will be how to *prioritise*. How can one take responsibility both for the day-to-day running of the school and for developing a clear sense of long-term mission – quite aside from managing the vertical and horizontal relationships covered in the following two sections?

The answer must be to delegate appropriately – an easy principle to enunciate, but harder to apply. A good example of a principal who makes this a key part of her leadership strategy is the head of Latseion Psyhico College, a Greek elementary school. Her main focus is a mission to bring together the financial, human and knowledge resources needed for effective curriculum innovation. She makes a clear distinction between leadership and administration. The latter, the daily bureaucratic functions, are delegated to a vice-principal.

Managing Relations with the Centre

The breadth of experience of managers in this report is an eloquent illustration of how the "decentralisation" of schooling takes highly varied forms in different countries, depending to a great extent on the prior experience of centralisation. In countries such as Greece, where educational management has been highly centralised in a hierarchical bureaucracy, the first taste of freedom for managers consists of relatively simple but unfamiliar things such as handling their own budgets and taking comparatively routine decisions without reference to administrative masters. In others, such as the United Kingdom, managers typically feel more widely responsible for the success of their school and for articulating its mission, although to some, this independence feels illusory in the context of the constraints dictated by accountability, curriculum guidelines and assessment.

In any context, it is often those managers that push their freedom to its limits who succeed; in a changing system, the limits are not always clear-cut.

In Greece, where there is also the beginnings of a retreat from centralisation, not all schools find it easy to take full advantage of the independence that appears to be on offer. Schools are encouraged to take initiative, but the principal of the Experimental School of Athens University has found that the law and regulations can limit her power to do so. There is a desire by innovative schools in Greece not to be led by regulations: the principal of Latseion Psyhico College, referred to above, sees her role as pushing curriculum reform well beyond what is laid down. But ultimately principals have to accept that they will be held accountable if they go beyond what regulations permit.

The Hungarian case illustrates a complex situation that school principals need to manage. School principals in Hungary are the employers of their staff. They need to satisfy their constituency, the staff, the parents and students. Among other things, the views of staff, parents and students influence the local government's decision to hire or fire the principal. School principals, fixed-term employees of the local self-government, engage in budget bargaining with their employer. Within its highly decentralised context, the central government utilises a number of financial and other indirect tools to steer the system where centre-local politics can often get into the scene. This complexity is significant when both local governments and schools are in large part dependent on the centre's financial resources.

There is an interesting contrast between Japan and the United Kingdom in terms of devolution and decentralisation. Although the central Ministry of Education in Japan (Monbusho) has a strong role in defining policies for the whole system, responsibility for education is divided between the central government, prefectural and municipal boards of education. In the United Kingdom on the other hand, local authorities started out with more powers than in Japan but the UK government has been devolving many of these powers to schools. In the latter case, managers often find that they need to recreate local networks at a local level partly to replace what was lost by the pooling of expertise in a local administration. This "horizontal" element of management is hence to some extent an alternative to "vertical" relationships which can aim to create co-ordination at a local level.

In Mexico, Nuevo Leon's project is bringing in changes at the system level where the State now has devolved responsibility in education downwards. The role of area supervisors is changing from that of administrative/controlling to one of facilitating. It is hoped that the area supervisors will, as a result, be better able to monitoring the implementation of the state policies, as well as assist principals and teachers in attaining their educational goals.

All of these issues have come together in complex and revealing ways in recent years in Sweden. School management culture in Sweden has undoubtedly travelled further than any other county in the study, from one of rules and regulations to goal-based result management. As a result, the degree to which schools take the lead in change, or conversely are driven by local authorities or by municipality-wide collaboration among schools, varies considerably. Hence a reading of the chapter on Sweden and the accompanying case studies illustrates eloquently the issues and possibilities opened up for school managers when central government genuinely loosens its grip on school management.

Managing Relationships outside the School

It is now universally accepted in OECD countries that schools must relate well to their surrounding communities if they are to be effective. In societies that have been undergoing profound economic and social restructuring, the school's role needs to be related directly to the changes that are taking place around it. What this means for school management is no less than a redefinition of the mission of the school. Its leaders become managers of "horizontal" relationships with others outside the school as much as directors of what happens inside it or enforcers of requirements handed down from above.

Three OECD reports in the 1990s looked at various aspects of this transformation: the closer partnership with business (*Schools and Business: A New Partnership,*

OECD, 1992); the relationship with consumers exercising choice of school (*School – A Matter of Choice*, OECD, 1994); and the active involvement of parents (*Parents as Partners in Schooling*, OECD 1997). Are these kinds of partnership simply supplementary to the activities of schools, or are they fundamental to the way that they work and are managed? Increasingly, it is the latter. One interesting aspect of many of the case studies in this report is the degree to which leaders are involved with external relations. At best this is not just a matter of being concerned with the school's image, but of involving others in defining its mission. In this role, school leaders must translate priorities that are derived from a broad coalition of interests into practical management of the school.

Several strong strands of this wider management task can be observed:

- The *involvement of parents* in constructing and implementing a change agenda. It often requires a big culture shift for school managers to accept that they must listen closely to parents, and some countries are taking only the first tentative steps. In reforming Mexico's elementary schools, for example, the very fact that the conscious support and understanding of parents is considered important marks a significant departure. In the transformation of some schools in the United States, the importance of working with parents is well accepted. This applies particularly to schools in deprived areas, such as the Parham school in Cincinnatti: less educated parents have traditionally felt less connection to the school, yet their involvement is the most crucial in terms of giving support to children's learning from beyond the classroom. However, such examples should not hide the fact that parental involvement and the degree to which parents have been able to feed into genuine decision-making remain patchy (OECD, 1997, *Parents as Partners in Schooling*, pp. 57-59). Perhaps one of the most valuable skills of school managers in the future will be to inform, understand and act on the view of the school clientele, while retaining a sense of educational direction.

- The *involvement of communities* goes beyond parents, to include various interested parties such as local companies and foundations, who are often more articulate than parents when it comes to articulating and negotiating their ambitions for schools. Sometimes those outside the school take the initiative, as in the Seattle Alliance described in the chapter on the United States. But the willingness to involve the community in a mission for reform must ultimately come from the school leaders. This has happened for example in schools in Gifu in Japan, where groups of citizens have been brought in as regular advisors, rather than just being asked their views on a sporadic basis.

- Greater *understanding of the social environment* can be important in deprived communities, and may be as crucial as educational factors in the way that change is managed. For example both the foundation and management of the Johann de Witt College in The Hague, Netherlands are based around the special needs of a deprived and largely immigrant community, in terms of support both inside and outside the school. It has developed partnerships with a wide range of local services, from mosques to the police force. Multi-service co-ordination has also played an important role in the Francis Combe School in the United Kingdom and in Parham Elementary and Birchwood Schools in the United States.

- A *widening of the curriculum* to include work based around communities and experience. One approach to school change, taken by the dynamic director of the de Stuifhoek Primary School in the Netherlands, is to transform it into a "school for experience". This meant adopting an experiential approach to learning which has created an atmosphere of stimulation and excitement aiming to engage all students. In rural Wisconsin, USA, New Paradigm Partners are similarly bringing education to life through hands-on learning, in this case across a range of schools. Its strategy is heavily oriented towards projects based in local communities and therefore directly involving non-teachers in education rather than asking them to look in from the outside. These are two examples where managers have taken adventurous decisions to make such learning central to what is offered at their schools, rather than simply adding it on at the edges. The extent of such transformation remains limited both by the constraints imposed by school systems and by the courage and imagination of school leaders, but the examples illustrate that the potential rewards are high.

Bibliography

BARTH, R.S. (1990),
   Improving Schools from Within, Jossey-Bass, San Francisco, CA.

OECD (1989),
   Schools and Quality: An International Report, Paris.

OECD (1999),
   Education Policy Analysis, Paris.

SENGE, P. (1990),
   The Fifth Discipline: The Art and Practice of the Learning Organisation, Doubleday, Garden City, N.Y.

Chapter 4

Emerging Issues, the Process of Change and New Directions for the Learning School

"Decentralisation and deregulation allow for greater freedom and flexibility for municipalities, schools, teachers and students in working out their own pedagogical solutions to problems within the framework of national goals. But it takes courage and clear-sightedness on the part of politicians, local school directors/superintendents and school leaders to use these opportunities successfully."

(conclusion to the chapter on Sweden)

New Roles

Each of the countries in this study would like, in its own way, to translate a willingness to reform into a capacity for innovation. Additionnally, the trend towards decentralisation acknowledges that the dynamic for transformational change in schools must come increasingly from within the school community.

However, the very terms "school" and "school community" are no longer as precise as they once were. In some countries, the schools' functions are being re-defined and they are becoming multi-service establishments, incorporating child care and pre-school as well as formal schooling and recreational services, as in Sweden. This creates a "seamless web" with children easing naturally from one learning experience to another.

Apart from their instructional role, schools have always been agents of sociali-sation, morality and citizenship. They helped foster what has now come to be known as "social capital", those features of social life – networks, norms and trust – that enable participants to act together more effectively to pursue shared objec-tives (Putnam, 1995). This role has, arguably, become even more important as the social capital generated by families, neighbourhoods, communities and other net-

47

works tends to shrink in many countries. Given the increasing number of broader stakeholders' involvement and influence on school management, schools have the potential of strengthening "social capital" of its own that fosters values for social co-operation and social interactions (OECD, 2001).

Teachers are not social workers, yet schools are increasingly expected to address social issues such as violence, bullying, environmental, gender and ethnic issues. In some cases, schools may do so in very specific ways through, for instance, multi-culturalism programmes or through courses in civic education. They may choose to do so in unique ways such as setting up a social inclusion unit or a Family Service Centre, as in the Francis Coombe school in the UK. In the Netherlands, co-operation between schools and community services has been enhanced, by integrating special needs and primary education, preventative/pro-active youth care, and social welfare services.

Schools also have to prepare young citizens to live in an increasingly knowledge-driven world, characterised by globalisation and the use of ICT. Thinking skills, problem solving skills and team-working are competencies that are increasingly prized and put pressure on schools to move away from an overly didactic approach. School staff are expected to change their traditional ways of teaching and running schools through greater use of ICT. They are expected to become "knowledge managers" themselves and "knowledge facilitators" for their students and their learning. The change is slower than anticipated but there is no denying the potential of ICT to alter significantly the manner in which schools go about their daily business.

Increasing social and parental demands are matched at the political level. Education has moved up the political agenda with, for instance, both candidates in the US presidential election in 2000 promising to make it their number one priority. Local politics are now impacting more directly on school management due, in large measure, to decentralisation and devolved management. At both national and local levels, education is seen as the key to unlocking not just social but also economic problems.

New Leaders

It is not just the role of school that is less clearly delineated than in the past – new school leaders are also emerging and working in different ways. In countries like Japan and Greece, the principal is usually a promoted teacher but, as the chapters on the United States and Sweden show, he or she may be drawn from other backgrounds such as the military, business, pre-schooling or recreational pedagogy. Some countries, particularly the United States and Flanders, find it difficult to attract suitable candidates for what is seen as an increasingly onerous job.

The principal is at the interface between system level demands, defined centrally and politically, and the school level requirements. He/she is also at the interface between demands of managerial leadership versus instructional leadership. The immediate administrative needs may drive out the more important demands of pedagogic leadership. This is recognised in some countries. For instance, Japanese primary and lower secondary schools have at least one administrator each while in Sweden a number of municipalities are in the process of appointing administrators to take over certain responsibilities in order to allow principals concentrate their energies on pedagogic leadership. However, these are the exceptions rather than the rule in most of the countries studied, with the result that principals have to juggle their various responsibilities as best they can.

Increasingly, the principal's role and responsibilities are being shared with other stakeholders including other teachers, students, parents, governors, business people, foundations, and local municipalities. The principal is, in effect, the head of a wider coalition of school interests than in the past. The relationship between the different parties varies from country to country and the fine line that previously separated advice from decision making is being blurred. In countries, such as Sweden, student councils have an important part to play in helping to shape individual school management policies. Swedish schools are also placing increasing importance on teams of teachers sharing responsibilities for organising and running schools. In other countries, different stakeholders, such as school governors in the United Kingdom, have an important voice in the formulation of policy.

Meanwhile, some countries allow greater scope for business or foundations to shape, both directly and indirectly, what happens in schools. The Seattle Alliance (see the chapter on the United States) helped recruit an Army general as Superintendent of the local public schools and he succeeded in turning them around. In some countries, foundations are giving large amounts of money for school innovation, staff training, technical assistance and the purchase of ICT. Such generous donations are certainly welcomed by the schools, especially if they come at a time of cutbacks in public expenditure. But they do raise questions about educational policy slipping further out of public control. A new mechanism to ensure quality public services within the market orientation and privatisation context is yet to be developed.

All too often the management components – financial, human resources, instructional, relationships with other stakeholders, etc. – are addressed in a fragmented way rather than strategically. Asset management, including educational facilities management, also needs to be managed strategically, as underlined in recent OECD reports (OECD, 1999b, 2000). This raises broader issues of more effective financial management mechanisms in the public sector. When management units become smaller because of greater autonomy for schools and diminishing educational system management layers, such as the case of the Local

49

Education Authorities (LEAs) in the UK, economies of scale are no longer attainable. The deployment of resources, including management knowledge, expertise and skills, in an effective and financially viable way, is becoming a key issue.

All of this highlights the need for principals and those at the system level to receive training. In the past, and still in some countries, principals in particular were given minimal, if any, training. Chapter 3 has shown how the school improvement movement of the past 20 years has put great emphasis on the role and training of principals. Pre-service and in-service training for principals has assumed a much higher priority in some countries where principals are recruited widely, than in others where principals are promoted teaching staff. Apart from less clearly delineated schools and school leaders, there is also an increasing acceptance that the task of managing schools is becoming much more complex. To this end, the National Standards for Headteachers in the United Kingdom list a comprehensive set of leadership and management tasks in five key areas:

- Strategic direction and development of the school.
- Teaching and learning.
- Leading and managing staff.
- Efficient and effective deployment of staff.
- Accountability.

New Tensions

A generalised problem is the tension, described in Chapters 1 and 2, between the desires for schools to take charge of their own destiny and the need for them to be accountable for their outcomes. In Sweden, the municipalities have been given greater powers but some teachers complain that decentralisation has stopped at the town hall, while in the United Kingdom the powers of the Local Education Authorities (LEAs) are being steadily eroded and responsibilities pushed down to the school level.

In general, however, schools are being given greater autonomy in areas such as budgetary and human resource issues. One such area is merit or performance related pay, which is already in operation in Sweden and the US. It is being introduced in the United Kingdom and is on the agenda in the Netherlands. In most cases, the decisions about who should or should not get such additional pay are a problematic exercise for principals. Teacher unions have strongly opposed the individualisation of salaries, but in Sweden some union leaders argue that the process has brought up the average salary – more significantly, they do not see any return to the annual incremental salary rises.

While principals are given this, not always welcome, autonomy, they also, on the other hand, have to meet increasing accountability demands set externally and nationally. Countries are looking at ways of exercising central control over increasingly autonomous schools (OECD/CERI, 1999). Procedures for setting a central curriculum, for inspecting schools or for assessing pupils and publishing results at a school level are all pressures that encourage school managers to conform to a well-defined set of norms. Indeed, assessing and ensuring the quality of schools is a growing preoccupation in OECD Member countries (OECD, 1995 and 1999a).

Schools are not unique institutions in having greater responsibilities thrust upon them. An OECD Public Management Committee (PUMA) publication describes how many countries have tried to introduce a fundamental shift from a centralised, hierarchical, rule-driven administration to one characterised by devolved management and market orientation, where emphasis is given to concern for results rather than to mere procedures (OECD, 1995).

As managing schools is becoming much more complex, school managers are getting more "professionalised". At the same time, other stakeholders are becoming involved in school management in many countries. Professionalisation versus increasing number of lay persons' involvement and influence on school management has started to pose some complex questions, such as power and control, as well as the gap of management knowledge and skills between the two groups.

Encouraging parents to act like consumers and make choices in a freer market can intensify these pressures. This can lead sometimes to schools having a fear of being different, lest the difference makes the school look bad. Reforms, such as decentralisation and the introduction of market forces, that are not necessarily intended to stifle a sense of self-determination, can potentially do so. While a competitive approach can enhance innovations and raise standards, competition can also widen the disparity between those seen as successful and those less so. This raises issues of equity and also of the mixed messages sent to the schools' clients – the students. They see that schools are promoting inclusiveness, co-operation, teamwork, etc., among their staff and students, yet there is an unresolved dichotomy between this collaborative orientation on the one hand, and the competitive culture that many schools find themselves in on the other.

The Process of Change

None of the countries in this study has found it easy to achieve transformation and there are several reasons for this. One problem is the obvious one that bottom-up change by its nature is harder to make universal than top-down whilst it is contradictory to command school managers to become innovators. But this does not prevent governments and others from attempting to encourage the conditions in which innovation and innovators can thrive.

51

They have not always done a good job of it. In some countries, the relaxation of central regulation has been rather partial, so managers told to innovate continue to come across rules which limit their capacity to do so. Mexico's innovation in using top-down resources effectively to encourage bottom-up renewal may be the way to go. In other countries, the culture of schools, education systems and, indeed, of public sector management in general, has been slow to change. Long-standing management traditions, styles and practices in some countries have tended to breed deep-rooted passivity and inertia and even an unwillingness to disturb the status quo in intermediate levels of authority and in schools where transformation of the traditional culture itself requires time and effort. "Lying low" is considered preferable to risk-taking in such contexts.

A frequently heard comment in schools that manage to change is that "success breeds success". This is true, but the process of change and development can be slow. The movement towards more school autonomy allows schools greater freedom to analyse and respond to the educational needs of their students. But unless leadership is exercised at the school level to promote this goal, autonomy may simply perpetuate existing practices. Stakeholders need an understanding of the process.

Teachers, especially those in secondary schools, have had a tendency to perceive their classroom activities in isolation from, rather than in relation to, school policies and goals. Subject-related training, which has traditionally focused on the compartmentalisation of disciplines, has fostered this approach to teaching. As a result, teachers can be resistant to adopting more co-operative teaching approaches. This is less true generally of primary schools where there is already a greater emphasis on teamwork and child-centred teaching.

The chapters on the United Kingdom and Sweden contain good examples of where determined leaders in secondary and primary schools question existing practice and engage their staffs in a process of challenge and change. The Cincinnati public school case study also demonstrates how teachers, through their trade unions, can be brought into the decision-making process and play an important role in transforming the school environment in difficult socio-economic circumstances.

However, getting teachers "signed-up" to a process of renewal is one thing, but it needs to be accompanied by appropriate strategies to review progress. Reviews or appraisals or evaluations take different forms in different countries – traditionally the emphasis has been on the individual teacher's performance, now it is increasingly on the school's outcomes as a whole. The role and functions of inspectors in some countries have also moved in that direction. In some cases, teachers' less than desirable working conditions, such as very low salaries, highlight issues such as motivation or quality assurance.

Research on appraisal shows that it is not working effectively in many schools. A MORI survey in the United Kingdom indicated that three quarters of teachers perceived no link between their appraisal and their professional development (MORI, 1995). A successful appraisal system may help to move the organisation forwards but it should also be recognised that "in far too many schools the outcomes of appraisal do not lead to action and are not being linked either to school development planning or teachers' own professional development plans" (Millett, 1996).

Yet, as the OECD's Public Management Committee has emphasised, evaluation is important in a results-oriented environment – it is part of a wider performance management framework. Presenting evaluation findings in an open fashion can create pressure to act on findings. At the same time, there can be a downside when the publication of headline results unfairly categorises schools in disadvantaged areas that are beating the odds. There is also a danger that more attention tends to go to immediate tangible results and positive image creation rather than quality improvement in line with educational objectives, which often requires time and space.

New Directions for Learning at School

How can policy makers encourage good leadership in school management, and take actions that help spread innovation? Part of the answer rests on a delicate equation between central direction and local autonomy, which is heavily influenced by political considerations. A basic principle should be at least to give managers "time and space" to become leaders, rather than plaguing their lives with endless circulars and regulations. Another variable is the degree of detail with which schools are held to account. If the political demand to make schools "accountable for outcomes" is taken literally, there could be considerably less interference with the procedures and processes by which these outcomes are achieved, as well as a careful analysis of whether the right outcomes are being measured.

Change within schools is inevitable, as it is in the outside, increasingly demanding world beyond the school gates. The schools are operating in a different milieu than a few decades ago. They have to cope with the impact of more serious social problems and are expected to undertake a greater social role in promoting civic understanding, health education, multi-cultural education, etc. At the same time, they are expected to assist young people develop the skills needed to survive and thrive in a rapidly changing world. School renewal or reform has to be an on-going process. It is as well to remember that "customers, competition and change have created a new world for business, and it is becoming increasingly apparent that organisations designed to operate in one environment cannot be fixed to work well in another" (Hammer and Champy, 1993). The same is true of schools.

School leaders have to help turn their schools into dynamic learning organisations and cannot allow obstacles to block growth and development. A school system that works well will incorporate collaborative learning as a pervasive ethos, from its top to its bottom. Local and central governments are having to learn how to *support* change in schools, rather than either over-prescribing it or standing back from it. Thus it is not just schools themselves, but whole school systems, that must become learning organisations.

So managing a school is not the same as managing a factory or a company. A school is part of a web of organisations and interests whose objective is to educate children. The managers at the centre of this web have a difficult task. But they must never believe that it is impossible.

Lessons Learned

The country and case studies that follow in Part II of this report contain some inspiring examples of where school management has indeed transformed education for the better. There is no one formula for doing so, but there are effective features to be found in some of the more innovative examples:

- Placing school management issues within a broad education system level framework is increasingly important. As illustrated in this report, education has become a hot political topic in many countries. This fact, coupled with public sector reform and constraints on public spending in many countries as well as technological revolution, all necessitate more than ever school management strategies developed at the system level.

- School managers are expected to assume increasingly complex and arduous tasks. Some countries are, however, confronted by shortages of school managers and/or management candidates. These need to be addressed as do issues related to management training and professional development. The responses should be set against the broad contexts of human resource management (including labour relations) and financial management. In a number of countries, management traditions, styles and current practice have not been transformed sufficiently to tackle the new challenges that schools and educational systems are facing.

- There is a sense of excitement among the stakeholders in many of the case studies – a realisation that change is possible, even in the most unlikely circumstances. But it can be a slow process. As an official in Flanders commented "it takes more time than in the private business, where you can see the results more quickly". The mastery of the skills for effective leadership and management of change also takes time to develop.

- Schools that are successful have a clear vision to which all the constituents have "signed-up". The responsibilities of the various stakeholders are also clearly defined. Changes designed with little involvement of those destined to use them are rarely as effective (Rowan and Taylor, 2000). In that sense every teacher is a school leader, as she or he has to lead students in their learning experience.

- Resistance to change is natural at both the school and the system level. Those involved in education are, almost by definition, verbal and literate people. They can learn the official language quickly but this does not necessarily mean they internalise it. School leaders have to find ways to motivate them. Merit or performance related money is used in an increasing number of countries, but improving motivation is more often about a sense of achievement, responsibility and self-fulfilment.

- The effective management of communications and perceptions is a key skill for a school leader. Different strategies are needed for different stakeholders. Leaders with insight not only consider the management of outgoing communications but also the manner in which communications are received and perceived by those communicated with.

- Some conscious efforts have been made in countries such as Mexico to integrate the research component in innovative projects. Yet, overall there was a surprising absence of that component, including formal evaluation on innovative projects. Relevant research is essential for informed policy development.

- It is striking from the case studies, how frequently team-working is cited as a key ingredient to the success of new approaches to school management. Leaders who form effective management teams have a more pervasive influence than those who rely on their own personal efforts. Time, space and a willingness to succeed are all required. However, teams that simply re-inforce but do not challenge old practices may give the illusion of change.

- When communities or schools take initiatives, they mobilise resources and demonstrate tremendous competencies in management. They also breed a sense of ownership and confidence to undertake further innovations and change. In such learning organisations, individuals and teams become reflective practitioners and are enabled to review their own situations and deal with problems or challenges as they arise.

- A dynamic leader often creates a momentum behind what he or she is trying to achieve. However, it is risky to rely on the charisma and energy of a single leader to sustain change within a school. The hardest task facing the charismatic or "hero" head is "letting go". When an organisation has progressed sufficiently it is time for other leaders to develop. The ultimate test of any transformation is its durability beyond its original instigator.

55

Bibliography

HAMMER, M. and CHAMPY, J. (1993),
Re-engineering the Corporation, Nicholas Brealey, London.

Millet, A. (1996),
"Management Update", Times Educational Supplement, 19 January.

MORI (1995),
Survey of Continuing Professional Development, MORI Polls, London.

OECD (1995),
Schools under Scrutiny, Paris.

OECD (1999a),
Quality and Internationalisation in Higher Education, Paris.

OECD (1999b),
Strategic Asset Management for Tertiary Institutions, Paris.

OECD (2000),
The Appraisal of Investments in Educational Facilities, Paris.

OECD (2001),
The Well-being of Nations: The Role of Human and Social Capital, Paris.

OECD/CERI (1999),
"Die Vielfalt orchestrieren – Steuerungsaufgaben der zentralen Instanz bei grösserer Selbständigkeit der Einzelschulen", German Speaking Seminar.

OECD/PUMA (1995),
Governance in Transition, Paris.

PUTNAM, R.D. (1995),
"Tuning in, Tuning out; the Strange Disappearance of Social Capital in America", Political Science and Politics, 28, pp. 1-20.

ROWAN, J. and TAYLOR, P. (2000),
"Leading the Autonomous School", Proceedings of an Anglo-Irish seminar on school autonomy, Society for Management in Education in Ireland.

Part II
COUNTRY CASE STUDIES

BELGIUM (Flanders)

Land area in square kilometers: 31 000

Total population (1998): 10 203 000

Per capita GDP (1999 prices): 24 300 USD

Percentage of GDP on education (1997): 4.8%

Amount spent per student (1997):
- – 3 813 USD (Primary)
- – 6 938 USD (Secondary)

Teacher salary range (1998):
- – 19 020-31 252 USD (Primary)

Note: Data above are for Belgium, but this report relates only to Flanders.
Sources: Labour Force Statistics: 1978-1998, OECD, Paris, 1999; *Main Economic Indicators*, OECD, Paris, April 2000; *Education at a Glance – OECD Indicators 2000*, OECD, Paris, 2000.

Country context

Belgium has one of the highest population densities in Europe with ten million people occupying just 30 000 square kilometres. From 1970 on, Belgium has become progressively a federal state divided into three distinct Communities: the Dutch-speaking Flanders with 5.9 million inhabitants and 58% of the population; the French-speaking Walloon region with 32% and a small German-speaking community. Approximately one million immigrants, of which about one half are of Turkish and Morroccan origin descent are also to be found in Belgium.

Flanders occupies, in many respects, a central position in Europe. Brussels is at the same time the capital of the Flemish Community, of Belgium and of Europe. Furthermore, the Flemish Community is at the crossroads between different European cultures and traditions and actively participates in a number of European programmes. It has a common history with the French-speaking part of Belgium, but a common language, and to a large extent a common culture, with the Netherlands, with which there are frequent exchanges of ideas and of experiences.

During the 1980s, Belgium experienced a dramatic decline in the manufacturing sector which was matched by a rise in service industries. Unemployment rates in Belgium have been amongst the highest in OECD countries. However, this is changing: unemployment figures have been substantially declining in recent years, reaching 9% in 1999. Unemployment in Flanders, at 7.1%, is below the national average and, unlike the Waloon region, tends to be cyclical rather than structural.

Freedom of education has been included in the Constitution since the beginning of the Belgian State. This principle consists of two pillars: free choice of school and educational freedom, namely the right to establish schools autonomously. However, this principle has been the cause of much conflict and struggle. The "School Wars" constitute a significant part of the cultural and political history of Belgium, both in the 19th century – with major flare-ups around 1850 and 1879 – and in the 20th century, particularly from 1951 onwards. This century of confrontation ended with the signing of the "School Pact" in the fifties. This was a pact between the political parties to ensure a distributive justice between the different educational networks. A law of 29th May 1959, referred to as the School Pact Law, has formed the basis for the organisation of all educational establishments, with the exception of the universities, in an educational system organised and grant-aided by the state.

Education is a priority in Flanders and the standards of education are above the average. According to the TIMSS international survey, the level of achievement of Flemish students in mathematics and science is one of the highest (OECD, 1998). Participation in pre-primary education is almost 100% whilst in secondary education it is very high. Compulsory education has been extended up to the age of 18.

Challenges Facing School Management

Three types of challenges are facing school management, the first one being more specific to Flanders, while the other two are to a large extent common to most countries:

- The diversity and the extreme *complexity of the social and institutional environment* are more characteristic of Flanders than of many other European countries. For one thing, there is a great difference of environment between large cities and rural areas. This complexity is further increased by the free choice of schools, and the dominant role of subsidised private schools, which strive to get a balance between meeting legal obligations and protecting the freedom they have. On the other hand, the multiplicity of school networks, levels of decision-making and players concerned with education, imply that management is very complex at the system level. At the school level, principals and administrators have to find their way through a maze of different regulations and procedures.

- *The school population and the demands of society are changing.* Young people are exposed to a new mix of cultures, and they often have to overcome emotional problems related to broken families. The school is expected to solve problems that society is struggling to cope with, such as violence among young people, which is appearing in large cities. For some children, the school is the only stable environment left with rules and protection. It can also play a major role in the integration of youth from immigrant families.

- The issue of accountability has come to the forefront in recent years. There is an increasing pressure on the school system, and on individual schools, to *demonstrate their efficiency and their quality* in order to obtain financial resources. At the system level, some Flemish researchers consider that "the frequent talk about human resources is a way to hide rationalisation and to restrict the amount of money given to education". At the school level, with the free choice of schools, parents are more selective, and more demanding, and there is more competition between schools.

Main Policy Approaches

The government policy is to reinforce the innovative capacity of the schools and to promote self- supportive organisations. This implies more autonomy, more participation of the stakeholders and a process of self-evaluation. These priorities are reflected in the budget allocated by the Flemish government for in-service training of teachers and school heads.

Whereas previously the Belgian State was traditionally rather centralised, the Flemish Community has officially moved towards a more decentralised system for community schools by giving more autonomy to the local school councils. The other two school networks – subsidised private schools and provincial or municipal schools – have always had greater autonomy in educational matters. There is a tendency to give more resources to the schools and fewer responsibilities to the "umbrella" organisations.

The promotion of self-evaluation by the schools is also high on the political agenda. This is felt to be lagging behind at the moment, compared to external evaluation. Research is encouraged and several instruments are being developed. Also related to this is the new approach of school inspection, which regards self-evaluation of schools as complementary to external evaluation by the inspectorate. Self-evaluation is thus a new task and a new challenge for school principals. Those who attempt to promote it, including school inspectors, are aware that no method is valid for all schools, given their diversity. They also realise that the process, which starts with the collection of various data, should not be too complex and that it could pose a problem for the smaller schools.

It is also government policy to increasingly involve the different stakeholders in the management of education. According to the law, teachers, parents and representatives of the community are represented in the various institutions concerned with the different levels. In addition, parents' and teachers' unions are encouraged and supported by financial and human resources, and it is a government policy to promote participative management of schools, as will be seen with the case studies.

Framework

The educational system is based on the principle of freedom of education (art. 24 of Belgian Constitution). Schools can be created and organised without being in any way connected to the official authorities. However, schools wishing to issue recognised diplomas and obtain subsidies from the State or Community must comply with legal and statutory provisions. Individual schools are grouped in 3 large educational networks, each network having its own "umbrella organisation":

- The network of community schools (former State schools), which must conform to special regulations concerning neutrality, received, in 1998-99, 14.4% of the pupils in mainstream basic and secondary education.

- The network of provincial and local schools (or grant-aided official schools), which is attended by 16.6% of the pupils.

- The network of grant-aided free schools groups, which may or not be based on religious principles (though most of them are Catholic), receives 69% of the pupils.

A major difference between the networks is related to the fact that the third one has the right to refuse pupils, in other words, to select those that it wishes to enrol. This right has been recently limited by a "Decree on Primary Education". A pupil cannot be refused admittance, "on the basis of criteria that are improper and violate human dignity". Nevertheless a difference remains, which can be seen by some as a handicap for the public schools, while others consider that it is their specific role to accept children coming from socially and culturally disadvantaged groups.

The evolution towards more autonomy is more drastic in the network of community schools, the subsidised private schools are used to being more autonomous. Decisions concerning the Community schools are shared among three levels: the central level, where the authority is the Council of Community Education; the School Group, where the specific educational policy is designed; and the school. The school head is assisted by a school board, which has only an advisory role.

In terms of finances, the Community is obliged to subsidise the schools run by different organising bodies, whether they are private or public. Schools are not allowed to charge fees for their normal educational activities.

Teaching salary costs are financed on the same criteria for all schools. They are based essentially on the number of students and the level and type (general or vocational) of education. However, they may vary slightly, as it is assumed that there are some economies of scale. As a result, some schools may find it advantageous to split into separate schools, at least from an administrative point of view. This may be purely formal and they may in fact continue to work together. Indeed, there is also a tendency to set up groups of schools which co-operate closely.

For municipal or provincial schools, additional funding may come from the intermediate level, which means that the financial situation of a school may differ according to both the wealth of the municipalities and provinces (small cities have more limited capacities) and also to their political priorities, which may change over time. Other resources may come from European programmes, or from the Ministry of Welfare, when there are specific social needs. They may also be obtained by schools implementing particular programmes, such as: children with special needs; children from immigrant families; or for the implementation of new technologies. These additional funds do not represent more than 1% of the overall budget for education.

Establishing the rights and responsibilities of the state (*i.e.* the Flemish Community) versus the educational providers is a delicate exercise. There is ongoing concern among policy-makers to achieve a careful balance between central goals, standards and targets (the "attainment targets" or "core-curriculum") and school-based planning for curriculum implementation. Therefore, checks and balances have been built into the decision-making process. All stakeholders have been involved in the long process of developing the two core curricula published in 1996 and 1997.

These aims and objectives are expressed in terms of broad competences to be achieved. Part of these competences are subject-related and the other part are cross-curricular. The time devoted to each subject is not laid down and can vary between schools or school networks, though not to a large extent, because the objectives to be achieved are the same. This change has been interpreted as a shift of emphasis from the definition of the process (which is left largely to the schools) to the goals and objectives to be achieved.

More specific curricula may be developed by the organising bodies or by the umbrella organisations of the different networks and become compulsory for the schools. A detailed study plan (syllabus) has to be worked out by the schools or by the organising bodies. It has also to be approved by the Ministry of Education.

Since 1997, primary schools are requested to write their own "work-plan" which covers a wide range of areas, such as: the objectives and the educational project of the school; its organisation; the didactics; the mode of assessment; and the school rules. This is particularly important in view of the fact that there is no longer an officially required division in year groups, subjects or degrees. The time-table is not imposed and the graded system can be abolished, so that the provision of education can be more differentiated and adapted to specific groups of pupils.

At secondary level, there is no national system of examination. At the university level, entrance examinations only concern studies in medicine, dentistry and civil engineering. Specific tests are organised by the network of Catholic schools at the end of elementary education. Many people agree that national tests are not only unnecessary, but would be harmful. It would encourage schools to focus their teaching on the preparation of examinations, rather than on the overall learning process. There is no state control over their content of text books, but publishers and textbook writers use the core curricula and core study plan as the basis for their work.

In Flanders, a document on school regulations is signed at the beginning of the school year, which constitutes an agreement between pupils/parents and the school regarding mutual rights and duties. This document plays an important role in regulating the relationship between the two parties.

Whether they work for public or subsidised private schools, teachers are civil servants and are paid directly by the central administration. Their status, their salaries, and their employment conditions are negotiated at the national level between the Ministry of Education and the unions, which are quite powerful. At the time of the visit, teachers' salaries were a hot issue. Unions were pressing for a salary increase, arguing that there was a shortage of teachers in some areas (maths, computer science) where private employers offer much better salaries. But the Ministry of Education argued that the comfort of teachers and their working conditions were at least as important and determine, to a large extent, the quality of education.

The teachers' unions reject the demands for greater differentation of salaries, which are currently based only on qualifications and seniority. The opportunities for promotion are very limited.

Until recently, staff selection for schools in the Community network was centralised. Now, schools are the employers and recruit teachers and non-teaching personnel on a regional basis. In addition, some large secondary schools can employ personnel for middle management (deputy school heads, advisors and co-ordinators). The subsidised private schools have always been autonomous in staff recruitment.

Schools have an obligation to prepare a plan for the in-service training of their teachers. A budget is earmarked for this purpose and its amount is being increased. The choice of programmes is left to the school principals, after consultation with the teachers.

School teachers used to be supervised by individual inspectors, whose tasks consisted of writing a report on the work of teachers. A completely new system was established in 1991, whereby the focus was no longer on individual teachers, but on schools as organisations. Teams of three or four inspectors visit schools for one week and undertake a comprehensive survey. The process of inspection follows the CIPO method, which implies an analysis of the *context, the input, the process and the output.* It includes a comprehensive analysis of the coherence between the objectives stated by the curriculum and by the school workplan and the work that is actually being done.

Inspectors have informal meetings with teachers, parents and pupils. Previously they gave advice to former State schools on pedagogical matters. Now they are no longer expected to interfere in this area, which is left to the schools and their organising bodies. It is for the latter to provide pedagogical support through their advisors. It may be difficult to clarify the division of responsibilities and the degree of co-operation between inspectors and pedagogical advisors.

One of the tasks of school inspectors is to promote self-evaluation in the school. This should serve as a starting point for their own external evaluation. Relating the two approaches implies that the criteria used by inspectors should be transparent.

The reports of the inspection team, which are the equivalent of an audit, are discussed by the principal and the teachers and serve as a basis for improvement of the school. They are public instruments and may be asked for by the parents, who can take them into account in making their choice of school. Every year, a synthesis of all inspection reports is published as a State of Union in matters of education.

Case Studies

For the last twenty years or so, there has been a tradition of in-service training of school heads in Flanders. There was a variety of courses, often focused on administrative matters. Today, there are two different situations:

- In some municipal schools, as in schools in the City of Antwerp, principals are obliged to follow a training course before being appointed. In community schools there is a certain amount of obligation to get a certificate after an examination or to follow a training course before being appointed.

- The subsidised private schools want to keep their complete freedom to recruit school heads on their own terms while refusing any legal obligation prior to their nomination. However, they are in favour of in-service training for newly-appointed principals.

Pedagogisch Centrum, Antwerp

Established in 1964, this centre is under the authority of the City of Antwerp and works only for the schools which are in the district (employing altogether 4 000 teachers). It has 22 staff members, most of them former teachers. There is only one other similar centre in the country, located in Ghent. It is innovative because it provides initial training for teachers who want to become principals in primary and secondary schools. It also organises a follow-up programme for newly-appointed principals.

The Governing Board of Antwerp has for some time required the candidates for a position of principal to successfully complete a special training course. They should also have a teaching degree and pass a written and oral examination, which includes administrative subjects, exercises and work on a case study.

The initial training course is organised every other year, and lasts for two years. For the current course, 64 candidates have been accepted. Some of them are not planning to become school principals. They find the course interesting and useful, especially for leadership and project preparation training, when they take a middle management job or become inspectors. A few others may not complete the course. Altogether, about 40% of the students will actually become principals at the end of the course.

The emphasis of the course is on human resource management and how to implement change, with a view to creating a learning organisation. Simulation games, video tapes, and role play are used. The total duration of the course is 120 hours spread over two years. It includes:

- A compulsory part of 70 hours, with 16 hours focusing on the Educational Department of Antwerp, 42 hours of weekend training on conflict-resolution, communication and leadership styles, plus 12 hours of work on an exercise.

- An optional part of 50 hours, to be chosen among seven modules: multi-culturalism; educational leadership; lifelong learning; differentiation; policy-making; networking; and quality improvement.

Trainers belong to the centre, but they are also advisors from the city administration. They have to go to the schools and are familiar with the local situation, which may be a starting point for discussions and analysis of case studies. For instance, preparing future principals to handle situations of aggression and violence is very important. Visits to other schools are also essential, because teachers and principals tend to stay in their own school and usually do not know anything about the others.

The follow-up programme is aimed at supporting newly-appointed principals of primary, secondary and special needs schools. Its two-year duration corresponds to their initial contract. There are seven half-day meetings per year and a lunch with all participants at the end of the programme. The follow-up programme is based on the recognition that transferring the concepts learnt in the course into daily practice is always difficult. Even more emphasis should be placed on this problem, by organising meetings between the newly-appointed principals and more experienced colleagues.

The best result of the programme is to create contacts between participants. "You need a social context for the professional learning of adults. You have to start from the problems that they perceive and to relate them to broader issues, rather than the opposite" as one participant commented. The participants often wish to continue this relationship after the end of the programme, not so much to get more information, but rather to have an opportunity to talk among themselves on an informal basis. Organising such meetings is currently difficult, because they are "drowned in the daily work". It is necessary to find the time, and to convince the administration, to support such contacts.

Centre for Adult Education, University of Antwerp

The Centre for Adult Education is an autonomous institute within the University of Antwerp. It provides post-academic educational programmes and undertakes research. At the request of the umbrella organisation of Catholic schools, it started a programme for newly-appointed school principals and vice-principals in the 1970s. Later on, the programme was subsidised by the Ministry of Culture and extended to other networks.

The programme is demand-oriented in that it attempts to mobilise the trainees to work as a group and as a learning organisation. The emphasis has shifted since the 1980s, when it started to focus on quality management and change. Today, the organisers consider that priority should be given to preparing schools to assume their responsibilities and missions with regard to the new social and cultural concerns (immigration, internationalisation, environment, values). The other priority is new technologies.

The programme is spread over a period of three years and includes, each year, a 3-day residential seminar and 8 other meetings. From the beginning, emphasis is put on group work as the participants have to know each other and constitute a group by themselves (which is the purpose of the residential session). At the end of the course, the participants are required to evaluate the contents, the methods and the teachers. The evaluation is used to constantly revise the contents of the programme, which includes information on legislation and administration, but is largely focused on leadership, problem-solving, communication and evaluation.

Here again, there is a demand for a continuation of these meetings, "the only place where principals say that they can relax from the pressure and learn from each other" to quote one participant.

The Institute for Paramedical Professions, Ghent

This is a public school, placed under the responsibility of the city of Ghent. It has 130 teachers and 600 students in regular middle school classes (grades 7 and 8), pre-vocational and vocational classes for medical occupations, and special classes of general education for children from immigrant families who do not master Dutch.

There are six departments located in different buildings, each with a distinct activity and a semi-autonomous management, under the responsibility of a co-ordinator. There is a staff meeting every week to ensure efficient co-ordination, and a lunch with all co-ordinators, which focuses on a specific topic is held on Tuesdays. The principal has been in charge for ten years. He has established an innovative and participative style of management. Innovation does not follow a top-down approach but is the result of a local initiative, leading to a new project when there is a problem. The participants are normally volunteers.

Participation implies that a maximum of freedom is left to the co-ordinators and to the teachers. The teachers see this freedom as an advantage which also benefits the students. For the principal, it should be clear that a democratic and tolerant approach does not lead to a complete "laissez-faire" attitude. Group work is encouraged rather than imposed, motivating staff members to set up informal groups to develop activities and projects which attract others and serve as an inspiration for pupils.

As many of the students are socially disadvantaged or are members of immigrant families, there are remedial teachers for pupils with learning problems. Social education and making the school as attractive as possible are considered most important. Building a personal relationship with the pupils is esssential, especially for those who need to be motivated to study and have no possibility to prepare lessons at home. Activities are organised with them during lunch time and every effort is made to establish contacts with the families.

The students' council, which has representatives from each class, meets sometimes with a teacher, who acts as a go-between with the other teachers, and sometimes without a teacher. One teacher commented "their demands are reasonable, they do not ask too much: revolutionary ideas come from the teachers, rather than from the pupils". They are said to be happy in the school, "many of them do not like the class, but they like the school". There is a special atmosphere in the school and for some of them it is their second home. As a whole, pupils are very active in organising fund-raising activities, such as concerts, flea-markets or barbecues.

Vocational education is provided, based on an integrated method: pupils work on projects adapted to real situations, and both teachers and students work in teams. Every student has a mentor during the whole process.

The vocational department is intended particularly for children with social and behavioural problems, who do not like school. For such children, it is important to create a home atmosphere. Small groups of 10 to 13 pupils are organised on the basis of projects. They run their own bank account with the money raised from different activities. There is constant discussion with the students, either at the group level, or on an individual basis. Listening to the pupils is seen as important, not only from a humanistic or social point of view, but also as an efficient way to motivate them for learning. The students' council meets regularly, setting its own rules. The group and the individual students feel responsible and have a sense of ownership in the school. Thanks to this approach, behavioural and discipline problems, which are frequent at the beginning, disappear after a few months. Some pupils even find leaving the school and continuing their studies in a more traditional context difficult.

The middle school department (general education and 1st grade of vocational education) is the only one in the country, at that level, to follow the Freinet principles of pedagogy. Learning is based on experience, creativity, emphasis on aesthetics and equality, and elder pupils help the younger ones. Some of these principles are also implemented in other departments, although they are not considered as belonging to the Freinet type of school. The department also emphasises project work, on-going evaluation and communication. It organises class meetings with a pupil as president. Students' representatives and parents are also invited to staff meetings. Pupils participate in an e-mail network with other Freinet schools, in Flanders, France and the Netherlands.

The teachers who choose to belong to this department have to be open-minded since many teachers tend to focus only on the preparation of examinations. For the school as a whole, the integration of teachers into its special management style depends to some extent on their own initiative. Most of them are satisfied with this management style and therefore there is no need to formalise the integration procedure.

Middenschool: H. *Hart*, B*ree*

This is a Catholic school located in a small town near the Dutch border. It provides only the first grades (7 and 8) of secondary education to 400 pupils, with a staff of 52 (46 teachers). 10% of pupils in grade 7 have learning disabilities and follow a special programme. In grade 8, there is a pre-vocational stream to prepare some of the pupils for their future career choice. The school has relocated recently to a new building, where three schools with different cultures have merged. The principal has been in this job for ten years.

The management style and the work of the school are based on an "Educational Project" developed by the staff, in co-operation with the parents and students. It defines the aims, objectives and values which are referred to constantly. On the basis of this document, which is revised every two or three years, other documents are prepared every year in the same participative way:

- The design of educational priorities, such as: learning how to learn, co-operative learning, progressive evaluation and participation of pupils.
- The school work-plan.
- The in-service training plan.

The Governing Board includes representatives from the religious congregation and local people. Participation is ensured through a "participation board" and by three committees of parents, of teachers and of pupils. The principal is also assisted by co-ordinators and by leaders of informal working groups.

There are seven teacher coordinators who, in addition to their teaching load, assist the principal by co-ordinating specific activities including subjects (*e.g.* mathematics teachers); pedagogical organisation; time-tables; planning of tests. In addition, the school is divided into 4 groups of 4 classes each and there is a "cluster manager" for each class. Each class also has its own tutor, who is the first contact with the pupils in case a problem arises.

Finally, there are also *ad hoc* working groups in such areas as: sports; festivities; European activities, etc. All teachers are expected to participate in at least one working group. In the beginning, only some teachers participated, while others tended to be critical. Now they all appreciate, and get to know each other better.

The relationship with the parents is changing too. In the past, they were met on an individual basis in connection with reports, complaints or negative evaluations. Now a broader view of the student population is taken with parents participating in the school as collaborators. Twenty parents, who are volunteers, meet six or seven times a year with the principal and are active in the work of the school.

The students' council includes representatives from each class. It elects a chairperson, vice-chairpersons, secretaries and a treasurer. The members receive two days of intensive training in communication skills. The council meets at least once a month and has three areas of responsabilities:

- Information on the objectives and the work of the school.
- Advice on school regulations, the organisation of extra activities, the time-table, the organisation of tests, etc.
- Decisions on the playground and on the use of the students' council budget.

Decisions are taken by consensus and not by vote. Two teachers attend the meetings, but they do not participate in the discussions. There are also two speci-alised councils for sports and environment issues.

Additional responsibilities assumed by the teachers imply more training. The in-service training plan is prepared with their participation and is related to the educational priorities defined yearly. Tutors receive three days of training focused on life-skills and issues such as relationships with pupils' families, violence, drugs, etc. Talking to the parents requires a special skill and training may help.

Evaluation, which used to be the work of the principal at the end of the year, is now an on-going process which involves all the staff. Achievements are assessed with reference to the objectives set by the various annual documents. Evaluation reports are used as a basis for improving work for the future. Every year, there is an evaluation meeting with the principal.

Innovation and Effectiveness

Self-evaluation is a policy orientation adopted by the government, but its implementation is left to the school leaders. Participative school management is largely a local initiative. Both are part of a broader policy, which includes several inter-related priorities, including evaluation, responsibility, continuing training of the staff, and an increasing school autonomy. All of them are expected to improve the quality of education and the attractiveness of the schools. In the context of this study, two questions arise: the effectiveness of these innovations and their transferability throughout the country.

Effectiveness could be seen from different points of view. Concerning the school achievements, a teacher from the paramedical school pointed out that a pleasant atmosphere and a personal relationship with the students considerably increased their motivation and therefore their performances. There has also been an interest in Flanders in measuring the quality of education by using instruments which are based on industrial quality concepts. But a rather cautious approach

71

seems to have been followed. For one thing, teachers are not familiar with this type of language. More importantly, a simple transfer of those concepts to the field of education would raise fundamental problems. The goals pursued by a school are very different from those of a private enterprise and the results cannot be assessed over a short period.

With regard to the dissemination of innovations, it is clear that in a context of increased school autonomy, the success depends to a very large extent on the school leaders and that the most innovative schools are often managed by charismatic personalities. On the other hand, comments heard during the visits only confirm what can be found in the international literature: the range of responsibilities of school-heads is increasing, and their burden is becoming heavier. They are faced with a huge number of tasks for which the majority of them are not prepared. They are said to be isolated between the policy-makers and the school staff and often left to themselves to face the problems.

This raises at least three problems, which are common to many countries but may be spelled out in specific terms in the Flemish context:

- How to recruit good leaders? As mentioned earlier, the teaching profession as a whole does not seem to be very attractive. It is even more so with the principals, whose salary is not very different from that of a teacher, despite the additional workload and responsibilities. Finding enough candidates of good quality may become a problem. But salary is not the sole element to be taken into consideration, working conditions and appropriate support are also important.

- Training is the first way to help principals and it is crucial. Valuable experiences are illustrated by the first case studies. It is interesting to observe that in both cases, training is focused, not on administrative and technical matters, but on management of people and on the relationship with the school environment. However, some people feel the need for an evaluation of existing programmes in order to produce a well-structured programme available for all. But it is understood that the private networks do not want to make it a preliminary requirement. They insist on keeping their freedom to define the selection criteria.

- Principals feel isolated, and the case studies illustrate remedies such as promoting group work in the school and networking with their peers.

But there is limited time available for meetings and contacts for the school leaders and their staff, who participate on a voluntary basis. Teachers are not expected to stay in school outside their teaching hours (20 to 22 hours per week).

According to the paramedical school, the main challenge is to motivate the staff to introduce innovations. Some of the school principals recognise that all teachers are not enthusiastic about a participative style of management. A tension may exist between two types of teachers: those who are more eager to listen and to dialogue; and those who are biased towards structure, order and discipline.

The principal of the middle school in Bree has succeeded in persuading practically all teachers to participate in at least one group activity, but it has taken a long time. One of her staff members recalls that, "at the beginning, she saw it as a passive gathering of non-coherent organisation; but now she sees it as in-house action-research and evaluation, sharing information and professionalisation". Similarly, while developing a school workplan may be seen as an additional burden, it also provides a very good opportunity to think and work in a team and to prepare a framework that the school has to fill.

Staff members of the same school have stated the conditions under which they think a participative culture can flourish. The school leader should:

- Be a convincing missionary of the school mission.
- Have a strong belief in the promotion of each participant and a strong commitment to realise the most optimal conditions for all.
- Have strong organisational qualities to make a learning organisation possible.
- Recognise that team members have specific tasks and responsibilities.
- Attend courses and participate in debates about innovations in education.
- Take into consideration the recommendations of the review of the policy plan.
- Be a dynamic, enthusiastic, flexible coach, proficient in social and communication skills.

The process of innovation seems to be primarily a matter of transforming the school into a "learning organisation". It requires some personal qualities of the leaders which can be developed through training. It implies changing the culture and the attitudes, which takes time. According to an official, "it takes more time than in the private business, where you can see more quickly the results". He also stresses that changing human relationships cannot be an entirely informal process, it requires organisational support.

Attitudes concern not only the staff but also the parents. Immigrant families often do not like too much freedom in the school. Although the Freinet principles practiced by the paramedical school looked particularly attractive, only a minority of parents are willing to put their children in this type of class. Most of them are more concerned with success at examinations.

The significance of the Flemish experience should be seen in relation to its specific context:

- Flanders is a country open to the outside world. Also its culture does not seem to be based primarily on a hierarchical relationship but instead favours co-operation and group work.

- In view of its small size (and of the comparatively small size of the schools), people tend to know each other and have a comparatively easier relationship, which facilitates the dissemination of innovations and more personal contact with students.

- The multiplicity of school networks, and the fact that most of the schools are private and subsidised means they enjoy a considerable degree of freedom. The Flemish authorities are permanently trying to strike a balance between central steering and respecting the freedom of the schools. Therefore, checks and balances are built into the decision-making processes. At the same time, the different levels and centres of decision-making and the various regulations are a source of confusion, and potential conflict which makes the work of school leaders more complex. Some see a need for more transparency.

On the other hand, the diversity, the multiplicity of structures and decision-making centres may contribute to the flexibility of the system. The government policy of decentralisation should promote innovation. What the most innovative leaders are asking for is simply the freedom to experiment. They say that you should not be afraid to innovate, but some of them feel that the government does not realise how difficult it is.

Flexibility and experimentation should be seen against the specific background of the Flemish approach to the regulation of education and the concepts of evaluation and of inspection. This encourages competition between schools striving for quality, rather than a central system of planning and examination.

Bibliography

BRAECKMANS, L., MAHIEU, P. and van HOREBEEK, G. (1998),
De schoolleider in beeld. 25 jaar directie-opleidinge ("Focus on the school-leader. 25 years in-service training of principals"), Garant, Leuven-Apeldoorn.

CLEMENT, M. and VANDENBERGH, R. (2000),
"Teachers Professional Development: A Solitary or Collegial (ad)venture?", Teaching and Teacher Education, 16.

DEVOS, G. (1995),
De flexibilisering van het secundair onderwijs in Vlaanderen ("Flexibility in secondary education in Flanders), Acco, Leuven-Amersfoort.

DEVOS, G., VERHOEVEN, J.C., van den BROECK, H. and VANDENBERGHE, R. (1999),
De rol van de schoolbesturen in het schoolmanagement ("The role of the school governing board in school management"), Garant, Leuven-Apeldoorn.

LAUMEN, R. (1992),
Reorganisatie van de inspectie van het onderwijs ("Re-organisation of the school inspectorate"), Tijdschrift voor Onderwijsrecht en Onderwijsbeleid, 2, pp. 75-82.

MICHIELSEN, P. (1998),
Schoolleiderschap. Op zoek naar identiteit ("School leadership. Looking for an identity"), Ministerie van de Vlaamse Gemeenschap, Departement Onderwijs, Brussels.

MINISTRY OF THE FLEMISH COMMUNITY, EDUCATION DEPARTMENT (1997),
Secondary Education in Flanders. Core Curriculum. Final Objectives and Development Aims of the First Cycle of Regular Secondary Education, Brussels.

OECD (1998),
Education at a Glance – OECD Indicators, Paris.

PEETERS, K. (1992),
Na scholing nascholing. Naar een professionalisering van de nascholing voor leraren ("Towards of a professionalisation of in-service-training for teachers"), Garant, Leuven-Apeldoorn.

PEETERS, K., van CAUWENBERGHE, A., SCHOLLAERT, R. and COUCKE, H. (1996),
Spiegel-effecten. De Vlaamse decretale navorming doorgelicht ("An evaluation of the Flemish legal regulation for in-service training"), Garant, Leuven-Apeldoorn.

VAN HOYWEGHEN, D. and HOSTENS, G. (2000),
Education in Flander, Ministry of the Flemish Community, Education Department, Unpublished document, Brussels.

VANDENBERGHE, R. (1995),
"Creative Management of a School. A Matter of Vision and Daily Interventions", Journal of Educational Administration, Vol. 33, pp. 31-51.

VANDENBERGHE, R. (1998),
"Thinking about Principals: How they Cope with External Pressures and Redefinition of their Role", *International Journal of Educational Research*, 29.

VERHOEVEN, J.C., JEGERS, M. and van HEDDEGEM, I. (1997),
Participatieraden en lokale schoolraden in Vlaanderen: de eerste jaren (Participation councils and local school councils in Flanders: the first implementation years), Garant, Leuven-Apeldoorn.

GREECE

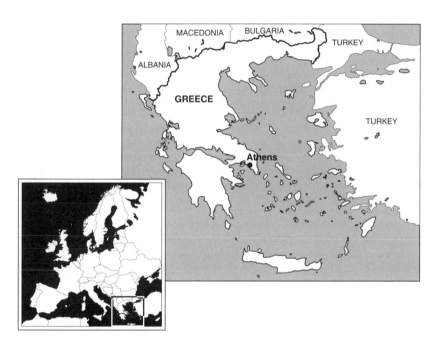

Land area in square kilometers: 132 000

Total population (1998): 10 507 000

Per capita GDP (1999 prices): 14 800 USD

Percentage of GDP on education (1997): 3.5%

Amount spent per student (1997):
- – 2 351 USD (Primary)
- – 2 581 USD (Secondary)

Teacher salary range (1998):
- – 19 280-28 521 USD (Primary)
- – 19 871-29 165 USD (Secondary)

Sources: Labour Force Statistics: 1978-1998, OECD, Paris, 1999; *Main Economic Indicators*, OECD, Paris, April 2000; *Education at a Glance – OECD Indicators 2000*, OECD, Paris, 2000.

Country context

To understand recent changes in school management in Greece it is necessary to consider political, economic, demographic and social changes that have occurred since 1945. A Civil War in the mid-1940s was followed by a constitutional monarchy that lasted until 1967, when it was replaced by the military dictatorship that ended in 1974. Since then, Greece has been a presidential parliamentary republic with a written constitution. Given this history, it is not surprising that words like "authority, control, inspection and management" need to be used cautiously in any discussion about the governance of educational institutions.

Economically, Greece has moved rapidly from being heavily dependent on primary resources, such as agriculture, fishing and quarrying, to a more diverse range of employment, including tourism, commercial and manufacturing industries. These changes have impacted on schooling as increasing prosperity has led to higher parental and student expectations. These have been expressed in higher participation rates in upper secondary schools and institutions of tertiary and higher education and the expansion of full-time and part-time private schooling (see the case of study of Latseion). There has also been a greater demand for vocational education at secondary schools and beyond.

Demographically, the last fifty years have been characterised by population growth, rural depopulation and urban expansion and periods of emigration. This has involved the in-migration of returning migrants and the immigration of persons from neighbouring countries. Cities have grown in area and population density resulting in school overcrowding (see the case study of Eighth Lower). The demand for more schools in the cities, while enrolment has declined in rural and island communities, has posed quite different problems for educational planners.

Since the establishment of the modern Greek state in 1832, Greece has had a long tradition of a highly centralised, tightly regulated system of education. Legislation determines the organisation of schools, the national curriculum, the funding arrangements for schools and all aspects of school staffing. In recent decades, the government has sought to decentralise, deregulate and de-bureaucratise public administration, in general, and education, in particular.

Challenges Facing School Management

Greece has three levels of schooling: primary (compulsory for students aged 6-12 years); lower secondary (compulsory for students aged 12-15 years); and upper secondary (optional for students aged 15-18 years). The upper secondary level has, since 1997, been divided into two types of schools: general secondary (*eniaio lykeio*); and technical and vocational schools (*technika epaggelmatika ekpaideftiriai*). All schools in Greece, including secondary schools are admininistered by the Ministry of National Education and Religious Affairs. School attendance for the nine primary and lower secondary years was made compulsory in 1976. For all schools, the central government has: defined the content of the national curriculum; recommended appropriate teaching methods; published textbooks; allocated funding; legislated for participation by various stakeholders in schooling; determined student examinations; and has taken responsibility for the organisation of schools, including all aspects of staffing.

The main challenges relate to government intentions to decentralise and deregulate the education system, as well as the interest shown in some schools to take a more pro-active role in their management. There have been difficulties both in the delegation of administrative duties from the Ministry to the Prefectures, and in the linkages between the prefectures and individual schools. The tradition of schools having to seek governmental approval for any changes they may wish to make has inhibited school-initiated innovation. The central government has been slow to introduce innovation at the local school level.

Traditionally, principals have been administrators who are expected to follow decisions taken at central level. They have had no specific training to become principals. They are appointed at regional level and the selection process, controversially, allows local communities, parents' associations, as well as elected teacher representatives to participate. In schools the only authority the principals have had is related to discipline and to co-ordination of school activities. There have been several attempts to break with tradition but the structures and the system have proven very resistant to change. This is not to say that there is a lack of awareness of the challenges facing schools in preparing young people for a fast-changing world or to ignore the attempts to give greater managerial responsibility to principals and other stake-holders in the schools. As part of its moves to give schools more autonomy and accountability, the Ministry wants principals to take on more of a managerial role, as opposed to their more usual administrative duties.

Main Policy Approaches

The decentralisation of various aspects of school administration was expressed by government legislation passed during the 1980s. A new framework for education, introduced in a law in 1985 (Law 1566/1985), allowed regional and

79

local authorities, as well as representatives from teachers' unions and parents' organisations, to participate in decision-making processes (Kassotakis and Lambrakis-Paganos, 1994). The introductory report to this law emphasised the importance of decentralisation, and provision was made for the transfer of funds and responsibilities to Prefectures. In addition, ownership and management of school property were transferred to public bodies. The law also extended the participation of the key education stakeholders, such as parents' and teachers' unions, in the management, planning and control of schools (Introductory Report, Law 1566/1985).

While the media and various stakeholders welcomed this legislation, it proved difficult to implement. This applied not only to education but also to all aspects of public administration in Greece. As shown in numerous research projects undertaken by Greek social scientists (Kazamias and Kassotakis, 1995), the centralised structures were quite resistant to change. It is interesting to notice that, according to one of these projects, centralisation was still quite strong in public administration in the early 1990s compared to previous decades (Sotiropoulos, 1993).

While various administrative schemes requiring wide participation were adopted, this did not include the transfer of authority and responsibilities to schools or local authorities to engage in policy-making. The role and status of key stakeholders, such as parents, teachers and local communities, remained extremely limited, while the role of the school principal continued to be that of an administrator with no substantial authority at the school level.

During the 1990s, there have been renewed calls for substantial decentralisation and transfer of powers to the regions and the schools themselves (Markou, 1991; Andreou and Papakonstantinou, 1994; Kazamias and Kassotakis, 1995). Recent educational legislation (1997) attempted to pass some responsibilities to regional and school levels. In particular, recommendations were made regarding school self-evaluation and these have been of considerable importance in redefining the responsibilities of school principals. It must be emphasised that the move towards school self-evaluation is a deliberate attempt to avoid re-establishing a system of external school inspection, a discredited practice which was in place until the beginning of the 1980s and which applied strict political and moral control.

The most recent legislation (Law 2817/2000) addressed the government's decentralisation agenda. Recognising that there were difficulties in the transfer of funding from Prefectures to individual schools, the government proposed the grouping of the 54 Prefectures into 13 groups, each headed by a new director. However, in June 2000, the new Minister of Education decided to abandon the grouping of Prefectures. The new plan is to decentralise the whole administrative structure of education in order to be more effective. It is important to note (as the case studies show) that some schools are gaining experience in handling school budgets through funding for national and transnational projects provided by Greek and European Union sources.

With regard to the curriculum, the Ministry has identified three dimensions that need to be acknowledged – the European, the national and the local. It was suggested that the national curriculum be modified in order to allow 20% of it to be responsive to local needs. However, this innovation has not yet been put into practice, with the exception of some history courses in certain regions. With regard to the European dimension, there was a need to balance movements towards harmonisation in the European Union with the interests of local communities. It was recognised that, in the upper secondary school, there was a need to enrich the curriculum through the introduction of new courses and subjects. For each course, textbooks had to be written and new examinations introduced. In the budget for 2000-2001 the central government budgeted for the modernisation of the general, technical and vocational curriculum and a reduction of content for student examinations.

Framework

As has already been stated, the central government takes full responsibility for all aspects of school staffing. School principals are appointed at a prefectural level for a contractual period of four years. The appointment decision has to be approved by the Ministry. Central to the selection and appointment process are the teaching competence, qualifications and length of experience of the candidates for promotion. Usually, a principal will have been a vice-principal who applies to be included in the prefectural list of potential principals. There has never been a provision for the formal, professional training of principals. A very recent development, in response to principals' interest in self-evaluation, and recent government pronouncements, has been a new provision by the Greek Open University. Distance learning modules in school management can now be studied on a voluntary basis by principals, teachers and other personnel who may be interested.

The responsibilities of principals and vice-principals are specified by law. Most of these duties would be described as administrative. They require the principal to ensure that the following central requirements are being met in the school:

- Co-ordinating various activities in the school.
- Checking the legitimacy of these activities.
- Representing the staff (at local or regional level).
- Keeping the records of both students and staff.
- Managing the site (campus, facilities, equipment).
- Managing the budget of the school.

81

It should be noted that the budget only concerns the maintenance of buildings and some student activities. Local municipalities are directly involved in school management, controlling the flow of financial resources to the school and setting limits on the authority of principals. It should also be noted that principals are expected to teach classes on a regular basis. But their hours spent in teaching are limited due to their administrative tasks. Each school has a Teachers' Council that has some responsibility for issues related to student discipline, and day-to-day problems that may occur in the school. Outside the school and beyond the municipalities, parents (according to 1985 legislation) have the right to form a union in every school and, through that union, participate in some limited aspects of school administration. More specifically, a representative of the parents' union participates in a School Council along with the principal, the deputy-principal and a representative of the students' union. The School Council advises on the management of the school's day-to-day operations (*e.g.* communications, hygiene, etc.). The School Committee, made up of the principal, a community representative (*e.g.* the Mayor) and representatives from the parents' and students' unions, is responsible for budget management and fund-raising.

Recently, some pilot schools were able to participate, at their own request, in projects financed by the Europeen Union, with the aim of improving their infrastructure and the running of the school. The results seem to be positive, as shown by the case studies below.

Schools may innovate but they do so under close scrutiny and regulation. In the case studies, three of the four schools are participating in the Reorganisation of Premises Project. This project, started in one school in 1995, has now been extended to many more schools with formal approval required from the Ministry. The project focuses on lower secondary schools concerning the change from general students' classrooms to subject specialist classrooms.

Traditionally, every class has had its own classroom to which specialist teachers came to teach. By abandoning this, it was hoped that principals could end the serious and pervasive damage to school premises and equipment. Indicative of the centralised nature of the Greek educational system, schools wishing to participate in the project had to meet stringent criteria relating to: the number and size of classrooms; the amount of free space to accommodate students' lockers; and the support of the school's teachers' association and the parents' association. This project has given principals the opportunity to make important decisions at the school level. It is one of the rare occasions that principals have been given authority, responsibility and additional financial resources to implement a specific project.

Private schools in Greece, both primary and secondary, are much more autonomous than state schools. Although they are required to conform to state requirements for the curriculum and the use of textbooks, they are able to enhance the curriculum and purchase extra resources. They have their own budgets, can hire and fire princi-pals and teachers and institute their own planning and control mechanisms. Any majeur changes to the curriculum must be approved by the Ministry of Education.

The framework established for the governance of schools in the public sector gave principals the choice, in the words of a lower secondary school teacher: "to close the office door and stay closely with the government's minimum require-ments or open the door to find opportunities for improving the school." From dis-cussions with practitioners in the schools it would appear that great emphasis is placed on the importance of the principal as a classroom teacher with a range of personal qualities and skills, particularly associated with inter-personal communi-cation. There is less emphasis on managerial skills concerning: budgets; staff development; delegation of duties; curriculum innovation and evaluation; and the management of change. It is against this background that the following case studies of four schools illustrate aspects of new management approaches in Greece.

Case Studies

Eighth Lower Secondary School in Athens

This is an inner city, multi-cultural school located in one of the relatively deprived areas of Athens. Opened in 1931 as a model school for the city of Athens, it gained private funding for the purchase of specialist teaching equipment (e.g. scientific laboratory equipment) and for the maintenance of the buildings. At the time, the area was characterised by open spaces and floral gardens, scenery difficult to envisage in terms of the current densely populated, traffic congested environment.

Some of the students of the 1930s became distinguished scholars and politi-cians, including prime ministers. During World War II the school was closed and the buildings served military purposes. In the Civil War it became a base for one of the sides. In the 1950s there was a need to re-establish the school as a compre-hensive (13-18 years) secondary school, and it regained its good academic, cultural and sporting reputation.

However, major changes in the local community were to alter radically the nature of the school. More prosperous families moved to the outer suburbs to be replaced by poorer residents. Urban expansion was accompanied by an influx of migrants from the former Soviet Union, Albania, the former Yugoslavia and from parts of Africa and the Middle East. The school lost its local community support. The increased size of population led to a demand for new schools and for the improve-ment of existing buildings, but the necessary public funding was not available. The result has been that the school site is now occupied by eight discrete schools, oper-ating in three shifts: morning; afternoon; and evening. There are elementary schools, lower secondary schools (day and evening) and upper secondary schools, each with its own principal and teachers.

During the visit by the OECD, the principal presented a photographic record to illustrate the graffiti and vandalism that characterised the classrooms and public spaces at the time of his appointment two years earlier. He described graphically the threat to personal safety that had been posed by the presence of drug dealers, the damage to students' lockers and the stealing of school equipment by intruders. He suggested that there had been a reluctance on the part of school staff to change things, as they felt that any solution was doomed to failure.

The principal emphasised that at the time of his appointment, in 1997, on a four-year contract, the school was at its lowest ebb, epitomised by the "lock-outs" of staff by the students. Of these students, nearly half were non-Greek speakers of foreign origin, some of whom had difficulty adjusting to the cultural norms of the Greek community.

Faced with these major problems – multiple use of the restricted site, deteriorating classrooms and public spaces in the school, loss of equipment, juvenile delinquency and local crime – the new principal took a number of steps to try to rectify the situation. He sought support from the municipal authority to clear up the damage in the school and encouraged parents to take a positive interest. An awareness of the "Reorganisation of School Premises Project" led to an application to the Pedagogical Institute to participate in improving the school.

What is particularly interesting is the role of principals in project initiation and management. In this school, given the multiple usage of the site, it was necessary to gain the support of other principals, teachers and parents. It should be noted that the school failed initially to meet the criteria for participation in the project (*e.g.* it had more than one shift). The Pedagogical Institute also needed assurance that all of the principals on the site were keen to engage in the project. It was agreed that the shift problem could be put aside but gaining the necessary consensus of principals proved more difficult. A single School Committee, comprising representatives of parents, teachers, students and principals for all of the schools, supported the project application. Eventually, in 1999, after a year of negotiation, it was agreed that the sum of three million drachmas would be made available to the site, divided into three equal parts among three of the schools. These principals had to agree on how they would manage the project budget.

One year later, some of the project outcomes were clearly evident. The amount of graffiti, while not absent, had been considerably reduced. The buildings were secure, with new locks and alarm systems in the classrooms. It was now possible to store video equipment and teaching materials in classrooms. Steps had been taken to define subject-based classrooms to house specialist subject-related teaching materials. Students' lockers, that lined the school corridors, were generally more secure.

The school had also been engaged in other funded projects. At the time of the visit a new library, located in a converted storage building and funded as part of a municipal project, was being stocked with furniture and books. In addition, the school had received special funding to buy scientific and ICT equipment.

The principal emphasised that, on this site, co-ordinating resources was a key role for each of the principals. Clearly, there was a need for effective co-ordination if the resources made available from the Reorganisation of School Premises Project were to be used fully. This co-ordination extended beyond the principals to the municipality, the parents, the teachers and the students. The principal also spoke about the need for principals to be resilient and persistent in their search for support and funding, while not being discouraged in the face of difficulties. In particular, he referred to the need for principals to be reflective, with a clear sense of direction and vision. He argued that "education was not about the value of drachmas but about the value of the child as an individual".

Second Lower Secondary School of Agia Paraskevi

Located in a prosperous Athens suburb, this school has 293 students (aged 12-15 years) and 33 teachers. It has an attractive site in the foothills of Hemitos with trees and bushes surrounding modern buildings. The school was refurbished and extended in 1995, coinciding with the engagement of the school in the Reorganisation of School Premises Project.

The vice-principal, who had been employed at the school for eighteen years and had been the vice-principal for twelve, described vacations he had spent in the United States where he had visited secondary schools. He had been impressed by their organisation and resources. In particular, he observed subject specialist classrooms, an arrangement then lacking in his school. The introduction of specialist classrooms and the provision of specialist equipment were evident in the way the school had used the three million drachmas that had been made available in 1995-1996 by the Pedagogical Institute for the Reorganisation of School Premises Project. It had been designated as a pilot school in this project and was regarded as one of most successful participants. The proposal to be a participant in the project had to be approved by the Ministry of National Education and Religious Affairs. Initially ten schools were selected as pilot schools and 100 schools across Greece were engaged in the project.

The subject specialities of the classrooms were clearly evident. Each classroom had specialist furniture, teaching materials with appropriate storage space and display areas. The music room was laid out with music stands and the walls were lined with musical instruments. These instruments, enough for a whole class, had been bought with a special grant made available by the local municipality who wished to create a school band for special functions. In addition, there were specialist rooms for such subjects as science, mathematics, ICT, history and languages.

It was emphasised that it was essential for a principal to have a vision for the school that "was shared with the teachers". By giving teachers specialist rooms, it was argued that teachers were able to put their own personality into their work. Classrooms and their resources were respected, and damage was reduced. There was a remarkable absence of graffiti or other forms of vandalism in this school. The improved level of security afforded by the reorganised classrooms encouraged the Parents' Association to fund the purchase of teaching materials.

It was also essential for a principal to have more awareness of sources of funding by working closely with the municipality and other groups in the community. In this school there were four examples of how a school was able to enhance its resource base:

- The school had a theatre, with a crescent of seating and a well-equipped stage, located in a separate building at the school entrance. These facilities were shared with the local community and adult education classes were held in it. It provided a valuable link between the school and the local community and special funds were made available by the municipality to support it.

- Another community resource was the basketball court, used as a public open-air cinema during the summer, for which the school receives payment.

- The school had allocated space for an office and consultation room for a vocational guidance officer who served a number of schools. The school benefited not only from having this specialist on site but also from funding for the rooms.

- The school was one of the pilot schools in a library project. Funds from this project had enabled the school to refurbish a former storage area for a new school library. Staffing for the library was provided by the project for one year and funding was also available for appropriate furniture and publications.

The school was also one of six pilot schools in the "Self-evaluation Project" that was scheduled for two years from 1998 to 2000. The project was co-ordinated by the Pedagogical Institute and involved teachers, parents and students in the evaluation process. Guidance to the schools in developing school-evaluation methodologies was provided in a handbook (Solomon, 1999) published by the Pedagogical Institute. This identified evaluation criteria and techniques. The function of the self-evaluation project was school improvement: self-evaluation was seen as a less threatening alternative to a system of external inspection.

In addition to these national projects, the school also engaged in a number of smaller scale projects associated with parts of the curriculum (*e.g.* the Globe environmental project). The school had recently participated in an international video-conference as part of another curriculum-based project.

It was clear that this was a very active school and the enthusiasm of the senior staff and teachers to innovate led to many new developments being tried out in the school. It was stated that "Success breeds success". For the principal and vice-principal there was a need to have both a vision for the future of the school and the capability to co-ordinate the various activities. The school met the requirements set out in legislation but sought to enhance the curriculum by going beyond the minimum specifications and adding extra-curricular activities. The vice-principal spoke about the need for teachers to be inspired by senior staff. It was important for the school to be seen by the teachers as a "whole organisation" in which they are a team. But the importance of the individual was not neglected. To quote the background paper produced for this study: "There seems to be a sense of a common purpose that is respected by all stakeholders…Parents are now more actively involved in many activities and they definitely support the project. They also give small donations for equipment such as music stands, costumes for drama performances, etc. The president of their association feels that it is partly their responsibility to keep the school at the top."

Experimental School of Athens University

As in a previous case study, this school occupies a site that is shared by more than one school. Located in the central business district of Athens, the school is situated on a busy street. On the site is an elementary school for some 210 students with its own principal and a unified lower secondary and upper secondary school. There are 130 lower secondary students and 141 upper secondary students. Despite its title, the school had, since the legislation of 1985, no close connection with the University of Athens. The School Committee was comprised of representatives of parents, teachers and students and did not include a representative from the university, although a Professor of the Department of the Science of Education was nominated as overseer of the school. It was a state school receiving its funding from the municipality. Until six years earlier, the primary and secondary schools operated as a single school. The school has a good reputation related to its examination results and there is excessive demand for places. Students are chosen by lottery, replacing a system of selection by examination that had been followed until the 1980s. This selection system only applies in a small number of experimental schools. Other establishments are obliged to receive students from clearly defined districts.

The principal emphasised that a major effort was needed in the school to bridge what appeared to be a considerable gap – the needs of the school and the limits for change set by the law. The target was to meet the legal requirements and then go beyond them but it was difficult to innovate in a centralised system. The

87

Ministry had invited proposals for changes but the administrative and bureaucratic arrangements meant that it was difficult to obtain the necessary approval to initiate changes. Innovation was always risky as there was the threat of being held accountable if the tight lines defining legal requirements were violated.

The school is seventy years old and, not surprisingly, the premises are one of its weak points. Participation in the Reorganisation of School Premises Project was seen as a good opportunity to refurbish the school and improve the atmosphere and, hopefully, the effectiveness of the school. As in a previous case study, the principal presented a photographic album showing the state of the buildings in 1998. Corridors and classrooms had been covered in graffiti, there were patches of damp and mould and furniture was damaged. All of this had changed, by the time of the visit, as a result of funding from the project administered by the Pedagogical Institute. The school had received 3 million drachmas for the lower secondary school, 3 million drachmas for the upper secondary school plus another 4 million drachmas.

The size of this budget raised some interesting issues. The principal, who had been recently appointed, had argued that it was important for a principal to be a practising teacher. She had suggested that there was a danger that heads could become full-time administrators. Indeed, as a result of the need to manage the budget, she had been obliged to withdraw from all teaching in the current year so that more time could be devoted to the budget. It was interesting that she had not received any training in either project or budget management.

At the time of the visit the school was assessing the first stage of the project and all key stakeholders in the school (senior staff, teachers, students, parents, other staff) were participating.

The school was also engaged in a number of other funded projects. The principal referred to the "Connect Project", a transnational programme in which ten other Greek schools participated. These schools were linked with schools in Italy and the project was concerned with using new teaching methodologies focusing on culture and tradition. The school was also engaged in a number of student exchange projects, and was a pilot school in a national ICT project.

It is important to emphasise that participation in innovative projects is provided for by the law. While the law does not state that school should innovate, encouragement is given for schools to do so.

Latseion Psyhico College (Elementary School)

This is a highly prestigious private school located on a spacious site on the north east fringe of Athens. It has 641 boys and girls (aged 6 to 12 years) and there are 53 teachers, mainly women, supported by secretarial staff. Designed as a two-storey secondary school, it was opened as an elementary school in 1995. The new buildings have many interesting features including: wide corridors and hallways; a courtyard and pillared atrium; a theatre; well-stocked library; a large dining room; sports facilities; and a number of specialist classrooms. During the visit, pupils were observed in one of two ICT rooms, a music room, an art room and a language room. Specialist teachers were employed for several subjects and reference was made to subject departments.

The school is part of a co-ordinated system. Pupils move from the elementary school to a lower secondary school and then to an upper secondary school. This school system is associated with a parallel three-part system, the Athens College, which has been established for many years. Both school systems are the products of private funding charging substantial fees for each pupil. In addition the school is supported both by the Greek-American Foundation and local sponsorship. A Board of Trustees in the United States oversees the schools and there is a local board of trustees for the two schools. Much of the administration of the schools is the responsibility of this board, including the allocation of an annual budget to each school and the appointment of the principal and teachers. In addition to administrative co-ordination, there is some curriculum co-ordination across the schools. For example, there is an administrative co-ordinator for the English language, located in the upper secondary school, who works closely with the English language co-ordinator in the elementary school.

The principal of the elementary school is a former teacher in the school who was selected by the board to become principal four years earlier. She emphasised the importance of curriculum innovation within the framework stipulated by the central government. Important factors that facilitated curriculum innovation in this school included:

- Availability of financial resources.
- A highly qualified teaching staff.
- Provision of funds to support staff development through in-service training.
- A longer school day that provided room for curriculum enrichment.
- Specialist teaching facilities and good curriculum resources.
- External support from overseas and local organisations.
- Availability of expert consultancy.
- Participation in transnational projects funded by the European Union.
- Curriculum leadership from the principal.

The principal related how, before her promotion, she had an extended visit to England, where she encountered new approaches to elementary education. In particular, she became interested in the project methodology that embraced co-operative learning, group work and individualised learning. When she returned to Greece, she experimented with this in the school encouraged by the former principal who had been enthusiastic about curriculum innovation. Other teachers in the school took an interest in this work and, in 1981, a group teachers drawn from private and public schools began to meet on a regular basis to discuss aspects of "open education". Experts were invited to attend some of these meetings. The group decided, in 1985, to establish a magazine titled "Open School" which, at the time of the visit, had some 1 000 subscribers. Conferences and workshops were organised that focused on the successful development of the project methodology.

As a principal, she sustained her enthusiasm for curriculum innovation. As part of its American connection, a team of two or three consultants from Harvard University visit the school, on two or three occasions, each year. She explained that they had suggested the creation of a central core of teachers to provide curriculum leadership. While accepting the notion of a group that would provide leadership for other teachers, she wished to change the membership of this group, annually, so that innovation could be shared among more and more teachers.

It is important to emphasise that the principal made a clear distinction between educational leadership and administration. The former included promoting an educational philosophy and called for a vision for the school. The latter was concerned with day-to-day bureaucratic functions and these she had delegated to a vice-principal. Establishing the linkage between the educational vision and curriculum innovation, within the government's curriculum framework, was seen as the most important role for the principal. She wished to encourage teachers to engage in, and share, initiatives within an educational frame defined by a generally accepted educational philosophy within the school.

Also, she needed to balance innovation with consolidation. She was aware of the need to gain the support of parents for innovations. She described how the school had organised a "learning fair" for parents to demonstrate to them how the school was developing new approaches to teaching and learning.

Another important role for the principal was leading the self-evaluation of the school. The board of directors required the school to engage in self-evaluation and, as part of this, the principal prepared an annual development plan. Associated loosely with school self-evaluation was the "supervision" of teachers. The principal formally observed lessons and read the plans of the teachers followed by evaluative discussions concerning the observations and planning.

"Supervision" can also be considered in the context of staff development. As indicated above, opportunities were available for teachers in this school to engage in in-service training provided both inside the school and elsewhere. Teachers could be released to follow postgraduate courses, or participate in courses provided through the school's links with other private, sometimes international, schools. Opportunities were also made available for student teachers to do practice teaching at the school and teacher fellows, from the United States, visited as interns.

Fundamental to all of the discussions was the definition of the principal's role in terms of educational leadership rather than administration. The principal defined her work in terms of the relationship between good classroom management and good school management with people coming first and administration second. That the school should meet the requirements of the government was emphasised but there was scope for going beyond those requirements. Curriculum innovation and school self-evaluation, combined with teacher supervision, illustrate how this exceptional school was able to promote change within a centralised system.

Innovation and Effectiveness

In the context of a highly centralised education system, Greece is seeking to find ways to give individual schools more responsibility and authority for certain aspects of their organisation. There is some evidence, from the private sector, that well-qualified and well-remunerated teachers, working with an abundance of high quality material resources, can improve school performance. In schools in much less prosperous circumstances, there is also evidence that the successful implementation of projects to improve the learning environment for students and teachers can give scope for self-management. However, in most public schools, problems and difficulties persist and there are important weaknesses in the area of school buildings and equipment.

Schools engaged in the Reorganisation of School Premises Project and the Self-evaluation Project demonstrate that tangible outcomes are being achieved in a very short period of time. It should be noted that schools volunteer for these projects, indicating that the principals and associated stakeholders have an interest in school improvement and in taking on new responsibilities.

With regard to the Reorganisation of School Premises Project, the transfer from student classrooms, to subject specialist classrooms in lower secondary schools, marks a profound change in the use of school premises. It is claimed that the change has led to: improved teacher and student morale; more effective delivery of the subjects in the national curriculum; security of teaching equipment; and a greater involvement of parents in schools.

With regard to the Self-evaluation Project, the pilot schools have been given the opportunity to try out ideas that have strong support from the Ministry of National Education and Religious Affairs. Self-evaluation is preferred to any system of external inspection and the pilot schools are being challenged to demonstrate that they are capable of devising and implementing methods of self-evaluation that include the evaluation of senior staff and individual teachers.

Given the support for these projects from the Ministry, it is likely that they will prove to be sustainable. The projects were co-ordinated by the Pedagogical Institute, a governmental organisation concerned with curriculum matters, and this organisation had published the guidelines for the Self-evaluation Project. How the findings from the two projects would be disseminated throughout Greece was unclear. It was difficult to find evidence at school level of any external evaluation and, there appeared to be no formal direct contact between the schools engaged in the two projects.

A similar sense of isolation was evident in the private school visited. There appeared to be very little contact between this school and state schools in Greece. Indeed, there appeared to be more contact with other international schools, located elsewhere in Europe, than with local schools.

Greece is taking the first steps in redefining the role of the school principal. Decentralisation, deregulation, democratisation and modernisation are terms that are used by various persons within the educational system as umbrellas under which the changes are being discussed and introduced. There was evidence of policies in financial and curriculum matters being developed by the Ministry that sought to give individual schools scope for innovation, decision-making and accepting new responsibilities. Pilot projects were in place that gave principals and other stakeholders the opportunity to gain experience that facilitated the shift from a broadly administrative, systems' maintenance role for principals to a managerial, systems' improvement role. There is evidence in the schools visited of successful outcomes achieved in a relatively short period of time. Effectiveness in innovation, however, depends also, on the way stakeholders are motivated by the principal (or vice-principal) to pursue a "common goal" in organisational improvement.

Bibliography

ANDREOU, A. and PAPAKONSTANTINOU G. (1994),
Εξουσία και Οργάνωση – Διοίκηση του Εκπαιδευτικού Συστήματος, "Authority and organisation – Administration of educational system", Nea Synora, Athens.

FRANGOS, CH. (1979),
Προϋποθέσεις και προοπτικές για μια εκπαιδευτική μεταρρύθμιση, "Preconditions and perspectives of an educational reform", O Politis, Jan-Feb.

GLINOS, D. (1925),
Ένας Άταφος Νεκρός, "An Unburied Dead", Athens.

GREEN, A. (1990),
Education and the State Formation, Martin's Press, New York.

KASSOTAKIS, M. and LAMBRAKIS-PAGANOS, A. (1994),
"Greek Education and its Legislative Framework", in N. Tulaziewicz and G. Strowbridge (eds.), Education and the Law, International Perspectives, Routledge, London, pp. 94-109.

KAZAMIAS, A. and KASSOTAKIS, M. (1995),
Ελληνική Εκπαίδευση: Προοπτικές Ανασυγκρότησης και Εκσυγχρονισμού, "Greek education: Perspectives for reconstruction and modernisation", Sirios, Athens.

MARKOU, G. (1991),
Ησύγχρονη εκπαιδευτική πρόκληση και η εκπαιδευτική πολιτική των ελληνικών κομμάτων, "The contemporary educational challenge and educational policy of Greek political parties", Logos kai Praxi, p. 45.

MASSIALAS, B., FLOURIS, G. and KASSOTAKIS, M. (1988),
"The Educational System of Greece in World Education Encyclopedia", Files and Fact Publications, New York, pp. 479-507.

MINISTRY OF EDUCATION (1985a),
Introductory Report, Law 1566/1985.

MINISTRY OF EDUCATION (1985b),
Law 1566/1985.

MINISTRY OF EDUCATION (1997),
Law 2525/1997.

MINISTRY OF EDUCATION (1997),
Law 2817/2000.

SOLOMON, J. (1999),
Εσωτερική Αξιολόγηση και Προγραμματισμός του Εκπαιδευτικού Έργου στη Σχολική Μονάδα, "Internal evaluation and planning of education in school units", Pedagogical Institute, Athens.

SOTIROPOULOS, D. (1993),
Κρατική γραφειοκρατία και λαϊκίστικο κόμμα: Η περίπτωση του ΠΑΣΟΚ, 1981-1989, "State bureaucracy and populist party: The case of PASOK, 1981-1989", Sighrona Themata, 49, pp. 15-19.

HUNGARY

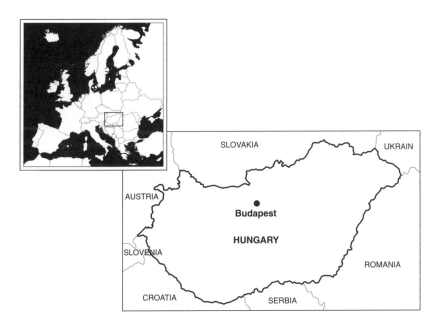

Land area in square kilometers: 93 000

Total population (1998): 10 114 000

Per capita GDP (1999 prices): 10 900 USD

Percentage of GDP on education (1997): 4.5%

Amount spent per student (1997):
- 2 035 USD (Primary)
- 2 093 USD (Secondary)

Teacher salary range (1998):
- 5 978-12 526 USD (Primary)
- 7 535-14 265 USD (Secondary)

Sources: Labour Force Statistics: 1978-1998, OECD, Paris, 1999; *Main Economic Indicators*, OECD, Paris, April 2000; *Education at a Glance – OECD Indicators 2000*, OECD, Paris, 2000.

Country context

During the last decades, Hungary has experienced a process of transition, which has had far-reaching consequences for the economy and society as a whole. But it is important to underline that this process has been initiated much earlier than in the neighbouring countries. In the 1980s, a gradual process of democratisation and of decentralisation was introduced and the private sector became increasingly significant. Dynamic entrepreneurs began to appear and intellectuals were quite aware of new ideas and developments on the international scene.

It is not so surprising, therefore, that when the change of regime took place, around 1990, Hungary went through the transition process at a particularly rapid pace. Drastic measures of privatisation and economic reform were undertaken as well as far-reaching institutional changes involving a large degree of decentralisation. During the early 1990s, economic re-structuring and the loss of export markets (especially in the Soviet Union) had serious adverse effects on the standard of living. There was a deep economic recession, with unemployment, poverty and inequalities between regions and social groups appearing for the first time.

The stabilisation programme adopted in the mid-1990s was followed by an economic recovery. The growth rate of the GNP has been high during the latter part of the decade but problems of poverty and inequality cannot be solved overnight. Restrictions on public expenditure had to be maintained which continued to have a serious impact on all government activities.

Changes which have taken place in the field of education, have been reviewed extensively by the earlier OECD report on *Transition from School to Work*. All aspects of the educational system have been affected by these economic changes particularly the organisation of schools and the curriculum content. In view of its relationship with a changing labour market, the re-orientation of vocational and technical education has received considerable attention.

In the whole system, teaching methods have been usually perceived as rather conservative. But according to international surveys, the average performance of Hungarian students is very good in science and mathematics while reading performances are not so satisfactory. There are wide and increasing inequalities, for example the recent International Adult Literacy Survey data published by the OECD shows that Hungarian adults are not at the same high level as the students (OECD, 2000). There are wide and increasing inequalities among regions and among families of students with different backgrounds. The most important trend affecting the school system is the drastic demographic decline of the school-age population.

Challenges Facing School Management

From the beginning of the 1990s, school management has been faced with different types of challenges related to economic conditions; demographic changes; and curriculum and programme.

The number of young people, aged 15 to 19, went down from 856 000 in 1966, to an estimated figure of 655 000 in 2000, and is expected to further decrease to 613 000 in 2005. Consequently school and class sizes, already traditionally small, are becoming even smaller. More than 800 general basic schools (primary and lower secondary levels combined – eight grades altogether) have fewer than 100 pupils. According to the OECD report on *Transition from School to Work*, the average pupil/teacher ratio in 1996 was 12.2 in primary schools and 10.4 in secondary schools, compared with 18.3 and 14.6 for OECD countries as a whole.

The main challenge for school management is the serious shortage of financial resources which is still being felt despite the recent economic recovery and the increased expenditure on schools. While they constitute an important element of the budget, teachers' salaries have not kept pace with inflation nor with the increasing income level in the business sector. The typical gross starting salary for a teacher is 40 000 Forints per month (or 30 000 net). Many teachers have a low level of motivation and must take a second job to survive. Attracting male teachers is difficult which partly explains why females account for 82% of teachers at the primary level and 67% at the secondary level. Some of the most enterprising teachers are leaving the profession. Although the number of teachers is high relative to the decreasing number of students, there may be shortages in specific areas (*e.g.* foreign languages or new technologies) where better salaries are available in the private sector. After paying the teachers' salaries, most schools have very little money left for other expenses such as equipment and supplies.

The system of school financing is a two-tier one: normative per capita distribution of money by the state to local self-governments on the one hand, and budget bargaining between self-government and schools on the other. As enrolment decreases there is a distinct possibility of school closures. While both the municipalities and the local populations resist such closures, it would be an economically rational decision to merge some of the smaller schools. To attract students, schools appeal to parents through improved academic achievements, better working conditions for teachers, and more attractive programmes. School managers find themselves in an increasingly competitive world.

As indicated above, the teaching methods and programme in Hungary have been considered to be somewhat conservative. Innovations are required for at least three main reasons. First, the demands of the labour market. Second, far-reaching changes in the institutional, social and cultural environment. Third, with the accession of Hungary to the European Union as a major objective, there is a need to meet the European standards in every field, including education.

In response, different innovative approaches have been adopted:

- For more than a decade, schools have been able to apply to a number of funds for innovation.
- Since 1993, there have been no compulsory central teaching programmes.
- Between 1995 and 1998, the Soros Foundation distributed 1 billion florints per year in grants to schools to support innovation.
- Since 1996, an amount equal to 7% of the funds transferred to municipalities has been spent on educational development, a large portion going directly to schools.
- Every school has been given the freedom and the obligation to create its own programme.

The reform of public administration and public financing is reflected in the emergence of a self-governing system in which very strong rights have been allocated to the teaching staff. Ownership of schools has been transferred to politically autonomous local self-governments (maintainers) having very broad jurisdiction in education. The powers of teaching staff have a determining influence on the nature of school level management.

Main Policy Approaches

The start of the transition period to a market economy has opened the way to strong demands for reform while offering a unique opportunity for innovation. However, policy-makers consider any reforms as progressive adjustments, in a process of slowly changing direction. They also emphasise that, despite several changes of government during that period, there remains continuity in the basic commitment to innovation.

The Hungarian education system has been subject to a variety of influences over time. Centralisation prevailed before World War II and even more so afterwards during the Soviet-type administration. Decentralisation was initiated in stages beginning in the late 1960s and further extended by the 1990 Public Administration Acts. A complex system of "shared responsibility" has been adopted and maintained by different governments, although a few areas, such as curriculum, are currently being centralised.

Curriculum reform has been stepped up since the 1993 Public Education Act (PEA) which introduced a two-tier system of content regulation – one dealing with national level framework documents and the other with school level documents. A National Core Curriculum was introduced two years later, supported by in-service training for teachers. The PEA was amended in 1999 with provision for a revised

Framework Curriculum which puts certain limits on the previously wide autonomy of schools.

Meanwhile, the quality improvement policy of the Ministry of Education is based on four pillars: strengthening the role of the state in the field of financing, emphasizing planning at the local level, supplementing the regulation of content by framework curricula, and developing a national system of evaluation, supervision and quality control. This includes Comenius 2000, an ambitious programme aimed at quality improvement throughout the education system as a whole.

The government has also adopted an "expert system" with nationally accredited experts who can be contracted by schools or municipalities for evaluation tasks. A similar pattern was followed later *i*) in the area of in-service training of teachers with nationally accredited experts participating in the evaluation of training programmes and *ii*) in the development of school level quality assurance systems with accredited experts being contracted by schools as consultants providing support (see the case studies). In line with the overall re-structuring of the economy through a drastic privatisation of industry, it was felt that the private sector would provide a better and more rapid approach utilising resources more efficiently.

During the initial stage, foreign expertise was used, but there was a preference for Hungarian specialists. Some of the researchers, who had worked previously within the public sector, became independent contractors. One of the factors which contributed to the introduction of the private sector, was the availability of quality assurance experts, who were flourishing at the end of the 1980s but who were looking for new markets by the 1990s.

In summary, school management in Hungary has many unique features. For approximately a decade, it has been one of the most decentralised education systems in the developed world, if not the most. Secondly, schools and school leaders have undergone an exceptional learning process to operate successfully in a radically changed environment. Thirdly, it has seen the emergence of an interesting set of policy instruments and measures for assuring coherence within a decentralised context.

Framework

The basic characteristics of the administration of public education can be summarised as follows (Balasz *et al.*, 1999):

- Public educational administration is highly decentralised and the responsibilities are shared among ministries.
- Horizontally, the responsibility at the national level is shared between the ministry directly responsible for education and other ministries (finance and interior).

- Vertically, the responsibility is shared between four levels: central (national), regional, local and schools.

- At the local and school levels, the administration of education is integrated into the general system of public education.

- At the local and regional levels, the public administration (including education) is under the responsibility of politically autonomous bodies.

- The role of the regional level is limited, whereas the responsibilities of the municipalities at the local level are very broad.

- There are a large number of municipalities (some 3 100, among which more than 2 400 maintain at least one school), but their average size is small.

The sharing of responsibilities is in three main areas: finance; curriculum and programme; and staffing.

The allocations for education in the State budget are transferred by the Ministry of the Interior, not directly to the schools, but to the "maintainers" (*i.e.* the municipalities for the public schools and the churches and other maintainers for the private schools). This state support is mostly based on the per capita normative grants, fixed annually by the Budgetary Act. They refer to the number of pupils, but also to a number of other criteria (grade, type of school, minority group, etc.). Extra provisions are provided when a large proportion of the student population is commuting from outside the municipal boundary. The level of grants is the same for private maintainers (mostly churches) and for the municipalities, in charge of public schools.

Although the allocations from the State budget refer to a number of educational objectives, the municipalities are free to spend the money as they see fit. In fact, these allocations cover approximately half of the educational expenditure of the municipalities. The other half consists of the municipalities' own resources and of State grants intended for other purposes. In addition to the normative grants, additional budgetary allocations finance specific development costs. School maintainers have to file an application, which specifies the type of activity and the plan for its implementation.

These allocations represent 7% of the state's educational subvention to local municipalities. This figure might seem comparatively low, but it is much higher if it is seen from the point of view of the budgetary flexibility of the school. It is said that the ability of a school to undertake special projects determines, to a large extent, its resources. Some schools also have limited possibilities to raise additional funding by renting rooms or organising special fee-paying courses. In addition, vocational schools receive a substantial contribution from employers (a percentage of the payroll) either directly, or through a Vocational Training Fund.

Teachers are public employees, but they do not have the same status or pensions as those of the civil servants. Their salaries and employment conditions are regulated by the Public Employees Act. They cannot be fired, except in very unusual circumstances. They are recruited by the school principals, on the basis of their qualifications, their experience, and a personal interview. Principals are free to fix a higher salary than the minimum set up by the law, but usually no money is available for that. They would obviously prefer to recruit an experienced teacher, but younger ones get a lower salary, saving some money for other expenses. The municipality hires school principals who are appointed for a five-year to ten-year term. Teachers, parents, trade unions and students' representatives are consulted, but the municipality makes the final hiring decision.

The Public Education Act of 1993 established a two-tier system of shared responsibility for curriculum regulation. The state defines the parameters while the school fills in the details. The maintainer decides grades to be taught and the organisational structure of the school. This has provided an opportunity to extend the programme to another level, to attract more students. The increased complexity of the system causes some degree of confusion to the public.

Case Studies

The case studies selected by the Hungarian authorities were focused, not so much on individual schools, but rather on national programmes. These programmes are intended to illustrate three aspects of an innovative and coherent approach to educational management, including a shared responsibility for curriculum, in-service training and quality improvement.

The Preparation of School-based Strategic Documents and Curricula

Even before the transition period, a number of schools were already allowed to experiment by being exempted from the national curriculum. A new policy of shared responsibility was to be introduced progressively in accordance with the 1993 Act. A National Core Curriculum was established in 1995. It provides guidelines for the course of studies, up to grade 10, with the following key features:

- It refers to broad areas of knowledge, and not to specific subjects.
- It does not relate to specific school types, as each school is free to decide the level of education and the grades that it will provide.
- It sets attainment targets for every other grade, thus leaving some flexibility to the individual school.
- It does not define the number of lessons, but only a proportion within broad areas.

101

The National Core Curriculum requires each school to determine teaching hours, subjects and teaching methods. All schools have to make decisions on these aspects – an entirely new situation for most of them.

A number of nationwide training courses for school-based programmes was organised by different institutions, such as the 20 County Pedagogical Institutes. In addition, the Soros Foundation assisted with team-oriented training for school groups (usually the principal and two or three teachers, but it could include representatives of the municipality or parents). The training was held four times a year, in an intensive way, with homework tasks to be completed in between. The training was practice-oriented with no fee or financial reward for the participants.

The programme stimulated bottom-up innovations and involvement of the school staff. Participants created an association of self-developing schools and became part of a network, using the Internet. It was estimated that, although the number of participants was small (100 schools and 300 teachers), the schools, together with pedagogical institutes and other educational institutions, became an important vehicle for spreading reform. The network of participating schools also contributed to the promotion of other innovative programmes. Finally, "a kind of common culture and language of school-based innovation has emerged from this project" (Balasz, 1997).

A survey undertaken in 1998 showed that approximately one third of schools was not successful in preparing a new curriculum and programme of an appropriate quality. The new government, elected at that time, felt that schools needed more specific guidelines. It is currently preparing a so-called "framework curriculum" which represents, to some extent, a move back to more centralisation. It determines the number of lessons to be taught for each subject (thus giving up the concept of broad areas), and the targets to be attained for every grade. In other words, it limits the schools' autonomy and their flexibility.

Whether the new approach means giving up entirely the concepts on which the National Core Curriculum was based, or is a simple adjustment is an open question. Schools are normally expected to revise the curricula that they have just adopted. However, schools where integrated subjects are taught, or schools running a programme already accredited, are not affected by the new approach.

In adopting a curriculum each school had three options: to develop its own curriculum; to adopt one of those which were offered by the national data bank; or to modify it to its own requirements. The data bank was established in 1996-97 by the National Institute of Public Education, in co-operation with a number of experts. It included about 700 curricula for the various subjects. They came from three sources: school experience; textbook publishing companies; or teacher training colleges. Experts determined whether or not they were consistent with the National Core Curriculum.

In general, school-level programme planning has been a complex initiative which has produced the following changes:

- Schools have become much more open to community involvement than ever before.

- Cross-disciplinary approaches have become more natural within the schools.

- Attempts to adopt the school level programme to the special needs of students have expanded.

- There has been a dramatic increase in the need for in-service training among teachers and principals.

- The traditional relationship between the staff and the principal has been radically altered.

- The sense of professionalism among principals and teachers has increased.

Examples of these changes and innovations are included in the school visits.

Buadörs Basic School

In this Budapest suburban primary school, with 700 pupils and 63 teachers, the first step in programme development was to clarify the objectives and the approach of the school. In the more advanced schools, it was undertaken in a business-like manner starting with the demands of the customers (*i.e.* essentially the parents).

The principal of the Buadörs Basic School was sent, with other teachers, to the weekly training session held over four weeks. They learned how to work in a team and how to assess the value of a pedagogical programme. They realised that teachers themselves needed some training in this new approach and in using the new-found freedom. Together, they conducted a survey among parents, teachers, and the municipality, to assess: their values; objectives assigned to the school; preferred teaching methods; and their expectations for the school within the next five years. Developing the child's personality emerged as the most important objective.

Vajda Janos High School

The Vajda Janos High School, in the suburbs of Budapest, was one of the schools which participated during the late 1980s in an experimental programme to develop a new curriculum and programme to meet local needs. The emphasis shifted from teaching to learning. To help students find their own interests, optional subjects with smaller groups of pupils were promoted. According to the principals approximately 70% of teaching contents is determined by the national

103

curriculum, the schools' own pedagogical programme development provides the remaining 30%.

To involve parents in the learning process, a parent/teachers' association was created to discuss the programme and the possible improvements. Particular attention was paid to children with special needs (social, family or psychological). The early stages of this innovative process were exciting with additional money available from research institutions. After some time, the initial excitement eased and with no more additional money, enthusiasm decreased.

During the mid-1990s, every school had to decide on its own programme. The Vajda Janos school was in a very favourable position in view of its earlier participation in a national experimental programme. It made an application for an additional grant for participating teachers to continue the work. With slight adjustments, a new curriculum was developed and shared with the national data bank.

In-service Training

In-service training of teachers (INSET) is a key element of the policy to modernise education, through the development of local initiatives. The 1996 amendment to the Public Education Act earmarked an amount equal to 2% of the state educational support for local municipalities for this purpose. Teachers are obliged to undertake at least 120 hours of training every 7 years. The key components of the INSET programme are as follows:

- Most of the state allocation for INSET is transferred to schools which can use this money to cover training costs.

- Schools are obliged to provide an institutional INSET plan based on their pedagogical programme.

- The individual promotion and remuneration of teachers are linked to participation in recognised INSET courses and qualification obtained.

- State allocation for INSET can be spent only on courses recognised by a national accreditation body.

- An open competition of all potential INSET course providers.

- A national methodological centre for INSET.

The development of INSET was conceived to promote quality, oppose conservatism and revitalise the traditional system by bringing in new and fresh training providers. It was also intended to compensate for the inadequacies of previous teacher preparation and training. The role of the central administration is limited to financing and to the setting of basic rules, while the main responsibility is given to the school principals. They are required to prepare five-year plans and yearly schedules for the professional development of their teachers, utilising training provisions available on the open market.

This process was adopted after several battles with the traditional training providers – universities and teacher-training colleges. The first decision was to give the money to the schools and not to the providers. It was assumed that schools could best access training related to their programme needs. Finally, it was decided that the monopoly of traditional providers was over and anyone could enter the training market, including private firms and individuals.

The final decision is based on an accreditation process directed by the National Accreditation Commission. Anyone can design a training course, but the course is accredited by a committee based on an expert evaluation. There are 350 accreditation experts who have been selected on the basis of their work and an extensive period of pre-service preparation. They comment on the methodology of the course, but the schools decide the relevance of the contents. Real competition is now going on between universities, pedagogical institutes, private firms or consultants. The role of the latter is still comparatively marginal, but it is estimated that competition has forced the more traditional institutions to modify their contents and their methods. The demands made by the teachers are slowly changing from rather traditional subject courses, to a demand for new teaching methods, team work and other forms of innovation.

Most of the cost of accredited training is paid by the central budget. The rest may be financed either by the municipality or by the school. For example, the Buadörs Basic School receives 15 000 Forints per teacher per year. Using this, the schools can cover 80% of the training cost, the rest being met by the individual teacher; in special cases, related to national priorities, 100% of the cost can be recovered. The school makes its own training plans with the principal and staff deciding on the nature of the training.

With the new responsibilities given to school principals, their training has become even more crucial. Among the training options is an innovative Dutch-Hungarian programme, which was introduced, during the early 1990s, in Amsterdam for school principals. The development of an INSET programme was followed by a programme for the pre-service training of school principals leading to a recognised degree and international accreditation. Emphasis is given to communication, group work, and problem-solving and participants are required to regularly evaluate the programme.

Comenius 2000 Quality Improvement Programme

Following the introduction of a variety of quality assurance programmes undertaken by local schools, a national programme, the Comenius 2000 Quality

Improvement Programme was introduced with the aim of providing a national framework for the school level initiatives.

This innovative and rather unique programme is based on the assumption that the quality concepts, which have been widely used in industry, could be transferred into the field of education, with some adaptation. Drawing upon experience gained from existing local quality assurance programmes, the Ministry of Education, assisted by experts and consultants from different backgrounds, has developed a methodology contained in a "manual of quality development".

The programme operates at two levels, one at the institutional level (*i.e.* the schools) and the other at the maintainers' level. At the school level there is a three stage progressive process for education quality beginning in the year 2000. The first stage focuses on an assessment of local needs in order to form a school-community partnership for programme planning (*e.g.* timetable development). The second stage involves setting up a total quality management (TQM) system for continuous improvement including the following elements: focus on partners; process control; development of an organisation culture. The third stage will disseminate the programme throughout the whole system by including 400 pilot schools, assisted by consultants selected by tender.

Specially-trained consultants are required to have an earlier experience in dealing with quality issues (usually in industry), but also knowledge of education. The selection takes into account the personal capabilities of the consultants, most of whom are part-time teachers employed by private firms. The Ministry of Education writes an agreement with each participating school and its consultant, whereby it will finance a given number of days of consultancy at a fixed rate. Schools can choose an accredited consultant from a Ministry of Education expert data bank created on the basis of extensive selection and training. A monitoring system was put in operation in order to control locally the quality of the consultant services. It should be noted that the introduction of TQM type quality assurance mechanisms is a major innovation with far-reaching implications both in Hungary and beyond. More details on the programme can be found in Pokorni (1999) and others.

Moricz Zsigmond Grammar School

This secondary school, in the small town of Szeatendre (30 miles north of Budapest), has 500 students (grade 9-12), 50 teachers and 27 non-teaching staff. It is a relatively affluent community where the majority of parents have higher education. The principal of the Moricz Zsigmond Grammar School has studied the American literature on human resources management and the Hungarian literature on total quality management and has written her thesis on these issues. She was concerned with the individualistic way in which teachers were working. To change this, she started a project on quality management in her own school, in 1998, before the National Programme was completed.

The project included work by the teachers with quality circles on evaluation and methodology. At the beginning, she had to convince the staff, since it meant additional work, but a number of teachers volunteered and now the majority are interested. When the time came to evaluate what had been done in the school, the principal felt that she needed the assistance of a consultant. The Comenius programme allowed for the financing of a consultant.

Eger Municipal Schools

Eger, a wine-producing northern town of 60 000, is in a relatively poor region of Hungary. Its primary source of revenue, personal income tax, has declined by 20% due to central government initiatives to redistribute funds to smaller and poorer communities. This has meant decreased resources for municipal activities including the education-related budget. The Socialist party is in power in Eger and claims that access to additional funding is very difficult while the Conservatives form the central government.

Quality improvement programmes are undertaken not only by schools. Municipalities may also launch their own project. Eger has set up its own programme, with the help of an outside private consultant. It includes self-evaluation activities by the schools and quality circles with representatives from different types of schools. Quality circles meet once or twice a month and discuss assessment issues and standards. One of the objectives is to harmonise the school practices and to facilitate the transition for the students who are in the process of proceeding from one level to the next. It is intended to create a partnership between schools following common goals.

Innovation and Effectiveness

Policy-makers emphasise the need for coherence between the different aspects of current decentralisation and the policy of involving private sector partners. Indeed, the coherence is particularly important, given the responsibility that Hungarian schools have in determining/establishing curriculum and programme, quality improvement, and training for teachers and principals. It is also recognised that launching pilot programmes takes less time than changing the institutions and reforming the system.

The changes of government have not affected the broad policy orientations; policy-makers are very keen to maintain the impetus and the enthusiasm which resulted from the new opportunities offered to principals and teachers. But experimentation also implies some degree of stop and go, as with the latest decisions concerning a limited re-centralisation and a return to a more traditional approach

107|

to the curriculum. This seems to have slowed down the efforts of a number of schools, which are now waiting for the new framework curriculum to revise the programmes that they had just adopted a few years ago.

As indicated earlier, the move towards decentralisation was initiated much earlier than the start of the transition period, but only a small minority of the key agents (school maintainers and principals) was prepared. And even today, in the words of one of the Hungarian experts, "when you decentralise, some of the schools (say one third) are innovative, another segment just follows and a third one is strongly resisting the change."

Whereas all schools were faced with the responsibility to adopt their own curriculum and programme, only some of them were able to do so. The new quality improvement programme is being piloted in around a tenth of the country's schools. In any case, Hungary is faced with the typical problem of how to spread the innovation on a national basis.

Several problems arise, with the most obvious one being the availability of financial and personnel resources. But the spreading of the programme is also related to the competence and attitudes of the key players at the decentralised levels. Competence is being tackled by training courses, but they have to involve all the players and not only those who are the most motivated and enterprising.

As mentioned above, disparities have tended to increase with the economic recession and with the modernisation of the economy. The question arises whether the policies and programmes adopted to modernise the education system and improve quality will increase or reduce the disparities between large and small schools and between rich and poor areas.

According to some of the school principals met during the visit, poor municipalities have less income of their own to make available to the schools. In order to avoid this, the government has taken specific measures in favour of the smaller and less privileged municipalities. Special grants for example may be allocated to smaller villages if they agree to co-operate among themselves. As Eger exemplified, however, local versus central political conflicts can impede progress.

But making an application for grants in order to get additional money implies that the staff of the municipalities and the schools have enough information and skills to take an initiative. Are these conditions likely to be fulfilled in smaller and poorer schools and municipalities? Smaller and isolated schools are also at a disadvantage with regard to the availability of in-service training for their teachers, due to size and remoteness of location.

It seems to be generally agreed in Hungary that competition in education is a good thing provided that it really operates freely. For instance, some training providers may have better connections and therefore a better chance to get clients. The accreditation system applied to in-service training and quality improvement programmes is conceived as a guarantee of fair competition. However, some people feel that in the field of teacher training it is somewhat static and inflexible, because the process is expensive and may discourage the smaller providers from participating.

At this stage, there does not seem to be much concern in Hungary for the possible negative implications of the participation of large international training companies, who could use their resources to control the market. At least regarding in-service training activities, monopolistic situations are not the problem for the time being. In fact, the large number of providers competing for programmes sometimes seems excessive and can be a source of confusion for the schools and teachers.

The free market system on which the quality improvement and the in-service training programmes are based, raise a few concerns. Within the free market system, the primary concern of the schools (as service providers) is to satisfy their clients (the parents and students), thus ensuring the survival of their institution. However, as some of the principals recognise, schools should take into account, not only the short-term views of the parents and teachers, but also the broader environment and longer term perspective. Are schools sufficiently equipped for that? Is there no need for more central direction and quality control of the outcome of activities run by the private sector?

Transferring industrial concepts and experts from industry to the field of education may raise a number of problems including cultural and terminology differences between two different worlds as well as the huge difference of income between school staff and outside consultants. Hungary is a good place to study the risks and dangers of linking education and the market. But it is also a good place to study the potential benefits of these links.

For the implementation of policies relying largely on local initiatives and the satisfaction of parents, school principals are more than ever in the forefront. In theory, at least, they have a wide range of responsibilities, which cover all aspects of school management. Those who have been particularly involved from the beginning in the promotion of innovations recall that period as an exciting one and feel that starting new projects the most positive aspect of their job.

Today, principals tend to say that they have to work under great pressure and that, although they are supposed to be responsible for everything, their freedom to act and their right to make decisions are quite limited. Some of them refer to a kind of schizophrenia in which they are caught when they try to satisfy the conflicting demands of the stakeholders. Their main concern is to look for additional resources, which requires a lot of initiative and an ability to bargain, especially with the municipality. They also must develop and implement the curriculum and programme. This is a clear departure from the old days, when principals simply had to make sure that the legislation was applied in the context of a centralised and bureaucratic system.

In summary, the new role of principals is demanding and difficult. Although their salaries are higher than those of other teachers, there seems to be fewer candidates for the job. Despite the emergence of innovative training programmes, there is still a lot to be done in the modernisation of their pre-service and in-service training, in order to better prepare them for their tasks. The fundamental question remains: to what extent can quality issues be addressed when teachers are very poorly remunerated within the entire school management context?

The situation in Hungary is truly unique because it is trying to transform a traditional, conservative, centralised schooling system into a modern competitive, market-driven, decentralised, educational service. It has been a difficult transition process in which a variety of strategies have been enlisted including: pre-service and in-service training; privatisation; and special incentive grants to motivate staff and inspire leadership. A number of countries may find their experience a useful laboratory to guide their own journeys of innovation.

Bibliography

BALASZ, E. (1997),
"The Network of Self-developing Schools: Case study of Hungary for the OECD-Japan Seminar", National Institute of Public Education, Budapest.

BALASZ, E., HALASZ, G., IMRE, A., MOLDOVAN, J. and NAGY, M. (1999),
Inter-governmental Roles in the Delivery of Educational Services, National Institute of Public Education, Budapest.

EUROPEAN FORUM ON EDUCATIONAL ADMINISTRATION (1995),
Local Autonomy and Shared Responsibility in Managing Schools, Budapest.

HALASZ, G. (1997),
The Reform of Financing Public Education, National Institute of Public Education, Budapest.

HALASZ, G. (1998),
The Changes of System Regulation in School Education in Hungary, National Institute of Public Education, Budapest.

OECD (2000),
Literacy in the Information Age, Paris.

POKORNI, Z. (1999),
"Comenius 2000, Quality Improvement Programme in School Education", Manual of Quality Improvement, Ministry of Education.

JAPAN

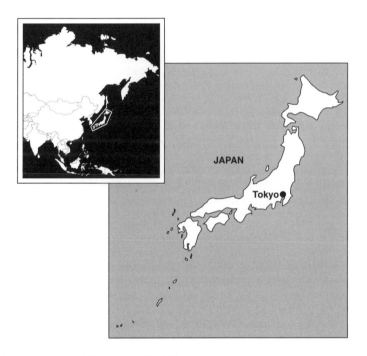

Land area in square kilometers: 378 000

Total population (1998): 126 486 000

Per capita GDP (1999 prices): 24 500 USD

Percentage of GDP on education (1997): 3.6%

Amount spent per student (1997): not available

Teacher salary range (1998):
- 21 899-52 867 (Primary)
- 21 899-54 465 (Secondary)

Sources: *Labour Force Statistics: 1978-1998*, OECD, Paris, 1999; *Main Economic Indicators*, OECD, Paris,
April 2000; *Education at a Glance – OECD Indicators 2000*, OECD, Paris, 2000.

Country context

From the 1960s, Japan has made massive economic progress based largely on manufacturing industries with a move towards tertiary industry. By 1997, only 5.5% of the working population were employed in primary industry with 31.9% in secondary industry and 61.8% in tertiary industry. A period of continuous economic growth came to an end in 1997, leading to calls for industrial and commercial restructuring. This coincided with increasing attention being paid to globalisation, particularly to the impact of new information and communication technologies which brought reforms in education.

Demographically, Japan has witnessed intensive urbanisation and consequent rural depopulation. The government is concerned with the implications of a falling birth rate, the trend towards nuclear families and an ageing population. Across the country, educational expectations have been heightened, with parents wishing to see their children attend prestigious schools followed by prestigious universities and, hopefully, by high status jobs. Increasingly, expectations have been high for both males and females. Social mobility, maintaining high living standards and education have been seen to be closely linked.

Traditionally, the centralised administration has been strong in Japan, but in recent years important steps have been taken to deregulate and decentralise many areas of the public sector, including education. A package of laws designed to promote decentralisation was passed in July 1999, with implementation beginning April 2000.

Such broad trends are reflected in national, regional and local policies for educational reform. In 1996, the second Hashimoto Cabinet designated educational reform, alongside governmental administration, the economic structure, the financial system, the social welfare system and the fiscal structure, as one of the government's major areas for reform. More recently, the Obuchi Cabinet took up education as a major agenda item and in March 2000 established the National Commission on Educational Reform, a private discussion group of eminent citizens advising the Prime Minister.

The Japanese state education school system consists of compulsory elementary schools (six years) and lower secondary or junior high schools (three years), voluntary upper secondary or senior high schools (three years), followed by universities (four years) or junior colleges (two years). In 1999, the Ministry of Education, Science, Sports and Culture (Monbusho) approved the establishment of a unified six-year secondary education system in three forms: unified secondary education both provided in one school; jointly established lower secondary and upper secondary schools; and coordinated lower and upper secondary education (municipal lower secondary schools and prefectural upper secondary schools are coordinated on educational programmes and exchange of teachers or students).

Challenges Facing School Management

The Japanese education system has been envied by other countries as Japanese students have performed very well in international tests. In recent years though, some disturbing trends in schools such as increasing juvenile delinquency, truancy/drop-outs, and bullying have attracted media attention and alerted the government and the general public, although the magnitude of these issues is not that big compared with other countries. In addition to the above, other concerns expressed by the Ministry of Education, Science, Sports and Culture (Monbusho) in 1994 included: excessive competition in entrance examinations; students' insufficient experience in a natural environment and everyday life; the excessive uniformity of schooling, violence against students and teachers; suicides resulting from bullying.

Responses to these concerns include attempts to reduce the pressure of school examinations and reform of the curriculum in the context of lifelong learning. Unified secondary schooling, a reduction in examination pressure and the amount of knowledge to be contained in the new Courses of Study, are currently being introduced. The five-day school week (replacing a five and a half-day school week) was introduced in order to develop children's "zest for life" in their community with a strengthened community-home-school relationship. Programme reform includes giving schools the opportunity to express their individuality, through the teaching of cross-curricular themes and encouragement for such topics as international understanding and environmental education. These reforms remain at the margin, as the core of the curriculum remains untouched. At the upper secondary level, there have been innovations in integrated programmes, in the development of credit-based programmes, extending student choice of subjects and study time.

An important challenge to schools has also been the requirement that schools should work more closely with their local communities. This is an essential part of Monbusho's decentralisation and deregulation agenda and is the focus of two of the study visits.

Currently school principals, who are at the interface between the education system level and the school level, are under a lot of pressure. Managing school staff has become an increasingly important aspect of school leadership. There has been a decrease in the employment of new teachers due to decreasing enrolment and an aging of the existing pool of teachers. Attempting to alter the age and gender profiles of teachers in individual schools is a concern for some senior staff. Less important is the management of school budgets that are determined by prefectures and municipalities.

For principals, the major challenge is to shift the balance away from the traditional role of school administrator, with a strong teaching profile, towards the new role of school manager. Appropriate training and professional expertise in curriculum management, staff development, external relations and financial control are required. Teachers need to pass an exam (administered by each board of education) to hold managerial positions, such as head teacher or principal. A variety of training courses is prepared by boards of education. Associations of principals organise their own training. Teacher unions organise training for non-managerial teachers and non-teaching staff. Special training principals is not mandatory in relation to their appointment by each board of education.

Gender equality is another issue, as official figures published in 1999 show that principals at all levels of schooling were predominantly male (85.5% in elementary schools; 96.7% in lower secondary schools and 96.8% in upper secondary schools), even though in theory, promotion opportunities are open to both gender. Like teachers, principals are subject to transfer from one school to another. However, many of them, following a seniority-based criteria, are appointed near retirement age and may remain in the same school until that age is reached, especially in senior high school. The post of vice-principal was enacted in 1977 and the senior teacher system was adopted in 1976.

The responsibilities of principals continue to be largely administrative. They are expected to organise the school on a day-to-day basis and be good mentors for the teachers. Principals usually share a variety of tasks with teachers. By doing so, the burden of the principal is reduced. Normally there is at least one non-teaching administrative staff member in each school at the primary and lower secondary levels.

Main Policy Approaches

With regard to school education, Monbusho's Programme for Educational Reform has three broad goals:

- To enhance emotional education from infancy.
- To realise a school system that helps children develop their individuality and gives them diverse choices.
- To reorganise schools taking into account individual school's autonomy.

The study visits reviewed these goals, though the focus was largely upon the nature of school autonomy and the linkages between schools and their local communities. In this context, a number of reform initiatives need to be understood: decentralisation of educational administration; increasing the discretionary authority of individual schools and improving the leadership of principals; and parental choice of schools.

With regard to the decentralisation of educational administration, two reports published in 1998 are especially important. Following the publication of the report of the Committee for the Promotion of Decentralisation, the Central Council for Education published its report titled *How Local Administration of Education Should be*. These were followed by the enactment in 1999 of the "Package of Decentralisation Bills". Key proposals for education were: review of school administration regulation; review of employment qualifications for school principals; review of modalities for the systems of co-ordinating and advising teacher and staff meetings; introduction of the School Advisor System; increased flexibility of class structures and improvement of the placement of teaching personnel; careful selection of research statistics and the abolition/reduction of guidance notifications.

The second reform initiative focuses on expanding the discretionary authority of schools and improving the leadership of principals. Until 2000, principals and vice-principals were required to hold Educational Personnel Certification (teaching certificate). The introduction of the Partial Amendment of the Enforcement Regulations of the School Education Law (January 2000) allows persons without this certification to be appointed to the position of principal or vice-principal. Associated with this has been a clarification of the role of school staff meetings. These meetings are a long-established feature of Japanese schools and reflect the importance attached to having mechanisms that enable the principals to arrange their schools on the basis of consensus. They have been defined as advisory, rather than decision-making bodies, serving to support the principal in the execution of his or her duties. Associated with this is the introduction in 2000 of School Advisors, one for each school. They are drawn from local communities, nominated by a principal and appointed by a board of education, as part of a move towards creating "open schools" (as described in the second site visit).

Freedom of choice of schools is the third policy initiative and is the focus for the third site visit. Traditionally, in the state (public) school system, students are required to attend schools located in the school catchment area in which they live. According to the proposal of the Administrative Reform Committee, in 1997 Monbusho issued a directive that allowed boards of education to adopt a more flexible arrangement, substantially expanding the opportunities for children to attend schools outside their school district in order to take account of parents' preferences and to make school choice more flexible. Consequently, there are localities, particularly in some districts in Tokyo, which grant almost automatic consent to parents who wish to send their children to a school outside their designated school catchment area. Some see this movement toward freedom of choice at the compulsory education level as an opportunity for schools to develop their individuality. Others see it as heralding the introduction of the principles of market competition in public school education. It should be emphasised that the majority of boards of education is not considering the introduction of such a system at the moment.

117|

Framework

Educational administration in Japan is based on legislation and regulations. Schools are classified as national, public or private, depending on their founder. National schools are established and administered by Monbusho. Public schools are established by local governments (prefectures and municipalities) and administered by local and prefectural boards of education. Private schools are established and run by incorporated organisations set up specifically for educational purposes. They are supervised by the Governor of the Prefecture in which they are located.

The major roles of Monbusho are: to establish a fundamental framework for the educational system; to create national standards; to support provision of education by local bodies; to promote proper implementation of educational projects.

Essentially, there are three hierarchical levels of educational administration: Monbusho at the centre, 47 prefectures and more than 3 000 municipalities. Prefectural boards of education administer and operate upper secondary schools, schools for students with special needs and cultural and social educational institutions such as lifelong learning centres, libraries and museums. Private schools come under the jurisdiction of the prefectures. Municipal boards of education administer and operate the compulsory elementary, and lower secondary schools, and local cultural and social educational institutions such as citizens' halls, libraries and museums.

Central to school administration are prefectural and municipal boards of education. In 1997, there were 47 prefectural boards of education and 3 421 municipal boards of education. The board members are appointed respectively by the prefectural governor or municipal mayor with the consent of the assembly concerned. In the same year, 68.9% of board members were more than 60 years of age and 79.6% of prefectural board members and 84.6% of municipal board members were men. At both levels, the role of the board is to decide overall educational policy for its locality. A superintendent, often appointed from a non-education background at the prefecture level, is backed by a secretariat to implement the policy.

With regard to the schools, the board of education (prefectural or municipal), that established the school, sets the School Management Regulations and the school conducts its day-to-day management based on these. School management regulations vary slightly between prefecture, but the basic content is similar and includes: school terms and holidays; the duties of principals; the duties of vice-principals; the duties of senior teachers; the job titles and duties of administrative personnel; the curriculum and educational materials; notification of school events with overnight stays; guidance digests and excerpts; and the duty to report the disciplining, expulsion and suspension of students by the principal.

Financial management rests with the boards of education, though local governments depend largely on the grants of local tax made by the central government. These grants are intended to rectify disparities in local finances and are included within the local government's general revenue. Principals have little, if any, budgetary discretion. Salaries of teachers and support staff in schools account for most expenditure. One half of the total amount is borne by the prefectural board of education that exercises the duties of personnel management. The other half is from the central government as an earmarked grant.

The 1998 report of the Central Council for Education (a Monbusho consultative body) proposed increasing the discretionary authority of schools, and adopting individual school budgets that reflect the distinctive educational activities of a school, based on a principal's education policy.

The employment of teachers is determined by drawing up a list of candidates who have passed a board of education's annual selection examination. Promotions to principal or vice-principal are also determined by boards of education. All teachers and administrative staff are subject to appraisal undertaken by local boards of education. Essentially, the school principal is the primary evaluator, with the local board of education the final evaluator. Local boards of education monitor the service of teachers in the compulsory system and provide confidential reports to the prefectural boards of education concerning the appointment, dismissal and career progress of teachers.

Transfer of teaching and non-teaching staff between public schools is carried out regularly (at least once every ten years). This is to eliminate differences between schools in the same area of jurisdiction, to further the professional development of teachers through experiencing a variety of schools and to avoid attachments to business persons that can arise in the case of administrative staff because schools are institutions with large budgets. The boards of education have authority over personnel transfers. However, transfers are commonly decided after taking the transfer wishes of individuals into consideration. School principals may submit their opinions on the appointment, dismissal and career progress of teachers to the board of education.

Based on the Local Public Service Personnel Law and the Law for Special Regulations Concerning Educational Public Service Personnel, the board of education has the responsibility to carry out training for relevant employees. Currently, newly appointed teachers receive "induction" training. For others, training is carried out according to years of experience or specific roles/functions based on the programmes provided by each board of education.

Under the 1958 Law Concerning Class Size and the Standard of Fixed Number of Educational Personnel in Public Compulsory Education Schools, a set personnel cost system was established. This law was introduced to rationalise class sizes and the placement of teachers. The number of teachers in a school is fixed by prefectural regulations. However, the 1999 package of decentralisation laws respected the independent decision-making of municipal boards of education. It revised the legal requirement for prefectural board of education approval of class organisation in municipal elementary and lower secondary schools, amending it to a consultation system. In May 2000, Monbusho announced plans to promote smaller classes for some subjects, such as English, science and mathematics in elementary and lower secondary schools, beginning in 2001. Currently, there is a legal maximum of 40 students per class and it was envisaged that, at the discretion of boards of education, classes of half this size would be taught selected subjects. In the context of falling enrolment, this change will permit more teachers to remain employed.

Experimentation in curriculum and other aspects of school life is encouraged, especially in schools designated as experimental, at national and prefectural levels. One of the schools visited (Nagara case study) was a prefectural experimental school. For such schools, special budgets are allocated. Schools volunteer to become experimental, an important decision for a principal and school staff.

Clearly, principals have a rather narrow scope for managerial discretion in budgetary and staffing matters, but there is more scope for local discretion with regard to aspects of the school curriculum. The curriculum framework is determined centrally and it is framed in Courses of Study based on the School Education Law. Within this framework, the boards of education are able to formulate their own educational curricula. The courses of study are revised on the basis of reports from the central government's Curriculum Council, and each school formulates a curriculum based on these. However, authorised textbooks and examinations for entry into upper secondary schools and universities are powerful influences on school curricula.

One of the areas where principals are being required to be more active is external relations. In this context, in addition to the essential formal administrative contacts with boards of education, relationships with the unions and local communities are important. The nationwide organisation of teachers' and administrative staff unions in public schools consists primarily of the Japan Teachers' Union and the All-Japan Teachers' and Staff Union. Principals and other managerial staff are not members of the unions. From the late 1950s until the early 1990s, the Japan Teachers' Union opposed central government education policies. In June 1990, following some union reorganisation, the Japan Teachers' Union proposed the slogan "participation, proposal, reform" advocating: social consensus; a policy of conferring with government; and a dialogue with the business sector. The change in the stance of this union has meant that school-based management can now be discussed in a more positive context. However, the All Japan Teachers and Staff Union, after merging with the left-wing faction of the Japanese Secondary

School Teachers Union in 1991, has sharpened its stance of opposition to government educational policies.

With regard to parents, most schools have a Parent-Teachers Association (PTA), that generally supports school activities for children, providing human and material resources, but not participating in school management. "The concept of opening schools up to their local communities or creating 'open schools' has been an issue since the 1970s. Turning this into a reality, however, has not been an easy task" (see Kawasaki case study). In Kawasaki and several other local communities, organisational measures, such as establishing an ombudsman system or local educational meetings to promote cooperation among schools, households, and the local community, have been gaining momentum.

Case Studies

District Educational Council in Kawasaki City, Kanagawa Prefecture

The heavily industrialised city of Kawasaki is located in the Kanagawa Prefecture that borders on the city of Tokyo. With a population of approximately one and a quarter million, it has 118 elementary schools, 57 lower secondary schools and 27 upper secondary schools. A distinctive and innovatory approach to community building and community-based schools was developed well in advance of the government's very recent legislation promoting decentralisation in education.

Since 1985 the city has been engaged in setting up Lower Secondary School Catchment Area Educational Councils (abbreviated to Regional Education Councils) as part of a programme of linking schools more closely with their local communities. These Regional Education Councils propose:

- Working toward building a network and reaching consensus on child-raising and residents' lifelong learning in the region through consultations with parents, teachers, and residents.

- Having residents participate regularly in the region's educational process, and having the opinions of residents reflected in school administration.

- Cooperating with and coordinating neighbourhood education-oriented groups (such as children's associations and community sports associations) to promote a new era of education in the local community.

- Promoting community activities in areas in which young people live, in order to support healthy development.

- Assessing the lifelong learning needs of local residents and supporting their learning.

In 1989-90, Regional Education Councils were set up on an experimental basis in three lower secondary school catchment areas. By 1997, all lower secondary

121|

catchment areas and seven administration areas had such councils. The focus of each council is on the inter-relationships between adults, children and their communities. The key words underpinning the organisations are networking, participation and consensus. In essence, they are intended to offer advice and support to schools but have no decision-making function.

Typically, the Regional Education Council has some forty members drawn from three broad categories: representatives of the PTA, neighbourhood associations and other organisations concerned with local children; persons drawn from residents' committees; teachers and administrative staff whose work relates to the education and welfare of children, and employees from youth centres, cultural centres and community centres.

Members are not elected. Generally they are nominated by organisations though it is possible for an interested resident to join the council after being nominated by twenty others. Creating such a council has not proved easy, since it requires the commitment of persons who are interested in the school and have the time to attend the various meetings. Further, it has been difficult to find appropriate places for meetings to be held.

The members select their own chairperson. They give their time voluntarily to the work of the council which is conducted through sub-committees. For example, one sub-committee has been drawing up a map of areas where children can play safely while another has produced a newsletter for members. An important activity has been the organisation of a work experience programme for about 100 students.

Kawasaki has promoted an educational programme that focused on human rights especially children's rights, in the context of moral and civic education. This was an important aspect of a broader concern with community education. In-service training opportunities were available for teachers with the principal deciding which teachers should benefit from these. There has been a link between human rights education and the work of the council.

Rinko Junior High School is located in an inner city industrial environment where the majority of the residents are blue collar workers. It has 300 students taught by twenty-two teachers (excluding a principal, a vice-principal and one teacher for health education). In 1997, the Regional Education Council and the principal emphasised the importance of improving the school's partnership with parents and the community. "Everything that the school does has to be for the benefit of the children" was the shared idea but it was difficult to achieve.

The principal emphasised that liaison with this council was an important role for him. He wanted the involvement of parents, arguing that for too long parents regarded schools simply as places that looked after children: "a crucial task for the council was to develop a systematic way for parents' voices to be heard." He saw the council as "a way of building bridges between the school and the homes of pupils, between school and community and between school and the local administration". He acknowledged that, with such a variety of interests represented in the council, it had proved difficult to reach agreements and establish a consensus. Success was dependent on the quality of the persons who participated in the meetings. As the principal asserted, "Active councils demand active members, especially residential members. Other members are engaged in other organisations and consequently are already quite busy". A residential member of the council, who is a retired teacher and had been nominated by twenty others, indicated that, of the forty members, fifteen were active core members. He emphasised that the council, and the various sub-committees, met frequently during school hours and this restricted the participation of persons with jobs, and parents of young children.

Continuity of membership has been an issue. Residential instability, members' time and other constraints and the transfer of teachers between schools, posed particular difficulties in the accumulation of the knowledge and skills essential for running this type of voluntary mechanism for an extended period of time.

The Council has received financial support in the form of a subsidy from the city, but the initial sum (of 400 000 yen) provided in 1996 has now been halved as a result of overall local educational budget cuts. The money was intended to cover such costs as guest speakers and the production of publications. It was paid directly to the chair of the council, who was expected to produce an annual budgetary report. The role of secretary is an important one and, in 46 of the 51 councils, this was undertaken by a teacher, assisted by one of five clerks appointed by the city board. These professionals were familiar with schools, and their administration, and provided the necessary expertise to facilitate the work of the council.

Issues raised in the Regional Education Council, that could not be dealt with adequately at that level, could be passed to one of the seven Administrative District Education Councils. These councils were able to co-ordinate the work of the Regional Education Councils. At the city level, all of these councils were seen as part of a broader concern for building up "community spirit" in a city with many social and economic difficulties.

Since Kawasaki was the first prefecture that introduced these councils, its experience is being evaluated by university researchers and will be influential in policy-making.

Gifu Prefectural Board of Education

Gifu is a city, located 396 kilometers west of Tokyo, which advertises itself as lying in the geographical heart of the nation. The prefecture has a population of 2 118 006 with 413 elementary schools, 205 lower secondary schools and 94 upper secondary schools. There are also nine universities in the prefecture.

123|

In an educational policy statement for 1999, the prefecture states: "In order to nurture those who will support the 21st century, the Gifu Prefectural Board of Education favours teaching to encourage originality (responding to students' abilities, personalities, interests, concerns, etc.) and a link between school, home and community to address problems such as dropouts and bullying." This is translated into three policy goals:

- To promote educational reform through community involvement.
- To promote enrichment through originality.
- To promote community life through sports and culture.

Evidence of how these policies were being interpreted was seen in visits to the Nagara High School and the neighbouring Nagara Elementary School. It is important to note that education receives the highest overall prefectural expenditure, which represented 24% of the budget in 1999.

In order to promote educational reform, the Prefectural Board of Education established the Frontier Plan "Education 21" Research Committee, in January 1997, from which it received proposals in March 1998. Mirroring discussions in Monbusho, these emphasised maximising the energies of places of learning, and gaining the understanding and support of the public to promote education that emphasises both individuality and "emotional education". For this study, an important proposal was: "To make school management more open to the public through such means as building a framework for gauging the views of parents/guardians and local residents."

In July 1999, the Gifu Prefectural Superintendent of Education announced an "Emergency Appeal" to all teachers in the prefecture to review the framework for school management. This review was targeted at the development of: well-disciplined schools; open schools; and dynamic schools. In order to achieve these, the following actions were implemented: the creation of School Councils in all prefectural schools; the establishment of Committees for Improving the Quality of Teaching Personnel; the creation of a school reform "Suggestion Box"; and the establishment of a School Reform Committee within the Gifu Prefectural Board of Education.

At Nagara High School a full meeting was observed of the newly appointed School Advisors. These comprised the school principal, as chairperson, a representative of the PTA, senior teachers and representatives from the prefectural board of education, and five citizen "advisors". The latter had been recommended by the principal to the board of education who appointed them. They were a student's mother, a university lecturer, a local businessman (a former student at the school), a representative of a community organisation and a fashion designer from a local department store. The two items on the agenda were a report of a group which had visited Utah in the USA in preparation for a student study visit focusing on music and geography, and the introduction of an English teacher who had been appointed to the school as part of a national language project.

Each advisor was given the opportunity to raise questions, and make comments about the presentations, or more general issues. Their role was also to provide advice on school management and school activities, particularly with reference to school-community co-operation. Advisors had access to the school's web site and could produce publicity materials relating to the school.

The selection of the topics for discussion in the School Advisors meeting reflected distinctive features of the school. The school prides itself on its English language provision, its international activities, its academic record and its sporting and cultural achievements. It has approximately one thousand students in the three upper secondary years, with 9 classes in each year. There are 62 teaching staff including the principal and two vice-principals. Most of the students go on to university education and it is the school's declared aim to send the whole of the graduating year to prestigious universities. In addition to the general curriculum (divided in the second year into science and humanities routes), the school offers a wide range of extra-curricular activities. The girls' choir has a distinguished record, having won the All Japan Chorus Contest seven times in consecutive years from 1989 to 1995.

Nagara Higashi Elementary School is a relatively new school established 27 years ago. It has 653 students divided into 27 classes with 26 teachers. Designated as an experimental school for curriculum development by the prefecture, it works closely with one of the city's universities. School management was discussed with reference to the role of the recently introduced School Advisors. There are two vice-principals, one with responsibility for the curriculum, and the other for pastoral matters.

The school's mission statement includes reference to the students' self-realisation and to the fostering of links with the local community. It places considerable importance on improving the quality of the teachers, who every three years make a formal presentation on their accomplishments. As in the high school, this elementary school has a strong international flavour. Two classrooms had been set aside for exhibits related to the school's exchange link with Hangzhou in China. This programme illustrates the scope that is available for principals to develop unique curricular and extra-curricular experiences for students. Curriculum space is provided through the compulsory cross-curricular component. This space, combined with a discretionary single teaching period per week, enabled the school to develop a range of community-related activities, including: traditional flower arranging for sixth year pupils; working with handicapped people in the fifth year; and a project on jobs related to the Gifu River in the fourth year.

School Advisors were appointed in April 2000, with five members nominated by the principal and approved by the board of education. The council comprised a former principal, a representative of a residents' organisation, a former PTA representative, a university lecturer and a former adult educator. The principal saw this council as offering support for the teachers in the development of the school's cross-curricular work.

Miyashiro Town Board of Education in Saitama Prefecture

Traditionally in Japan, at the compulsory elementary and lower secondary school levels, students are required to attend those schools in the catchment area in which they live. If, for any reason, parents/guardians do not want their children to attend the designated school, they can either send their child to a private school, or present their reasons for seeking an outside school to the board of education.

Recently, under Monbusho's guidance for the "flexible operation of the school catchment area system", the numbers of students attending schools outside their catchment areas have been increasing, particularly in metropolitan areas. This flexibility has resulted in decreased enrolment and the possibility of school closure or amalgamation. Schools, therefore, seek to gain a greater level of support and trust from their local communities.

Miyashiro is a small town of approximately 33 000 residents located on the northern limits of the Tokyo metropolitan area. It has four elementary schools and three lower secondary schools. Falling school enrolments reflect the decreasing birth rate. Between 1986 and 1998, the number of elementary school students dropped from 3 252 to 2 027, while lower secondary school student numbers fell from 1 977 to 1 241. By 2003, the number of elementary and lower secondary school students is expected to decline to 1 640 and 945 respectively. In response to these changes the municipal board of education decided to implement parental choice of schools, gradually. In restructuring its system, the town sought to introduce a school selection system, controlled by the administration, to ensure that no school would either be closed, amalgamated or become too small. The decision, to introduce parental choice in limited areas, was made before Monbusho announced the relaxation of its policy.

The key to parental choice was the designation of a small number of school catchment areas as "adjusted areas", so that parents or guardians could choose the elementary and lower secondary schools for their children. But the board of education administrators emphasised that time was needed for negotiation. Parents liked to have two choices – the designated school and one other. At no point was there any discussion about choosing schools outside the town or prefectural boundaries.

In setting up its system for adjusting areas, the Director of the Student Affairs Division of the Miyashiro Board of Education spent considerable time listening to the opinions of the residents. It was decided to establish adjustment areas in four locations comprising 17% of Miyashiro's total area. Elementary school, and lower secondary school students, living in the adjusted areas were similarly given the option of choosing a preferred school. There were 34 elementary school students residing in adjusted areas in 1997, of whom five elected to attend a school of their choosing. The rest attended their designated school. In 1998 there were 11 transfers in total and 7 in 1999.

Between May 1997 and February 1998, there were some twelve stages in the implementation of the school selection programme including: the designation of the adjusted areas; providing information to households; and receiving applications for selected schools. Linked to the school selection policy was the encouragement given by the board of education to each school to build on its unique strengths and promote its distinctive individuality.

This uniqueness was well illustrated in Kasahara Elementary School, a facility with distinctive architecture. The design of the building was modeled on Ryugu Castle, with two stories standing in spacious and attractive grounds. Wide and open corridors give access to well-appointed classrooms which are considered as students' "living space". A feature of this elementary school is the provision of appropriately equipped specialist rooms for music, the creative arts and science. The town's own financial resources over and above the Monbusho's school building grants made it possible. It was evident that the school was seeking very deliberately to enhance the curriculum in many ways. Curriculum leadership, coming from the team of principal and two vice-principals, was the key to this success. It is not surprising that the school received requests for children to be able to commute there from other school catchment areas. However, the numbers who have transferred to the school are still very small. The school does not have a parent-teacher association (PTA) and is currently exploring ways of developing a closer relationship with the community. One of the concrete steps is that some redundant classrooms have been transformed into a community-based vocational activity centre for physically handicapped people and into a community meeting place.

Innovation and Effectiveness

The three case studies highlighted school-community relationships in one way or another. However, these are complicated and multi-faceted both in their motivations and in their activities. They embrace curricular and extra-curricular activities, community development, school improvement and public relations.

The District Educational Council in Kawasaki City is a long-standing school – community mechanism to address a wide range of education-related issues with a strong bottom-up initiative and input from its residents. Unfortunately, it is rather difficult to judge the success of the innovations without evaluation data. The School Advisors were introduced in schools very recently so that it is too early to judge the merits and impact of their appointment. However, they mark a substantial step in the attempt to formalise the links between schools and their communities.

127|

Miyashiro's innovation on parental choice at the school level is so far very small in scale. Nonetheless, it is likely to figure more prominently in the future as decreasing enrolment impacts on all sectors of the school system. Decisions relating to the management of falling rolls are made outside the school but, for principals, the need to ensure their schools remain distinctive and successful, while communicating these features to the community, is likely to be increasingly important.

It is clear that enthusiastic schools or school boards are able to find some space for interesting, though not fundamental, innovations. Successful innovations are taking place, sometimes in the wake of central government policy-making, and sometimes at the grassroots level of individual schools or school boards. There is a substantial and influential private education sector in Japan. There seems to be some innovative initiatives in the sector but that was beyond the scope of the visit.

As a framework, the existing education system, with local and prefectural education boards, already has a number of decentralised management features. However, in practice hierarchical public management tradition has dominated until recently. Management by directives from higher levels of authority is changing, yet it has bred deep-rooted passivity at education board and school levels. Bottom-up initiatives are hard to spring up within the context.

Education boards retain most of the managerial responsibilities under the existing system: on human resources, decisions regarding the numbers of teachers who are to be appointed to school staffs or transferred from one school to another are made by the appropriate boards; on finances, school budgets are determined by boards of education and are largely defined by staff salaries. Subsidies are provided by municipal and prefectural boards of education to support particular school activities, assisting in the promotion of school individuality. Special funding is made available to support newly formed School Advisors.

At the school level there is already much concern with problems related to student behaviour, on the one hand, and ever increasing parental expectations for student achievement on the other. Adding responsibilities for curriculum improvement, staff development and establishing community relationships is inevitably seen by schools as a burden. This would require a radical redefinition of the role of the principal, from the sensitive mentor and careful administrator, to the efficient manager and human developer.

Principals are aware of the need to have professional development policies that include staff self-evaluation and in-service training. But currently there is no mandatory requirement for principals to receive training. Principals met in the study schools emphasised their role as educational leader while acknowledging the importance of fulfilling externally defined administrative and legal requirements.

Broad public sector reform has been putting pressure on the educational sector and on its move towards decentralisation and deregulation. It is recognised, at all levels of the system, that decentralisation inevitably means the transfer of resources and decision-making powers to prefectures, municipalities and schools. So far, financial resources have not been transferred.

It still needs to be seen how new educational objectives and modernisation of schools toward the 21st century will be reconciled with the current management practice in Japan. This includes a strong top-down structure, such as the nomination of school board members and school advisors, rather than an election as well as significant gender and age imbalance in management (the composite of principals and board members).

Bibliography

EDUCATIONAL COMMISSION FOR KAWASAKI CITY (1986),
Looking for Lively Kawasaki Education, Kawasaki City and City Board of Education.

KOSHINO, S. and FUKAMI, T. (2000),
Case Studies on the "Flexible Management of School Attendance Areas", Jinbungakuho (The Journal of Social Sciences and Humanities), Tokyo Metropolitan University, No. 308.

MOCHIZUKI, T. (2000),
"The School Council System in Gifu", Kyoshoku Kenshu ("Teacher Training"), May.

SANSEIDO (1999),
Kyoiku Sho-Roppo (Education Acts and Related Acts).

MEXICO

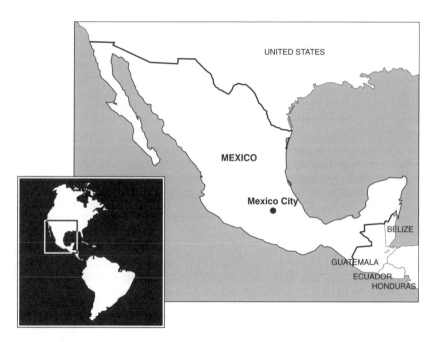

Land area in square kilometers: 1 996 000

Total population (1998): 95 675 000

Per capita GDP (1999 prices): 8 100 USD

Percentage of GDP on education (1997): 4.5%

Amount spent per student (1997):
- 935 USD (Primary)
- 1 726 USD (Secondary)

Teacher salary range (1998):
- 10 036-19 346 USD (Primary)
- 14 708 USD (Lower secondary, 15 years experience)

Sources: *Labour Force Statistics: 1978-1998*, OECD, Paris, 1999; *Main Economic Indicators*, OECD, Paris, April 2000; *Education at a Glance – OECD Indicators 2000*, OECD, Paris, 2000.

Country context

With a land area of almost 2 million square kilometres and a population of about 96 million, Mexico shares borders with the United States to the north and Guatemala and Belize to the south-east. It is a representative, democratic and federal republic with a government composed of legislative, executive and judicial branches. The country is divided into thirty-one sovereign states, as well as the Federal District in which the capital, Mexico City, is located.

Bridging both temperate and tropical regions, Mexico's terrain includes mountains, plains, valleys and plateaux. Snow-capped volcanoes slope down to pine forests, deserts and balmy tropical beaches. This diverse topography supports a variety of industries including manufacturing, mining, petroleum and agricultural production. As a member of the North American Free Trade Agreement (NAFTA), it has the United States and Canada as main trading partners. In economic terms, Mexico boasts a GDP of US $370 billion (US $8 100 per person), which ranks it 13th in the world. It has an annual growth rate of over 6%. Beginning in 1985, Mexico began a process of trade liberalisation and privatisation. From 1982 to 1992 government-controlled enterprises were reduced from 1 155 to 217.

Approximately 80% of the population is of mixed European and North American Indian or African slave ancestry (*metizo*) while 10% is of purely indigenous descent (*indigena*). Mexicans are predominantly Roman Catholic, Spanish speakers but more than 50 distinct indigenous peoples maintain their own languages and cultural traditions. The indigenous population is over-represented in the poverty statistics in which 28 million Mexicans are estimated to live in extreme poverty with a further 12 million classified as poor.

Both rural/urban and internal/external migration characterise the life of many Mexicans seeking improved employment opportunities. For example, the population moving from rural areas to municipalities of more than 2 500 increased by 13% from 1970 to 1990. Seasonal agricultural labourers regularly migrate with their families to northern farms searching for work. The number of Mexican citizens living in the United States was estimated to be 7 million in 1996.

Mexico has a very young population with 56% aged 24 or younger. In 2000, the population below the age of 14 represented a third of the total – falling to 28.4% by 2020. The number of pre-school children is declining at an annual rate of 0.7% while the demand for mandatory basic education among 6- to 14-year olds is experiencing an annual increase of 0.1%. It is estimated that the juvenile population, age 15 to 24, will reach 20 million by 2020.

Mexico has a vast educational system with about 1.5 million teachers instructing 28 million students enrolled in 208 000 schools during 1998-99. 90% attend primary and secondary schools, while 8% are enrolled in post-secondary institutions and 2% receive job training. Education has long been a political priority and was a major issue in the 2000 presidential elections which were won by the National Action Party (PAN).

Challenges Facing School Management

Traditionally, public education in Mexico has been a centralised, bureaucratic system related more to school administration than management. Teachers, principals and supervisors have academic responsibilities but the quality of their work and commitment has often been questioned. There has been a lack of teamwork in sharing experiences, problem-solving and decision-making. The local school has seemed more preoccupied with political issues, working conditions and regulations than educational improvement.

The School Technical Councils, designed to provide academic planning and evaluation, have spent most of their two-hour monthly meetings on administrative matters. Administrative functions and teacher absenteeism also have limited the time devoted to academic instruction and assessment duties. There has been a lack of parent participation in schools as teachers and administrators have not felt obligated to inform them about pupil progress or academic concerns. This system of education has been shaped by a variety of factors including: poor teacher training; rapid expansion of educational services; administrative demands; union relations; undefined tenure and retirement provisions; lack of training for principals and supervisors; absence of evaluation procedures; and limited access to the schools by parents and students. In order to transform and modernise the system, the Ministry of Public Education has strongly encouraged teachers, principals and supervisors to be active participants in educational renewal. This has involved a process of self-assessment at the local school level to identify needs and mobilise resources to satisfy these needs.

This has been a very difficult task as traditional bureaucratic attitudes and longstanding unsuitable practices are deeply ingrained in some Mexican schools. In order to transform schools from such a system to an educational management process focused on the needs of the learners, several changes are required. In school projects, personnel are now encouraged to work as a team to improve their educational environment and to be more accountable for the learning outcomes of their students. This must involve teachers, principals and supervisors redefining their roles. The objectives and organisational role of the School Technical Council must also be redefined to provide leadership in the transformational process. Finally, the relationship between the school and the family must be nurtured and strengthened.

Main Policy Approaches and Framework

In May 1992, the governments of the 31 states joined with the federal Ministry of Public Education (SEP) and the National Union of Education Workers (SNTE) to create the "National Agreement for the Modernisation of Basic Education". Under the Agreement the operation of basic educational services, previously provided

133|

by the Federal Government, was devolved to be the responsibility of each individual state. State governments, therefore, became responsible for the management of all pre-school, elementary and lower secondary schools, as well as teacher education services. Funds were committed to ensure the quality provision of these services. The responsibility for the Federal District (Mexico City) remained with the Ministry.

A major outcome of the Agreement has been the reorganisation of curricular content and instructional materials. The Federal Government redefined study plans and has continued to provide free text books for the six primary grades, as well as other educational materials and instructional resources for teachers. State governments have the authority to identify needs and establish educational services to meet these needs. Funds are transferred to the state governments who are responsible for improving the quality of education in the local schools. The Federal Government, however, retains the responsibility for the provision of study plans, programmes and basic materials. In January 1995, the Federal Government proclaimed the "1995-2000 Educational Development Programme", which further defines the objectives, strategies, and actions governing educational management as stated in Article 3 of the Constitution of the Republic.

Strategies and actions undertaken by the Ministry of Public Education have included the following:

- Increases in public spending with 4.5% of the GDP assigned to public education in 1997 (the most recent figures). Allied to these increases was greater access to schooling for children and young people at basic, upper secondary and post-secondary levels.

- The state governments managing 10% of the federal budget for education to encompass personnel training, construction, maintenance and equipping of schools.

- PROGRESA (Programme for Education, Health and Nutrition) a compensatory programme to address the needs of disadvantaged populations including indigenous peoples, farm and migratory workers, marginalised communities and special needs children.

- Basic curricular reform, to improve the quality of teaching and student learning in such areas as oral and written language and mathematical problem-solving.

- "Teacher Modernisation Library".

- The Federal Government proclamation in 2000 of the "Year of Reading" to improve literacy skills and promote a love of reading among people of all ages.

Mexico has also given greater priority to teacher training at both pre-service and in-service levels through such initiatives as the National Programme for the

Permanent Modernisation of Basic Education Teachers (PRONAP), and the Teacher Career Programme. In 1996, the "Programme for the Transformation and Academic Reinforcement of Initial Education Institutions" was introduced in consultation with teacher education institutions to undertake curricular and infrastructure reform aimed at improving quality and relevance. In addition, about 480 Teacher Centres were opened and equipped with satellite receivers, television, libraries and other facilities for learning. Other initiatives included:

- The creation by the state of Nuevo Leon in 1998 of the "Strengthening School Area Supervisors Educational Management Project" (see case study) to reinforce the technical and academic support which school area supervisors provide for principals and teachers.

- At the upper secondary education level, the strengthening of academic services, as well as the "Upper Secondary Education Pilot Project for a Relevant Education" (see case study) which will extend services to 20 000 students in 9 states.

- The National Council for Social Participation, established in 1999 by the Ministry, to encourage parental involvement in developing strategies to improve the quality of education.

Evaluation and research are also seen as important elements in school improvement. The external evaluation of educational achievement was introduced in 1995 by the Federal Government to test a sample of 500 000 students each year in order to establish national standards for different subjects and grades (e.g. reading comprehension and mathematics) at both the primary and lower secondary levels. Two years later, it introduced the "School Management in Elementary Education Project" (see case study) to explore factors which limit the achievement of Mexico's educational goals including study plans, programmes and the performance of teachers, principals and school area supervisors. Two further initiatives are worth noting:

- Distance learning supported through the EDUSAT (Satellite Education) net which will extend information services to 35 thousand lower secondary and primary schools and expand teacher education opportunities in 2000.

- Leadership by the Ministry of Public Education in adult education by co-ordinating services, adapting programmes and renewing support materials for job training and technological education for lifelong learning.

Traditionally, Mexico, as a republic, has three levels of government – federal, state and local – which are subordinate to the Constitution. Article 3 of the Constitution and the General Education Law form the framework for the national education system. It obligates the Federal Government to provide pre-school, elementary and lower secondary education for every citizen. Each state is required to maintain free elementary and lower secondary schooling for which attendance is mandatory. The General Education Law gives the Federal Government the specific right to determine study plans and programmes of elementary, lower secondary and teacher education for the nation. The same law grants the Ministry the responsibility for evaluating the education system and setting compensatory programmes.

In 1993, Article 31 of the Constitution was amended to legally require parents to send their children to both elementary and lower secondary schools. The General Education Law has stipulated the powers of the Federal Government through the Ministry of Public Education (SEP). SEP has the responsibility to raise the national quality of basic education, and to ensure equal access to educational services. The law also requires SEP to regulate a national system of teacher education, in-service training and professional standards for teaching staff to improve the quality of basic education.

The states are responsible for the delivery of basic education including indigenous and special education, as well as pre-service training and the ongoing professional development of teachers. Both levels of government are responsible for compensatory education for disadvantaged populations. The number of Mexican students receiving basic education at the pre-school, primary and lower secondary levels continues to rise. This has been as a result of the extending of basic education services to marginalised populations such as indigenous peoples, children of migrant workers and those living in remote areas. Special programmes have been developed to provide compensatory education for these students.

The law also defines the role of SEP in the promotion of upper secondary, higher education and adult education and training provided by both public and private institutions. There has been a general increase in young people pursuing studies at the upper secondary school level. It is expected that the educational attainment of those aged 15 or older will increase from an average of 6.5 grades in 1990 to reach nine grades by 2010.

Case Studies

Present education policy provides a framework for three case studies designed to improve the quality of education through innovations in school management. Two projects were initiated by the federal Ministry of Public Education – one at the elementary level and the other in upper secondary education. The third case study focuses on the role of area supervisors responsible for basic education in the state of Nuevo Leon.

School Management in Elementary Education Research and Innovation Project

A pilot project was established during the 1997-98 school year, as part of a movement to improve school management undertaken by the Ministry of Public

Education's Directorate for Educational Research. Two hundred schools in the states of Colima, Baja California Sur, Guanajuato, Quintana Roo and San Luis Potosi were included in the pilot project. The School Management Project focused on the work of basic education teachers in developing the intellectual abilities of children at the elementary and lower secondary levels. Its main purposes were: to find or design new instructional materials; to assess professional development strategies in order to transform teaching methods; to enhance student learning; and to promote a process of self-evaluation among educational personnel seeking to improve school performance.

Activities of the project were in three areas:

- *Innovations* to promote the transformation of the organisation and improve educational outcomes.

- *Professional Development* for school workers to acquire self-evaluation skills.

- *Research* to collect and organise information concerning each school's general characteristics and to review the process of innovation undertaken by the school.

Each school was required to assess educational needs according to goals contained in their study plans. Main obstacles to achieving these goals were identified. As a result, a "school project" was mounted in each school to address learning needs, overcome obstacles and evaluate results.

One obstacle to overcome has been the traditional "school culture". Within the 200 annual school days, (comprising 800 hours of instruction), as much as one-third of the time has traditionally been devoted to organisational meetings and civic activities as opposed to the teaching of students. Principals' duties have been mainly of an administrative nature rather than dedicated to improving the learning process. Parents and other community members have not been involved with the school nor have they been kept informed regarding student progress.

The project represents an intervention, not from the national level, but from local principals, teachers and parents, in developing their own process of self-evaluation to improve the quality of the school's learning environment. Tools to encourage this transformation have included materials and professional development.

Traditional approaches to national evaluation at the local school level have been mostly ineffective as the teachers' union tends to discourage activities which disturb existing practices. Therefore, schools have been reluctant to deal with findings and data gained from any form of external assessment.

The School Management Project emphasises a self-evaluation process of innovation geared to the needs of each school. Leadership is drawn from principals and area supervisors but especially from teachers. Professional development activities prepare local personnel to be active participants in selecting a self-evaluation process for the school using information gained from both local self-assessment and external assessment conducted by the state ministries of education.

Some anticipated results from the pilot project included the following dramatic changes:

- Introducing transformation of traditional schools into "new self-evaluating public schools".

- Emphasising the education of children in the classroom – not administrative and bureaucratic inertia.

- Trying mechanisms to ensure the right of parents to participate in the education of their children.

- Promoting professional co-operation between teachers and principals.

- Making teachers and principals more accountable for educational outcomes.

- Opening the school's self-evaluation process and its outcomes to public scrutiny.

- Redefining the role of the principal – educational leader not administrative bureaucrat.

- Encouraging these changes in school management on a school-by-school basis according to each unique set of needs.

The School Management Project started with five states with 40 schools in each state. A Project Co-ordinator and team in each state invited schools to participate and schools had to choose to join the project. They had to agree to its purposes and the self-evaluation nature of the process – not top-down direction from the state or federal governments. Participating schools received more educational materials and training but they retained autonomy in finding their own solutions to their own needs in improving the intellectual abilities of their students. Each individual school project must be open to parental participation in a more co-operative environment, which stresses a democratic "esprit de corps".

The project began in 1997 with 200 schools. By 2000, it had grown to 2 000 schools in 20 states. The original pilot schools became mentors for the newcomers. About 80% of project schools are now using the self-evaluation process. What does the school have to do to make a difference among teachers, principals, children and parents in coping with the national purpose? It is clear that a long-term commitment is required with a slow steady rate of growth. The project also needs institutional support – not only principals and teachers – but state ministries of education must be involved in supporting the change process.

If area supervisors are involved, schools are more likely to be successful in implementing the self-evaluation objectives. Some schools have a shortage of equipment and a need for improved facilities which also may impact on the success of the school project. However, now they can identify their needs and work towards improvements. The role of the principal has also changed from a keeper of administrative detail to a leader for educational improvement. Parents are more likely to be participating in project schools. Longitudinal case studies are recording the change process in individual project schools. About 30% of schools have had limited success because of a relaxation of commitment and teacher transfers.

During a visit to Colima, the School Management Project State Co-ordinator and his team of former teachers described their work in meeting with area supervisors, principals and teachers to discuss local needs and the objectives of the project. In general, there is a difference of opinion between school personnel who recognise the importance of a self-evaluation school-based initiative and those who see improved facilities, equipment, materials and salaries as a prerequisite to change. However, the need for an effective School Technical Council, where practitioners can gather to discuss teaching methods, student learning and "quality issues about education", was almost universally supported. In Colima, the Project Team assessed progress achieved during the two-year pilot period (1997-1999). In the 40 pilot schools, it was felt that initial resistance to the School Management Project among principals and teachers had declined. Teachers were feeling more involved in the life of the school and had learned to work better together as colleagues. They were listening to each other, sharing pedagogical experiences, solving educational problems and working to improve the quality of teaching. Evaluation of academic outcomes has led teachers to do more work on improving language and mathematics through school projects. The principal, previously preoccupied with administrative duties, has begun to be seen as a supportive educational leader.

A new role for parents was also emerging. Teachers began to actively seek parental involvement by making them more aware of changes in the school programme and teaching techniques. As a result, parents became more politically active as advocates for improved school facilities. The concept of shared responsibility among school personnel and parents was also seen in such activities as school maintenance, food preparation and the organising of special events (*e.g.* poetry contest).

Parents are also better able to appreciate the vital contribution of schooling in improving the future quality of life and employability of students. The improved relationships with teachers and the local school have helped parents to better understand the importance of literacy, numeracy and technological skills (*e.g.* computers) to the future social and economic well-being of their children and the Mexican nation.

Upper Secondary School Project for a Relevant Education

There are two main types of upper secondary education in Mexico: professional technical education and general education (*bachillerato*). Professional technical education, involving 14.4% of enrolled students, is a three-year programme to prepare students for a specific type of employment rather than university preparation. However, by completing six supplementary courses, technical education students can now achieve equivalency with a *bachillerato*. Technical qualifications are registered with the Department of Professions of the Ministry of Public Education (SEP). Examples of such technical institutions are the National School of Professional Studies (CONALEP) and the Centres for Industrial and Service Technological Studies (CETIS).

The three-year bachillerato can be found in two forms – the "bivalent" and the general or pre-university arm. The bivalent combines professional training in a technical setting with upper secondary studies to prepare students for advanced studies, preferably technological. Bivalent institutions existing in such fields as science and technology, industry and services, marine studies and farming technology now prepare 27.4% of students.

The general preparatory bachillerato includes: different schools linked to public and private universities; schools accredited by the federal government; and *colegios de bachilleres* and state preparatory schools. The general preparatory bachillerato stream now accounts for 58.2% of upper secondary students. Only half of Mexico's young people enter upper secondary schooling and of these about 55% complete their studies and enter university. In general, only between 16 and 24% of those students who entered upper secondary schools during the 1990s graduated from higher education. The high school graduation certificate has little value in the labour market.

In 1994, the Mexican Government approached the Organisation for Economic co-operation and Development (OECD) to conduct an examination of its higher education policy. The 1996 Review of Higher Education Policy in Mexico expressed a concern that the lack of diversification in the upper secondary and higher education systems, especially related to a weakness in technical education, placed the country at a strategic disadvantage. It recommended the creation of new or improved educational and training opportunities – particularly programmes of a short duration with the option to continue to higher levels.

As a result of the OECD review, the Ministry of Public Education prepared a background report addressing the diversification of the upper secondary school system and the first years of higher education. In 1998, the Pilot Project for a Relevant Education was established by the Vice-Ministry of Higher Education and Scientific Research. The Project has the following objectives:

• To improve teaching and learning in the upper secondary schools.

- To transform the orientation and contents of the upper secondary system to correspond to existing legal and academic frameworks of education service providers.

- To substantially upgrade the social value of general education programmes according to new practical and technical strategies.

- To attract and retain students, as well as to improve graduate efficiency.

- To raise the profile of the new programmes with local authorities and employers, so as to ensure jobs for graduates.

The pilot project encouraged a new approach to learning which would incorporate the students' own life experience in order to heighten their interest in gaining new technical and practical knowledge and skills. Learning through example would be emphasised with direct application to future employment. New strategies for assessment and monitoring the knowledge of students and teachers would be developed. Course contents would be reduced to enhance student active – learning rather than memorisation.

To the basic subjects of lower secondary education – mathematics, physics, chemistry, biology and social sciences – four new contemporary technological subjects were added. Civics and economics; machine and motor technology; information and communication; and health and environmental care were seen as an essential educational framework for Mexican citizens.

In January 1999, the pilot project began with ten upper secondary schools – all in urban areas. The ten schools were in different states, functioning under very different conditions of student population, teacher contracts, material, equipment and administration. A review of the pilot project by a team from the OECD from June 15 to 21, 2000 produced the following observations.

Although still in its early stages, the project seems to have made a difference in: teacher-student interaction; curriculum innovation; and familiarisation with computer technology. Teachers particularly value: the new curriculum materials; project-specific professional development; and the networking within and across schools. Students seem to like: the regular tutoring by teachers; access to computers; and more opportunities for question and answer sessions. The challenge now is to extend the positive results from the pilot project to improve the relevance of upper secondary education throughout the nation (OECD, 2000).

Field visits to pilot project schools consisted of Bachillerato 4 in the city of Colima and the Escuela Industrial Alvaro Obregon in the city of Monterrey. Each visit was conducted by the local federal Project Co-ordinator who, with a small team, is responsible to manage the coherence between all school initiatives and the objectives of the programme. The co-ordinator is also in charge of: the incorporation of new pedagogical tools specifically designed for the programme; monitoring of student progress; and keeping teachers informed about the programme.

In Colima, the Project partner is the University of Colima which manages upper education in 12 localities. The university provides a general baccalaureat and 10 technical options (*bachillerato tecnico*). Bachillerato 4 is linked to the university and the Director of Upper Secondary and Higher Education serves as the co-ordinator.

The attractive mini-campus was very well maintained with clean, freshly painted classrooms, a small library and internet-connected computers available on a self-service basis. A general meeting with project teachers was convened to review accomplishments and discuss future directions.

A set of pilot project standards was contained in a contract between the federal government and the University of Colima. Standards to be met included specifications for the library, laboratories, classrooms, washrooms, gardens and sports areas. Teachers and students, interested in a new way of teaching and learning, enrolled in the project on a voluntary basis.

Facilities include: twelve classrooms with screens; four television sets; overhead projectors; a computer-assisted design workshop; self-service computer lab; and a teachers' workroom with internet and project networking connections. The twelve teachers have specialities in such fields as: applied chemistry; metallurgy; informatics; topography; design; literature; history and English.

Teachers work on a collegial basis with the students to enhance their self-directed learning skills. In a meeting organised with students, study tours of local industries were described which better link the curricula and programme to future employment. Regular meetings are held with parents to explore the objectives of the programme and progress achieved.

A second upper secondary school visit was arranged to Escuela Industrial Alvaro Obregon in the city of Monterrey, capital of the state of Nuevo Leon. Nuevo Leon is an industrial region which faces a shortage of skilled workers. Part of a huge former factory was utilised to provide several classrooms constructed within the building. Local industrial employers have donated modern equipment to assist teachers in imparting practical skills geared to future employment needs. This workplace setting provides almost an apprenticeship on-the-job learning experience for students directly related to skill shortages in the industrial region.

The two schools in Colima and Monterrey were quite different institutions but both demonstrated positive features of the Pilot Project for Relevant Education. While the federal Vice Ministry Secretariat of Higher Education and Scientific Research has overall responsibility for the project, a strong working relationship between federal officials, local co-ordinators, principals and teachers is evident. The sharing of values, concepts and implementation strategies is enhanced by frequent meetings of university partners with project participants. Participants also share information, knowledge and assessment procedures through ongoing e-mail contact. Project staff are in continuous contact with teachers to collect their feedback on such innovations as the teachers' guide and the application of new curricular and programme materials.

Strengthening School Area Supervisors and Principals Educational Management through the School Project in the State of Nuevo Leon

This school management project, established by the state of Nuevo Leon in 1998, focuses on changing the role of the area supervisor to improve the quality of education in the schools. It was felt that change must first be achieved by convincing chief supervisors and area supervisors of the need for improvement so as to eventually gain the participation of principals and teachers at the local level.

Traditionally, the role of area supervisors has been neglected by policy but their support is essential if change is to be achieved in the schools. Their duties have been mostly administrative rather than providing academic leadership. As a result they were not always respected in the schools but they were feared for their political and administrative power. But, as former teachers and principals, they have the potential to make a much more important contribution to school management.

The original pilot project began in 1998 with a group of 57 primary and special education school supervisors (representing about 10% of the total supervisors in the state). They were first surveyed as to their attitudes concerning the current limitations on their technical and pedagogical functions. They felt it would be difficult, but not impossible, to make this change in role as they are persons with 30 to 45 years of service in the education system.

To achieve this transformation they felt a need for their own professional development programmes through the establishment of groups of supervisors meeting together regularly. They wished to strengthen the function of the supervisor with the addition of support personnel trained in modern technical and pedagogical methods. They also hoped to get closer to the schools through being more involved in local "school projects" designed to improve the quality of education in the classroom.

In 1999, a further group of 150 supervisors, at all basic education levels, was added to the project with the original group of 57 acting as mentors. The project now had three facets: professional development activities for groups of supervisors; specific technical support for those working groups; and follow-up procedures concerning their work in the schools. The professional development facet dealt with a better understanding of the reform process beginning in 1992, an updating of current pedagogical methods and an overview of current basic education curricula. Supervisors also learned about the planning process leading to the

143|

initiation of local school projects. The new supervisor's role is then to monitor the progress of school projects, and report to the state Ministry of Education concerning their need for additional resources.

The supervisor now becomes a facilitating source (as opposed to an authoritarian force) to bring the ministry's resources to bear on the educational needs of the local school through its own locally-initiated project. Supervisors act as enablers of educational improvement in the schools, thus gaining respect and raising their self-esteem. As a result of the success achieved in the first two phases, the state government has decided to extend the project to all 600 school supervisors in the 2000-2001 school year. There is some concern that such a rapid expansion would not be able to be sustained by existing project resources, technical support and follow-up provisions.

Anticipated results of the "Strengthening School Area Supervisors and Principals Educational Management through the School Project" are as follows:

- A change in the role of the school supervisor from pursuing strictly administrative duties to one of academic leadership through acquiring the pedagogical and conceptual skills needed to assist principals and teachers in improving the education of children.

- An improvement in the quality indicators and Ministry of Education institutional procedures to better support teachers and principals in their daily work.

A field visit was arranged to the Rebeca Cantd Ayala primary school in Monterrey. The area supervisor and principal conducted a tour of first, fourth and sixth grade classrooms. This was a morning school with classes from 8:00 a.m. to 12 noon. A different school occupies the building from 1:00 p.m. to 5:00 p.m. About 40% of teachers work in both schools.

The federal Ministry of Public Education (SEP) provides all texts, workbooks and teachers' guides. Children with learning disabilities (*e.g.* perceptual, autism, behavioural) are integrated into the classes. Children seemed happy and proud of their workbooks, which were marked on a regular basis by teachers who encouraged good performance. While supplementary reading material was quite limited, the children created wall displays and story boards (*e.g.* National Day, the Olympics). Academic progress is assessed on a regular basis (September, April and June) by the state Ministry of Education in addition to local testing and diagnostic procedures.

Innovation and Effectiveness

In 1992, Mexico began an ambitious series of reform initiatives to transform school management at the pre-school, primary and lower secondary levels of compulsory basic education. The relevance of upper secondary schooling has also been assessed and with it the need for better technical and vocational education within federal, state, independent and private institutions.

But, introducing change in a very traditional education system of 208 000 schools with 1.5 million teachers and 28 million students is a challenge of monumental proportions. For example, the rate of poverty, particularly among indigenous peoples and migrant agricultural workers, stands at 40 million (or 42% of the population). Only 50% of Mexico's young people continue beyond a grade nine level and only half of these complete upper secondary school and go on to higher education. The three case studies described in this chapter represent valiant efforts to better serve the needs of these disadvantaged learners, to provide more skilled workers for the country's burgeoning industrial sectors and to prepare young people to be productive citizens in a new technologically-focused, knowledge-based economy.

The 1995-2000 Educational Development Programme outlines a range of innovations that will have to be undertaken by different levels of government to bring Mexican education from the 19th to the 21st century. Increased spending by the federal and state governments to improve school buildings, purchase new furniture, equipment and learning materials and raise teachers' salaries has been a definite priority. The fact that many schools operate on a two-shift basis with teachers working from 8:00 a.m. to 5:00 p.m. underscores this need. The Federal Government has encouraged the educational renewal process through curricular reform and the publishing and distributing of some very attractive texts and workbooks, basically for primary schools. There is also a concerted effort to introduce and/or improve school libraries at the basic education level. Other essential innovations have been directed to the schooling needs of rural indigenous peoples and migrant agricultural workers. Children of these impoverished families have traditionally had limited exposure to educational services because of remote location or transient lifestyle. The Ministry of Public Education has produced special teaching and learning materials to improve their educational opportunities. For example, a computer information tracking system is now being implemented to ensure that migrant children continue their education wherever they may relocate.

Efforts at the upper secondary level in this regard are more modest. Material improvements, however, are of little consequence unless the existing school culture can be modified and educational leadership transformed to improve the quality of classroom teaching and learning. All three school management case studies address these concerns by mounting pilot projects designed to maximise the potential of the human resources to be found in Mexican schools and the communities they serve.

The SEP's School Management in Elementary Education Project exemplifies these objectives by focusing on the needs of teachers to be self-evaluators of their own learning environments. To enable this transformation to take place, the

145|

role of local school principals must be radically changed. No longer can they afford to be administrative gate-keepers. Instead, they must become transformational leaders who empower teachers to assess learning needs, plan and implement school projects and evaluate the results on an ongoing basis to improve classroom performance. Parents have been acknowledged as valued participants in the learning process. This self-evaluation design has involved innovation, professional development and action research. It began with 200 schools in 5 states, and has now been extended to 2 000 schools in 20 states. Top-down resources have been used most effectively to encourage bottom-up renewal. This is a model, which has a strong potential to be emulated by many other countries who face the kind of educational challenges to be found in Mexico.

The Pilot Project for a Relevant Education is another innovative initiative by the Federal Government in response to the needs of young people in Mexico's rapidly developing social and economic context. The key players include governments, employers, the universities and the upper secondary schools. A pilot project, involving classrooms in ten schools in different states was initiated to develop new diversified curricula, teaching methods, professional development and contacts with employers seeking skilled workers. The improvements seen in pilot schools were impressive in terms of classroom and library facilities, the use of computers and modern technical equipment to better prepare students for higher education and future employment. These innovations may serve as a benchmark to encourage the restructuring of a traditionally academic upper secondary system into one which attracts and retains students while preparing them for the challenges of a new technological age.

The final case study describes a basic education school management project initiated by the state of Nuevo Leon. The focus here has been to transform the traditional role of the area supervisor, from purely administrative functions, to a facilitator and monitor of educational improvement programmes at the local school level. This radical change in job description was achieved through the formation of professional working groups, the addition of technical assistance and the acquisition of modern pedagogical and evaluative skills to better serve the needs of school improvement projects. The result has been a new sense of self-esteem and professional purpose for area supervisors. Success with the original pilot project may lead to a totally new leadership role for all area supervisors in the state.

In conclusion, Mexico has introduced some very important innovations in school management which have the potential for replication in many other countries faced with the challenge to update and improve the quality of their educational provisions (*e.g.* Latin America). They have approached change as a grassroots, bottom-up developmental process rather than through a series of top-down directives, rewards and sanctions. It should be recognised, however, that as valuable as these experiences are, Mexico faces an immense challenge in scaling them up into effective reforms. It is the use of the carrot, not the stick, that seems to be working to improve Mexico's vast, complex, impoverished system of education. It is hoped that these innovations will be sustained to serve as a catalyst for continuous renewal as Mexico enters a new era of political governance.

Bibliography

CONSEJO NACIONAL DE POBLACIÓN (Conapo) (1999),
    The Demographic Situation of Mexico, Editions 1997 and 1998.

MINISTRY OF PUBLIC EDUCATION (1999*a*),
    Profile of Education in Mexico, 2nd revised edition.

MINISTRY OF PUBLIC EDUCATION (1999*b*),
    1998-1999 School Year Report, Mexico.

MINISTRY OF PUBLIC EDUCATION (2000),
    2000 Educational Sector Programme.

MINISTRY OF SOCIAL DEVELOPMENT (1996),
    National Migrant Agricultural Programme, Mexico.

NATIONAL INSTITUTE OF STATISTICS, GEOGRAPHY AND INFORMATICS (1995),
    Population and Housing Survey.

OECD (1998),
    Overcoming Exclusion through Adult Learning, Paris.

OECD (2000),
    "Quality, Equity and Relevance: Report on a Pilot Project to Reform Academic Upper Secondary Schools in Mexico".

SECRETARIAT OF EDUCATION (2000),
    Upper Secondary Education Pilot Project for a Relevant Education.

VICE MINISTRY OF HIGHER EDUCATION AND SCIENTIFIC RESEARCH, MINISTRY OF PUBLIC EDUCATION (2000),
    Upper Secondary Education, Pilot Project for a Relevant Education.

NETHERLANDS

Land area in square kilometers: 41 000

Total population (1998): 15 698 000

Per capita GDP (1999 prices): 25 100 USD

Percentage of GDP on education (1997): 4.3%

Amount spent per student (1997):
- 3 335 USD (Primary)
- 5 152 USD (Secondary)

Teacher salary range (1998):
- 24 593-35 494 USD (Primary)
- 25 762-51 956 USD (Secondary)

Sources: *Labour Force Statistics: 1978-1998*, OECD, Paris, 1999; *Main Economic Indicators*, OECD, Paris, April 2000; *Education at a Glance – OECD Indicators 2000*, OECD, Paris, 2000.

Country context

The Netherlands is the second most densely populated country (after Korea) among OECD nations with 15.7 million people crowded into 41 000 square kilometres. Fertile land reclaimed from the sea provides for a highly automated and efficient agricultural sector whose worldwide exports are second only to the United States and France. It also has a strong industrial economy led by food-processing, oil-refining, metalworking, chemicals and electronics. Almost 80% of the gross domestic product, however, is devoted to the services' sector which accounts for 75% of the labour force.

The Netherlands boasts an unemployment rate of about 5% – one of the lowest among OECD countries. However, a quarter of the labour force is either on social security or job creation schemes. Many new jobs created during the 1990s have been part-time. Women comprise about 50% of the workforce but the long-term unemployment rate among women with little education is four times that of the unemployed population as a whole. Persons of Dutch heritage comprise 96% of the population with the other 4% being of predominantly Turkish or Moroccan origin.

Two themes characterise schooling in the Netherlands. First, the national government maintains a stated policy to "decentralise and deregulate" the educational services. While overall financial support is provided by the Ministry of Education, 70% of schools are operated by the private, non-profit sector (e.g. denominational) leaving 30% to be administered by local municipalities (state schools). In fact, "the right of choice" is enshrined in national educational policy. Groups of parents, religious or pedagogical interests may establish and maintain independently managed schools financially supported by the Dutch government. In 1999, there were more than 7 700 primary schools with an average enrolment of 218 pupils or an average of 140 for those serving children with special needs. Secondary education consists of 700 schools with an average enrolment of 1 200.

The second theme might be described as "governing from a distance". To ensure accountability, the national Ministry of Education, combines deregulation and enhancement of school autonomy with "quality control" at the local school level. These were formulated after extensive consultation with all parties concerned with the field of education to form an ongoing complementary relationship.

The schools are provided at both the primary and secondary levels. Primary education serves children from age 4 to age 12, while secondary education is for students between 12 and 18 years. Both levels provide special education for pupils with learning disabilities. Secondary schools include education at the pre-vocational (VBO), junior general (MAVO), senior general (HAVO), and pre-university levels (VWO). Secondary vocational training is also provided at the assistant, basic, professional and middle-management levels for students aged 16 to 20 years (Ministry of Education, Culture and Science, 1998). MAVO and VBO are currently in the process of being transformed into VMBO or pre-vocational secondary education, which will also incorporate part of special education.

Country context (*cont.*)

Individual schools (and collectively managed groups of schools) are encouraged to be more autonomous through deregulated financial provisions covering pay and non-pay items of expenditure. VBO, MAVO and HAVO have the same "basic education" curriculum during the first three years of secondary school. Educational output is regulated through final exams with "attainment targets" to be maintained and measured through normative standards of the Inspectorates in Primary and Secondary Education (Kreuzen, van der Pluijm and Sleegers, 2000).

The result is a "loose-tight" deregulation versus regulation conflict. Schools, on one hand, are encouraged to be more autonomous in certain financial, facility and personnel management areas. At the same time, the national government has tightened its controls and expectations regarding curricular content, student achievement and school management. Schools, therefore, often function in a complex and sometimes apparently contradictory environment.

Changes in the social and economic environment have also impacted on the role of the school. Factors, such as the changing nature of work, socio-cultural realities, family relations and the growing freedom of young people, have required schools to develop new values and norms for children and adolescents. Another issue is the growing importance of Information and Communication Technology (ICT) in everyday life and future employment opportunities. The implementation of ICT, while a priority, has been difficult due to a shortage of equipment and teacher know-how. "Beacon schools" have been established to encourage the integration of ICT into the school curriculum and programme and to act as models for other schools.

Challenges Facing School Management

School management in the Netherlands might best be described as "a work in progress". Since the 1980s, the Dutch government has striven to decentralise and deregulate its educational service. The focus is very much on the local management of individual schools, or merged clusters of schools, under the same management structure. While the emphasis may be on local autonomy, the central government maintains strict control in the allocation of: a funding formula; a national curriculum; teacher salary scale; and standards related to student achievement and programme effectiveness. Thus, the local school is expected to demonstrate increased autonomy in the management of its financial grant, facilities and personnel, while the national government demands overall accountability in the output of education in Holland.

The striving for local autonomy, within a context of national accountability, represents contradictory demands for the school manager. Individual schools (or

151|

clusters of schools), are governed by a board of local citizens. This "governing board" is responsible for employing staff, maintaining facilities, and the provision of learning materials. Funding to local governing boards is allocated by the Ministry of Education on a per pupil basis dependent on the educational level of the school. The principal (head-teacher or school manager) is appointed by the governing board to which he/she is responsible for the day-to-day operations of the school, pupil achievement and the implementation of national policies.

Primary school principals (and vice-principals) receive administrative release time from their teaching duties – depending upon the size and educational level of their school. For example, the manager of a school with up to 145 students would normally be released about 13 hours per week while the manager of an average size school of 218 students would have almost 20 hours per week. Schools have budgets to buy more release time for principals, vice-principals or teachers with special assignments. Most secondary schools (average 1 200 students) have more than one full-time vice-principal. Schools do not normally receive secretarial assistance and the principal is responsible for clerical and other administrative duties. Care-taking services are purchased out of the overall school budget.

There is no compulsory pre-service training or certification programme for school managers/principals. They are appointed from the teaching ranks and are expected to improve their managerial skills as they gain experience. In 1994, a voluntary in-service training programme for primary school principals was established with financial support from the Ministry of Education. Secondary school managers have access to a variety of in-service training opportunities on an optional basis. The Netherlands School for Educational Management (NSO) has developed a pre-service programme for secondary school leaders (Kreuzen, van der Pluijm and Sleegers, 2000).

Because of the contrast between the ideals of local autonomy and the reality of national accountability, the role of the school manager is very complex and demanding. Schools are expected to implement a series of top-down political, educational and administrative policies, while maintaining bottom-up local accountability.

Main Policy Approaches

The Dutch government's policy of "governing from a distance" has meant greater responsibility for local school management, while it tightens its control of national educational outcomes. The national curriculum (basic education) mandates attainment targets and the descriptions of levels and skills to be attained.

Education is defined according to a series of normative standards concerning curriculum and programme content. "Quality instruments" include the "integral school monitoring programme" of the Inspectorate in Primary Education, and "quality cards" at the secondary level for each school. The results are published by national newspapers as league tables with the top 5 and lowest 5 schools. Meanwhile, the Inspectorate in Secondary Education is experimenting with intensive evaluative visits to record achievement at that level. Schools are also obliged to provide a "school handbook" supplying parents with detailed information on the school programme and its effectiveness. Public accountability for the quality of education is therefore mandatory.

Decentralisation and deregulation, however, have also meant that a formula budget based on enrolment is delegated to the local school and its governing board. Both direct "lump-sum" grants at the secondary level and the "job-budget" for staff allocation at the primary level give the local school autonomy in areas of financial, facility and personnel management.

Another decentralised development has been the "Local Educational Policy" giving the local community an active role and responsibility for programmes for the socially and educationally disadvantaged (including those for whom Dutch is a second language); compulsory education and drop-outs; educational advisory services; labour market programmes; teaching of immigrant languages; adult education and acculturation; school buildings; and greater freedom in the administration of public education. The larger cities have responded with expanded opportunities for newcomers and the poor with early and pre-school education, language instruction and drop-out reduction policies (Kreuzen, van der Pluijm and Sleegers, 2000).

A second important area of policy development has been the "merging" of institutional and administrative structures to improve efficiency and cost-effectiveness. Secondary education has experienced school mergers (from 2 000 to 700) to improve accessibility and their financial entitlements. In primary education some school mergers took place in the past but currently the central authorities have encouraged the creation of larger management units and professionalisation through financial subsidies to larger boards. Many schools have merged into larger administration systems.

These mergers and organisational changes sometimes have resulted in new managerial functions and levels ranging from building/location co-ordinators to central executive management teams. For example in some instances, three layers of management have been formed: the governing board; a central executive team; and the individual school managers. Divisions in responsibility may be changed profoundly leading to new supervisory roles and decentralised management structures (*e.g.* self-directing teams of teachers).

"Joint representative advisory boards" may function at the central merged-consortium level to advise governing boards on such issues as employment and staff allocations. More demands have been placed on advisory boards due to their

153|

increased influence in policy definition within schools. National authorities have initiated training for employee members of advisory boards, but not for other members (e.g. parents and students).

These administrative developments influenced the form and structure of participation. Professional staff, parents and students have taken a more active role on advisory bodies or participation councils to assist in co-ordinating local educational policy.

Reforms, initiated by the Ministry of Education, represent a third development. These centrally directed innovations are multi-dimensional in that they affect various levels within the school organisation. One such policy has been the integration of special needs children into regular primary schools, reducing referrals to special education facilities. These are children with special learning or behavioural problems (as opposed to the physically handicapped). Schools are encouraged to recognise differences among pupils and to develop a range of programmes for exceptional learning needs. Future plans call for the eventual integration of the handicapped (now in special education facilities) into regular schools (Arion Group, 2000).

Related to the above, the fourth area of development has been the relationship of the school to the local community and the world at large. Decentralisation has given municipalities a greater role in interpreting education policies and sharing services and resources with the school. Such co-operation is demonstrated in the integration of special needs children into regular schools and in community-school linked services such as preventive/pro-active youth care, and social welfare services.

Policy has also moved in the direction of smaller classes. Influenced by the success of the American STAR project, the central authorities have provided additional personnel funds and subsidised accommodation costs to reduce class size between ages 4 and 8. Finding classroom space, in schools with full enrolment, continues to be a problem (Kreuzen, van der Pluijm and Sleegers, 2000).

Secondary education has seen the introduction of the "basic education" curriculum. Students follow a compulsory programme in their first three years followed by a central achievement test. The upper forms of secondary education encourage more independent learning for students through the introduction of a "study-centre" or "second stage" once the basic education curriculum has been successfully completed. Pre-vocational schools offer four different "learning pathways". Both approaches promote active learning and content flexibility requiring teachers to facilitate, rather than direct, the learning process.

Parents are encouraged to be more involved in school governance, management and policy development. "Parental choice" promotes a wider range of learning options. The freedom of denomination, as laid down in the Constitution

(Article 23), gives parents the right to choose and manage schools (Goldring and Sullivan, 1996).

New demands for quality management from central authorities require schools to be accountable to parents and the local community for choices made and results achieved. There is a continuing struggle to ensure parental involvement in the work of governing boards and participation councils. Without parental involvement, policy expectations in such areas as community schools, broad schools and window schools are in jeopardy.

In summary, schools (with their governing boards and managerial staff) are confronted by a vast array of political, educational, moral, social and organisational demands and expectations. Satisfying this diversity of needs and these standards of performance form the basis on which principals, heads, and other management personnel are held accountable both locally and nationally. The complexity of the work of school managers continues to escalate, as they attempt to satisfy the often conflicting demands of top-down versus bottom-up accountability.

Framework

As previously stated, Dutch schools are organised in a decentralised system with management responsibility delegated to a local non-profit organisation or municipality. Each school (or cluster of schools) has a governing board which employs professional staff, maintains facilities and monitors the implementation of curriculum and programme. School managers are employed by the local governing boards to be responsible for site-based budget, facility and personnel management.

The traditional management style might be described as "teachers with special tasks". Their main focus remains the classroom teaching role with limited time devoted to managerial tasks such as the formulation of school policy and the coaching of teachers. This style is particularly apparent in small primary schools where principals have limited release time.

In the implementation of national innovative policies and local accountability, different styles of managerial leadership have evolved to meet these challenges.

Increases in local autonomy have resulted in a call for more "instructional leadership" which is seen as an effective means to promote quality control and public accountability in school performance. Characteristics of this leadership model include the following (van den Berg and Sleegers, 1996a):

- A professional approach to teaching as a role model to other staff.
- Co-ordination of the educational programme of the school to ensure the best use of teacher skills and experience.

155|

- Support for their teachers and encouragement for their ongoing professional development.

- Evaluation of pupils and the ongoing monitoring of academic performance.

- Maintenance of an orderly and peaceful learning environment.

Another leadership method, to deal with the complex and ambiguous changes faced by Dutch schools, has been "transformational leadership". Leaders are expected to be oriented towards the involvement, motivation and capabilities of all actors within the organisation. This method promotes the improvement and renewal of schools in the following ways:

- Professional co-operation among teachers.

- Professional development of teaching personnel.

- Support for teachers in effective problem-solving.

Transformational leaders demonstrate charisma/inspiration/vision to inspire staff to welcome innovations, be aware of their personal goals, and co-operate in developing an overall school mission. Leaders are attentive, respectful and understanding of teachers' feelings and needs. They challenge their teachers to develop intellectually, evaluate and improve their work, try new procedures, and share their expertise with colleagues. Change and innovation are enhanced, as the school becomes an organisation devoted to learning (Leithwood, 1992a).

"Integrative leadership" addresses the need for an expansion in scale and greater autonomy, particularly in larger educational institutions where leadership portfolios may be divided into separate departments. For example, financial affairs need not worry about organisational development or curriculum and programme. With integrative leadership, the principal of a larger school is expected to be responsible for both general administrative duties and the instructional leadership of educational personnel.

The integrative leader combines policies in personnel, educational and financial management. His/her personal leadership vision should encompass a complete picture of what the school stands for and how to accomplish its mission of continuous improvement. Needless to say, the conflicts between the general administrative and instructional roles continue to be a source of tension for principals in today's ever-changing, moral, political and social environment.

The styles of leadership described above are based on the school manager as leader in a top-down hierarchical structure. Another proposed model is to view leadership as a collective responsibility. Members of the professional staff, who have functional qualifications, would share the managerial responsibilities. Managerial functions (such as: organising instruction; promoting teacher co-operation; vision development; facilities management; professional development; encouragement

156

and recognition; standardisation of procedures; and monitoring the processes of change) would be the shared responsibility of the total organisation.

This perception of leadership, sometimes referred to as "interactionistic", obviously requires an advanced state of social interaction, trust and cohesion, within the organisation, rather than relying on the personal qualities of one designated individual. This leadership concept, whereby managerial responsibility is shared by several people in a school, is now being pursued in several Dutch educational institutions (Firestone, 1996).

Case Studies

De Stuifhoek Primary School in Made

De Stuifhoek is a Catholic primary school located in the town of Made. This school of 450 students and 26 staff is led by a particularly dynamic director. The process of innovation really began in 1977, when three schools were merged into one new building. In 1991, it was recognised that the traditional theoretical curriculum (mathematics, spelling, etc.) was too difficult for some children. It was decided to develop a new approach to education based on "learning experience" to better serve the individual needs of pupils (Kolb, 1984).

The community became the focus for education with visits to the town hall, factories, local merchants and historic sites resulting in student-centred projects, which combined both concrete and abstract learning; for example, constructing models of the town's streets and buildings, integrating social studies, mathematics, science and language into a multi-disciplinary theme. Students were encouraged to create their own learning projects.

In 1994, the central government offered additional funding to encourage "inclusionary education". De Stuifhoek became the "School for Experience" and an assistant director for education was appointed who has provided leadership in transforming the school into a "centre for experiential learning" to serve the individual needs of all students, including those with learning disabilities (but not physically handicapped). Consultations were undertaken with existing and former students, parents and neighbours to advise the school on its new policy. Assistance was also sought from professional organisations and an authority on inclusionary education at the University of Utrecht.

As a result of these consultations, three new goals were announced: involvement; well-being; and solidarity. Inclusionary education was defined as "a holistic approach to focus on the individual learning needs of all children including those with intellectual and behavioural disabilities". Today, a series of standardised tests (developed by the CITO Institute) is administered to assess academic achievement and readiness for promotion. A system of "learning contracts" between pupil and teacher has been developed. Parents are kept informed through parental interviews (3 per year) and written reports. Children who are not progressing are referred to a special education committee for remedial assistance. Parents also participate as members of the school governing board and the "parent and teacher advisory committee". About 200 parents are reported to be active volunteers in the school. The Primary Education Inspectorate conducts regular 2 to 3 day intensive visits (every two years) based on the "school plan". Results of these inspectoral visits are published by the Ministry of Education.

De Stuifhoek Primary School is a most impressive learning environment filled with activity and excitement. A friendly rapport exists between pupils and teachers who seem to very much enjoy this student-centred approach to learning. The building is well equipped with colourful displays of children's work. The vibrant atmosphere and sense of respect and caring displayed by children and teachers are a tribute to the principal's "transformational" style of leadership and concern for accountability to local stakeholders and national authorities.

Johan de Witt College, The Hague

Johan de Witt College was established in 1991 by merging several schools to provide secondary education in The Hague. It serves a total of 2 500 students (age 12 to 18 years) from four locations in various parts of the city. Each campus has its own leadership and educational policies. A central executive team of two persons has overall responsibility for the management of the four campuses. They report to a governing board made up of the Mayor and city council. The governing board and central executive are responsible for the instructional programme, financial affairs, personnel matters, day to day operations, and the implementation of national standards.

The visit took place at an inner-city campus providing vocational education to a group of 400 recent immigrants and refugees representing 70 nationalities (e.g. Surinam, Morocco, Turkey, Somalia, Iraq, Iran, etc.). The school's director described the basic instructional and vocational training programmes in technical education (e.g. auto and electrical repair); administrative studies (e.g. bookkeeping, retail sales); and health and care (e.g. nursing assistant) preparing students for service industry employment.

The school building was constructed in the early 1990s, utilising special incentive grants from both the Dutch and European governments, to better educate children of parents in low income inner-city neighbourhoods. Area residents were initially opposed to the project (e.g. traffic flow, crime, etc.), but were reassured that the elaborate security system, with television monitors and controlled access gates, would provide a safe and secure learning environment. (This was a particular concern for Islamic parents who feared for the safety of their daughters.)

The result is a modern, attractive, secure, extremely well-equipped (*e.g.* one computer for 3 students) vocational education institution.

The school is organised around the "broad school" concept serving a neighbourhood suffering from the effects of unemployment, poverty and crime (*e.g.* overcrowding, theft, prostitution and drug sales). Partnerships are forged with local services including law enforcement, social welfare, religious (area mosque), health, and truancy prevention. A "care committee" meets every two weeks to assess the learning needs of individual students. Another valued resource has been the neighbouring museum providing visual, performing arts, and cultural enrichment. The school's lobby proudly displays the logos of ten corporations which have made significant financial and in-kind contributions (*e.g.* computers, retail sales centre, automotive, etc.).

The programme of the school provides for the special learning needs of students with lower academic achievement and socially unstable backgrounds. The building of self-esteem is stressed to prepare students for employment. They are encouraged to be polite and show respect and appreciation. Some observers are critical, however, seeing the school as an artificial society which pampers the students and shelters them from societal realities.

After successfully completing the three-year nationally mandated basic education curriculum, students (and their parents) choose a vocational field (*e.g.* technical, administrative, health and care) to prepare for employment. All students take national standard exams administered by the central authorities. The Inspectorate in Secondary Education conducts a formal inspection every two years to assess progress in such areas as administrative affairs, curriculum and programme, teaching techniques and student health and safety. Parental contact is maintained with four parent interviews during the year. Parents are also encouraged to join with students and teachers as members of the "participation council". This involvement, however, is often difficult to achieve due to language and cultural differences.

In summary, this vocational education campus is a very impressive and well-equipped building. Security is seen to be a priority due to the low socio-economic nature of the neighbourhood and parental concern for school safety. The school's director seems to enjoy a friendly rapport with students. In addition to mandatory basic academic skills, a variety of customer service-oriented courses are available to students in preparation for employment. The school utilises several community services and takes an almost paternal interest in the welfare of the multi-cultural, multi-racial student body ("we take good care of them").

Foundation for Catholic Education "Henric von Veldeke" in Maastricht

The Hendric von Veldeke Foundation is an example of a central management organisation in primary education. In 1995, the Foundation merged 13 schools,

159|

with a total of 4 000 pupils and 250 staff, into a new "central management structure". This represented a three-tier system composed of a General Board (governing board); Central Management Executive; and a Central Council of Principals. The schools are scattered throughout the city of Maastricht and serve a variety of socio-economic areas. Each school retains its own character ranging from a classical group-centred format to more of an individualised student-centred approach.

The Central Executive consists of a chairwoman, as chief executive officer, and a vice-chairman responsible for financial and personnel matters. The Central Executive reports to the General Board on a regular basis regarding the quality of education. They are leaders in: educational innovation; the effective use of human resources; and ongoing professional development of personnel. Beginning in 1996, the Central Executive introduced three objectives to increase the quality of education: function differentiation; duties (tasks) differentiation; and payment differentiation.

Function differentiation involves a process of describing and valuing functions, through meetings with the professional unions, to strengthen and improve educational and administrative management. One outcome was the establishment of the role of "cluster head-master" with the responsibility for supervision of a cluster of schools each of which has its own location-leader (site manager).

Duties (tasks) differentiation defines a new set of professional roles creating such positions as: internal counsellor; remedial teacher; executive manager/co-ordinator; computer expert; and subject specialist (*e.g.* Dutch, mathematics, etc.). These specialised positions must be derived from the existing staffing provisions (job-budget) allocated to the Foundation by the national authorities.

Payment differentiation is perhaps the most controversial management innovation. Through existing government policy and consultations with the professional unions, criteria have been established for a system of premium pay and temporary extra increment (merit pay) for teachers demonstrating exceptional performance. Principals are trained in assessment procedures to designate the personnel receiving the salary premium, extra increment (half-year basis) or other benefit (*e.g.* professional visit, conference, etc.). The Foundation maintains a limited amount in the annual budget for payment differentiation (Kreuzen, van der Pluijm and Sleegers, 2000).

These innovations were introduced through an extensive process of external and internal communications. A brochure describing the objectives was published and advice sought from professional education, support and counselling institutions. Extensive consultations were also undertaken with unions; teaching teams; parents; and school participation councils.

The Foundation is committed to creating a "learning organisation" where talent and performance are recognised and rewarded and professional renewal is encouraged on an ongoing basis. The quality of administrative and educational management skills is developed and enhanced through a variety of training opportunities both external and "home-grown". The career development of teachers, subject specialists and school managers is a priority through "internal quality circles", specialised training, and continuing personal and professional reflection.

Innovation and Effectiveness

While education in the Netherlands is a study in contrasts there are several features that are particularly noteworthy.

Schools of Choice

The constitutional right of parents and other interest groups to establish and manage local schools has been a tradition for many years in Holland. Their experience has important implications for current experiments in school management in other countries (e.g. charter schools in the United States, grant maintained in the United Kingdom). They have demonstrated that local stakeholders not only have the ability to create schools responsive to their needs, but can manage them effectively. The fact that the central government facilitates their setting up and financially supports these schools, provided they meet national standards, is central to their success.

One example, in Rotterdam, is a group of Islamic parents (from several different countries and Muslim religious and cultural traditions) which has come together to found its own secondary school. The parents recognise that their cultural and religious experience is quite different from the Dutch norm. Some Islamic parents may not feel welcome in existing denominational or state schools. Such religious and cultural issues as head covering (for girls), accommodation for prayers, ritual bathing, dietary and other laws, flexible schedules, and gender separation may not be acceptable in regular schools. The proposed new school would address these issues and involve more parents and religious elders in the educational process (e.g. governing board, participation council, school volunteers, etc.). It is interesting that a non-Muslim school manager has been chosen as Rector for the new school.

School Management Training

There are a variety of training programmes available for school leaders at the primary level. The central authorities provide the tuition and replacement costs for two-year part-time in-service programmes for primary school managers. One example is an innovative in-service training programme established by the Fontys University for Professional Education. Its Centre for School Management, in co-operation with the Catholic Training Institute, has twenty programmes throughout

Holland for practising principals and vice-principals. The part-time residential course began in 1994 as a two-year voluntary professional development opportunity for principals. The central authorities agreed to pick up most of the tuition costs. In 1998, an 18-month programme for vice-principals and a one-year course for principals age 50+ were added. Participation in all of these programmes is on a voluntary basis (Verbiest, 1996). The objective of the programmes has been to see the school manager as an integral leader both in classroom and administrative practice in the following ways:

- Strategic leader (school and environment).
- Human resources manager (transformational).
- Quality performer (financial, academic achievement).
- Reflective practitioner (creative problem-solving to promote good practice).

The primary delivery method has been "Intervision". A group of course participants (from different areas) form a cohort coming together regularly to discuss problems, reflect on solutions and support each other. They learn to work co-operatively to develop an insight into good practice (*e.g.* self-directed learning, co-operative learning, reflecting on practice, transformational leadership, etc.). The first year of the course deals with leadership skills (*e.g.* situational factors, communication, basic leadership). During the second year they reflect on Senge's Five Disciplines (challenging, inspiring, enabling, modelling, encouraging) and the school leader as coach (Senge, 1990).

It is interesting to note that the participant cohorts often continue to meet after the programme is finished, as an ongoing professional support group. The life of the school manager can be a solitary and stressful existence. Holland expects to face a growing shortage of school managers as many teachers traditionally reject this career pathway. Compulsory pre-service and continuing in-service training might serve to attract and retain professional school leadership.

Community Schools

A definite commitment to the concept of the "community school" (open school or broad school) is evident among some governing boards in the Netherlands, particularly in large cities. In theory, such schools strive to make extensive use of community-based resources to improve services and opportunities for learning. Partnerships are forged with social welfare, health, immigrant support and law enforcement services. Cultural resources (*e.g.* museums, galleries, theatres, etc.) are used to enrich the learning environment. Community service and resource providers meet regularly to co-ordinate activities (Goldring and Sullivan, 1996).

Another area of community-school development has been industry-education partnerships. Employers may donate equipment, materials or funding to extend the programme of the school. Transition-to-work schemes are enhanced, particularly in vocational education institutions, through on-the-job placement.

Parental involvement is also an essential component of the community school. Parents may participate as school volunteers, serve on governing boards or be members of participation councils. Fund-raising represents another important contribution which parents may provide. While parent-led "schools of choice" are a tradition in Holland, it may be difficult to keep parents active in the life of the school on an ongoing basis, particularly in secondary schools. Improvements in communication and sensitivity to language and cultural differences might be ways to attract and retain parental involvement.

Information and Communication Technology (ICT)

Judging from the case studies, there seems to be a strong commitment to the implementation of ICT in Dutch schools. It is seen as essential that students gain modern information and communication skills if they are to compete for jobs and participate in society as a whole. The schools visited as part of this study were using ICT equipment in support of the learning process. The vocational education school was particularly well equipped (one computer for every 3 students), but the average is one computer for every 16 students. However, three challenges are faced by school managers in the integration of ICT into the curriculum:

- The availability of appropriate software to support educational practice.
- The ongoing upgrading of computer hardware.
- The professional know-how of teachers to use ICT effectively in the classroom.

Limited financial support from the central authorities in supplying ICT hardware, software and staff training on a continuing basis remains a problem. The introduction of "beacon schools", and a policy commitment by the current Secretary of Education, would seem to be important developments in better integrating information and communication technology into the provision of education in the Netherlands.

Student-centred Learning

A new emphasis on active, independent learning is now being seen in Dutch schools. While teacher-directed education is still the norm, there is a growing recognition that the individual learning needs of students must be accommodated. This requires a new role for teachers in facilitating the learning needs and interests of each of their pupils. The new emphasis is currently most often seen in the upper forms of secondary education through the introduction of the "study-centre" concept. Students are encouraged to undertake independent study projects after successfully completing the basic education curriculum.

163

Experiments in student-centred learning are also to be found in primary education. In particular, the De Stuifhoek School in Made demonstrated the "learning through experience" approach to meeting the individual learning needs of children. The introduction of personal learning contracts, and co-operative problem-solving in small groups, has laid the framework for a more inclusionary, holistic approach to education. The role of the school manager, as transformational leader, is essential to success in such a climate of innovation.

Accountability

Holland has a unique decentralisation/deregulation approach to schooling. Accountability is stressed at both the local level, through autonomy in school governance, and at the national level through the imposition of uniform curriculum standards and an inspectoral system of school assessment. This loose-tight accountability system represents a profound challenge for the administrative and instructional leadership skills of the school manager. The preparation and ongoing professional development of such leaders is of crucial importance.

In general, the Dutch system of education has many impressive accomplishments of which it should be justly proud. It has created and maintained a humane and caring approach to school management, which is responsive to local needs and interests. Schools are attractive, well-maintained centres of learning. Teachers seem committed to their profession and enjoy a strong sense of rapport with their students.

Noteworthy innovations observed included:

- Right of choice and freedom of school access.
- Bottom-up local autonomy with top-down accountability.
- Inclusionary education and student-centred learning.
- Co-ordinated use of community services and resources.
- Information and communication technological and other employment-related skills.
- Concern for the needs of newcomers and other socio-economically disadvantaged learners.
- National standards of school performance and student achievement.

The preparation and ongoing support of school managers, however, is an area of concern. Principals are expected to be accountable to both central authorities and local governing boards for student achievement and school operation. The result is a complex and sometimes turbulent environment.

Principals, especially in primary education, must wear two hats, combining administrative skills and instructional leadership. Depending upon the size of the school, central budgeting restraints and staff allocations provide limited release time from classroom duties to perform key administrative tasks (*e.g.* clerical, record-keeping, instructional support, team-building and community relations). The addition of ancillary administrative support staff in the job-budget would relieve the burdens on principals and allow them to spend more time on pedagogical leadership.

There is currently no mandatory pre-service training for this demanding assignment of school principal. In-service training in school management is not compulsory for principals and school leaders at the primary or secondary levels. These concerns could be addressed to support the needs of existing school leaders, as well as an incentive for future recruitment and retention of professional educational managers in this era of changing societal expectations and fiscal accountability.

Bibliography

ARION GROUP (2000),
Integration of Handicapped Children.

FIRESTONE, W.A. (1996),
"Leadership: Roles or Functions?", in K. Leithwood *et al.* (eds.), *International Handbook of Educational Leadership and Administration*, Kluwer Academic Publishers, Boston/Dordrecht, pp. 395-418.

GOLDRING, E.B. AND SULLIVAN, A.V. (1996),
"Beyond the Boundaries: Principals, Parents and Communities Shaping the School Environment", in K. Leithwood *et al.* (eds.), *International Handbook of Educational Leadership and Administration*, Kluwer Academic Publishers, Boston/Dordrecht, pp. 195-222.

KOLB, D.A. (1984),
Experiential Learning: Experience as the Source of Learning and Development, Prentice Hall, Englewood Cliffs.

KREUZEN, K., VAN DER PLUIJM, J. and SLEEGERS, P. (2000),
"Innovation in Education 2000, Background Report", OECD/CERI.

LEITHWOOD, K. (1992a),
"The Move towards Transformational Leadership", *Educational Leadership*, 49, 5, pp. 8-12.

LEITHWOOD, K. (1992b),
"The Principal's Role in Teacher Development", in M. Fullan and A. Hargreaves (eds.), *Teacher Development and Educational Change*, Falmer Press, London.

LEITHWOOD, K. (1994),
"Leadership for School Restructuring", *Educational Administration Quarterly*, 30, 4, pp. 498-518.

LEITHWOOD, K., TOMLINSON, D. and GENGE, M. (1996),
"Transformational School Leadership", in K. Leithwood *et al.* (eds.), *International Handbook of Educational Leadership and Administration*, Kluwer Academic Publishers, Boston/Dordrecht, pp. 785-840.

LEITHWOOD, K., JANTZI, D. and STEINBACH, R. (1999),
Changing Leadership for Changing Times, Open University Press, Buckingham/Philadelphia.

MINISTRY OF EDUCATION, CULTURE AND SCIENCE (1998),
Education in the Netherlands, February.

NETHERLANDS MINISTRY OF EDUCATION, CULTURE AND SCIENCE (1999),
Information Dossier on the Structure of the Education System in the Netherlands, Eurydice, Zoefermeer.

OECD (1991),
Reviews of National Policies for Education: Netherlands, Paris.

SENGE, P. (1990),

    The Fifth Discipline. The Art and Practice of the Learning Organisation, Basic Books Inc., New York.

VAN DEN BERG, R. and SLEEGERS, P. (1996*a*),

    "Building Innovative Capacity and Leadership", in K. Leithwood *et al.* (eds.), *International Handbook of Educational Leadership and Administration*, Kluwer Academic Publishers, Boston/Dordrecht, pp. 653-700.

VAN DEN BERG, R. AND SLEEGERS, P. (1996*b*),

    "The Innovative Capacity of Schools in Secondary Education: A Qualitative Study", *International Journal of Qualitative Studies in Education*, 9, 2, pp. 201-223.

VERBIEST, E. (1996),

    "Sources for the Learning of School Leaders", in Meso, *Journal for Educational Management*, 16, 89, pp. 10-20.

SWEDEN

Land area in square kilometers: 450 000

Total population (1998): 8 851 000

Per capita GDP (1999 prices): 23 000 USD

Percentage of GDP on education (1997): 6.8%

Amount spent per student (1997):
- 5 491 USD (Primary)
- 5 437 USD (Secondary)

Teacher salary range (1998):
- 17 974 USD-not available (Primary)
- 20 052 USD-not available (Secondary)

Sources: *Labour Force Statistics: 1978-1998*, OECD, Paris, 1999; *Main Economic Indicators*, OECD, Paris, April 2000; *Education at a Glance – OECD Indicators 2000*, OECD, Paris, 2000.

Country context

Sweden has been to the forefront of the IT revolution, not just in schools and the workplace but also in the home. The Swedes are among the highest users of the internet for business and personal use. There is a widespread recognition that even more rapid changes in communications and information technologies will reverberate throughout society and will have a profound impact on the manner in which family, school, recreation and work activities are organised.

The increase in usage of IT coincided with the recovery from the economic down-turn that had led to cut-backs in public expenditure as well as to higher unemployment in the early to mid-nineties. The unemployment rate has returned to around 5% while industrial production was up 11.6% in June 2000 compared with June 1999. However, the benefits of the improvements in the economy are not spread evenly among the 8.8 million people in Sweden, of whom 12% are either for-eign-born or first-generation immigrants. If anything, inequalities have grown.

Sweden has been moving steadily in the direction of greater decentralisation and deregulation. The municipalities or *kommuner* have been given additional powers but also greater responsibilities. They are obliged to offer pre-school education for children whose parents are working or studying. Pre-school centres, primary schools and recreation facilities are being integrated in many municipali-ties, with consequent changes for the manner in which the education system is organised.

There is a recognition – at official level at any rate – that teaching and learn-ing have to change in parallel with what is happening in the wider society outside the school. The day-to-day practice at school level inevitably takes time to catch up with the official rhetoric. But the acceptance of the need for change is reflected in some of the far-reaching decisions taken over the past few decades whose effects are still working their way through the school system.

Teachers are now employees of the municipalities, which have to weigh school needs with other demands on local budgets such as care of the elderly, libraries, childcare, etc. With the agreement of the unions, teachers' pay has become increasingly individualised. They are no longer automatically entitled to incremental pay raises. Instead these are awarded on the basis of criteria, includ-ing, a commitment to improve the quality of learning for their students. The intro-duction of market forces means that school leaders can be "head-hunted" to work in other schools in return for higher pay to a much greater extent than previously. In the nineties, the state opted out of direct negotiations on salaries, which became individual with negotiations between the teacher unions and the munici-pality association.

Challenges Facing School Management

School leaders in Sweden are the focal point for differing, and sometimes competing, pedagogical and administrative demands. These are mediated through the politicians in the municipalities. The municipalities are allowed complete freedom to organise the local education services within the framework of the 1985 Education Act and the curricula. These documents define the objectives to be attained by each student at the end of the fifth and ninth years of compulsory education. The municipalities have the responsibility to make it possible for every child to meet these objectives. The national goals are thus translated into local plans, influenced by whichever combination of politicians is in control of the town hall, as a result of elections held every four years. In many parts of the country, these elections have precipitated changes in the organisation of local schools. Karlstad, for instance, began re-organising its school catchment areas into more cohesive units in 2000. It also acknowledged the considerable pressures on school heads by creating a new post of administrative officer, so that the school leaders could concentrate on pedagogical work and other essential tasks such as leading the teachers' learning about teaching and learning.

One such task is the individualisation of teachers' salaries. This is a problematic exercise, especially in small municipalities where somebody already employed in the school becomes the leader with the responsibility for deciding, or at least recommending, the following year's salary structure. The increases have to be sanctioned by the municipality. Larger municipalities usually have directors, or superintendents of education, who may block or at least query the recommended raises. They may not agree that such raises are justified on the basis of the school plans for improvement in the quality of the learning experience for students. One director of education put his power and responsibility bluntly: "no plans – no pay increase." Such an approach ensures that school heads have to come up with realistic plans with their staff. If they fail to do so, the staff will want to know why not. Of course, it's not just teachers' salaries that are individualised – others are in the public service – but in the school context the issue has to be handled with great sensitivity and tact.

Sensitivity alone is not enough when the biggest challenge that the leaders face is changing the culture in their own schools to put the emphasis increasingly on students taking responsibility for their own learning. A team approach is encouraged, which can be wasteful and misleading if all it does is to reinforce old practices, without questioning their underlying assumptions. In some upper secondary schools, it can be harder to introduce effective teams for teachers who believe in a rigid classification of knowledge which, they feel, is best transmitted to students in forty minute blocks. The need for teamwork is stressed in a new agreement on school development between the unions and the government. It is

171|

also emphasised in leadership training programmes. But changing the culture of teaching and learning is only one part of the equation. The other is putting in place an evaluation system to ensure that the goals are being achieved.

In summary, school leaders need to have worked out and articulated their educational philosophy, values and vision. They need to be strong in the sense that they believe they can lead others to "internalise" and implement the changes in official policy. They need the self-knowledge to recognise their own skills and limitations, as well as the openness to acknowledge the skills of others.

Main Policy Approaches

In the past a "good" school leader in Sweden was one who was well versed in government rules and was a skilled administrator of funds and staff. Little pedagogical leadership was expected from the school head, other than the interpretation of the national rules. The management of the education system has changed, from one based on rules and regulations, to goal-based result management with the responsibility for delivery handed over to the municipalities. Some have adopted the philosophy of the learning organisation. Indeed, the pattern and policy of school management can vary from town hall to town hall. Even the very definition of school leaders, principals or managers in Sweden varies and does not always agree with the general European notion of one school principal for each school.

In many municipalities, there are school-leader teams responsible for a number of schools. This reflects the growing emphasis on teamwork, which underpins many of the developments in today's Swedish education system. Even the traditional isolation of teachers is being overcome in many schools where these teams are being created. The composition and functions of school-leader teams vary considerably from municipality to municipality. In some cases, teams are charged with responsibility for a number of schools. This is more common since the decision was taken four years ago to integrate childcare and recreation centres with schools. But teams can also be responsible for a number of similar type schools within a catchment area in a municipality. Weaknesses in one school in that catchment area could warrant special attention, for instance with the appointment of an extra person from the team, for a period of time.

Within schools, teams are sometimes composed entirely of subject teachers. In others, they are represented across most subject disciplines and are charged with organising the classes and social activities of groups varying in size up to 100 students of different ages – virtually running schools within schools. In the Skare catchment area of Karlstad and Elineberg school in Helsinborg, for example, the teams are given considerable autonomy and responsibility (see case study).

Teamwork is also encouraged among the students, who co-operate among themselves, and with the teachers. This can be done informally or through more structured student councils and conferences. The students thus have an increasing role in the decision-making process. This fits in with the belief that students should take on responsibility for their own learning. Each class at primary and secondary level is supposed to hold weekly "class councils" where the students and teachers discuss the inner workings of the class and make decisions about changes in the day-to-day routine. In Elineberg (see case study), for example, teachers are divided into teams that meet every Monday morning at 8:00 a.m. Each teacher then meets a group of students, which has been assigned to him/her and they discuss their weekly study plans. The outcomes of these individually tailored plans are reviewed in a further session at the end of the week. In the upper secondary schools the students participate in decision-making, including policy and budgetary matters. Normally there are ten people at these conferences – five elected students, three teachers, one other staff member and the school leader. Since 1997, pilot projects have allowed for a majority of students at these conferences. Students are made aware of their rights and they have a national representative body, which has organised events, including demonstrations against cutbacks in educational spending.

The team approach may be increasingly used in schools but there is still room in the leadership spectrum for a "strong" leader such as the Botvid upper secondary school where the head was sent in to rescue a school perceived to be in crisis (see case study). His strength comes, not from a traditional male-macho view of leadership, but is largely grounded in his vision for the school and his ability to enthuse both staff and students. The flexibility of the municipal authority to headhunt and pay somebody more money to move from one school to another is an important factor in allowing such leaders to develop and utilise their skills.

A further factor is the loosening of the regulations governing the appointment of school leaders. From 1913, there was a legal requirement that school leaders needed to have training as a teacher. But from 1991 onwards, the only requirement was the leader needed to have "insights" in pedagogy as there were no demands for any particular educational qualification. As a consequence of the integration of nursery schools and recreation centres, an increasing number of principals in the compulsory school are not trained primary or secondary teachers. This is in part a recognition that professionals from childcare and primary schools have much to learn from each other's different pedagogical training. Similarly, in the *gymnasium* the principal sometimes has experience of leadership from the private sector or the public sector (such as the military or psychology, etc.). There have also been significant changes in regard to gender as the majority of new school leaders are women. This reflects the very high percentage of women in teaching and childcare. The appointment of principals from what might be

173|

regarded as non-traditional backgrounds, is a challenge to those who have a hierarchical view of teaching, childcare and recreational activities.

Framework

At first glance, the school system in Sweden seems a rather simple structure. All pupils can start school when they are six or seven and are obliged to stay in school until they are 16, after which the vast majority go on to an upper secondary school – *the gymnasium*. About a third then go on to university studies, while most of the remainder participate in specialised vocational programmes.

The clear lines that once distinguished childcare, pre-school, recreation centres and primary schools are, however, beginning to blur. The local authorities are obliged to offer pre-school education, from the age of one year, to all children whose parents are working or undertaking studies. In 1999, the first preschool curriculum was established with the aim of constructing direct links between pre-school activities and the start of the compulsory school system. In the past few years, there has been a move towards integrating these services, so that there is a "seamless web" of learning opportunities for the young child and no abrupt transition from one "system" to another. It's not unusual, as the case study shows, to find young children in an integrated centre from early morning until 6:30 p.m. in the evening with parents paying for the pre-school/childcare and recreational services while the primary schooling is free of charge. There may be one leader, or a team, in charge of these integrated centres, depending on the decision of the municipality.

Sweden is divided into 289 municipalities or *kommuner*, each of whom is responsible for the quality of schools in its area and for payment of teachers' salaries. When the education system was decentralised a decade ago, the traditional supports from the centre were removed. The National Board of Education was replaced by a new agency *Statens Skolverket*, which is charged with the supervision of the national educational system. It adopted a "hands-off" approach to schools, setting out national goals but leaving it to the municipalities to adapt them, and to schools to find their own solutions to pedagogical problems. It was still "steering" but with a much lighter touch. One of the main ideas of *Skolverket* was to carry out national evaluations built on local evaluations. But due to the financial crisis in the mid-nineties the local evaluations were not carried out as expected and this created pressure for more national evaluations.

Municipalities reacted with different degrees of success to their new-found freedom and responsibilities. The early to mid-nineties were marked by a deep economic recession, which led to cutbacks in services, including education. Many municipalities made senior staff redundant, thus losing some professional expertise necessary for the changed circumstances. The economic corner has been turned and education is moving back up the political agenda for investment. In some cases, the teachers' unions complain that decentralisation has stopped at the town hall and has not percolated down to the schools. In others, such as Karlstad, there is a dynamic sense of engagement by the politicians, the officials and the schools. The quality of the local plans varies enormously, hardly surprising, given that there are so many municipalities. But the municipal politicians have learned valuable lessons over the years about the importance of good plans, if their schools are to meet national goals of quality and equality, and meet local demands for economic and social development. In the past, leadership was seen through the lens of the national rules – now it is up to the municipalities to ensure the quality of the students' learning experience. They have both the carrot and the stick in terms of control over the financial resources, which they make available to the schools.

Case Studies

Elineberg School

Elineberg School with an enrolment of 900 students (aged 6 to 16), is situated in a residential part of Helsinborg. In 1993, the school leadership reached the conclusion that the traditional way of managing a school with one head teacher, and a deputy head teacher, made it impossible to achieve pedagogical changes. It became one of the first schools in the country to introduce work teams.

In 1993, a group was formed, based on the view that there must be several people in the school, believing in and working towards reform. The starting point for the discussions in the team was not the subjects that the school offered, or how the day was organised, but the students themselves. The group focused in particular on one question: "what will be important to a fifteen-year old in thirty years time, that the school should provide today?" The answer to the question came from the group in the form of a summary consisting of several key words such as: *flexibility; environment/ecology; critical disposition; comprehensive view; ability to work independently; security/belief in the future; and preparedness for the multi-cultural society.*

In the next stage, two competence-development days were reserved for the teachers to find examples in which pedagogical methods could lead to the goals which lay embedded in these key words. The teachers were also asked to put forward suggestions for changes which needed to be made to the school's physical environment – the school had been built in 1966 in a typical sixties' style.

The discussions led to a number of teachers wanting to change over to a new way of organising their work with the pupils. This led to the formation of "work teams". The point of departure was that the teacher would be a tutor/mentor for the students, instead of simply conveying knowledge. These teachers saw their

175|

task "as creating learning situations for students who would take increasing responsibility for their own learning".

In Spring 1994, about twenty teachers, comprising about a third of the teaching force in the school, formed three work teams to try out the new ideas. Support from the educational administrators and the politicians in the municipality was readily available and crucial to the eventual success of the venture. The process was assisted by a refurbishment of the building, which gave a more open "feel" to the school, reflecting the new pedagogical aims. The local library, which served as a public and school library, was relocated to the school premises.

The leadership recognised the danger of the novelty aspect of the team approach wearing off and a return to old habits. It accepted the successes of the first enthusiastic teams, but recognised the possible shortcomings of others, that were to follow, once the team idea spread throughout the school. Collaboration does not spring to life, simply because people are brought together in teams. There were inevitable tensions between those who preferred the old ways of working and those who wanted to work the new way. This raised questions about the rights of teachers to refuse to participate in the new pedagogical organisation and the right of management to insist that they do. The school leadership maintained that if it had decided to conduct the school in a specific way, this must be accepted by the individuals who worked there. A handful of teachers left, partly for other reasons as well. The tensions took some time to resolve. A consultant was brought in to facilitate teachers, who had worked for years in isolation, to work together.

The teams began to gel into active units and now operate in such a way that a teacher who taught in the school fifteen years ago, would hardly recognise the working conditions today. There are ten teams of teachers under the general direction of a seven-member leadership group. Each of the ten comprises teachers from across most subject areas. They effectively run "schools within schools", taking responsibility for the educational and general welfare of perhaps 85 students of varying ages. The teams meet separately at 8:00 a.m. every Monday morning for an hour in which they discuss the week's activities and timetable. There is no longer the rigid division between subjects. Teachers can work together in small groups on a project with their students, or they can agree to devote a longer period of time than normal to one topic by approaching it collaboratively. They work in different ways with different groups at the same time. The exception are teachers of art, music and craft whose classes are time-tabled across the school.

Each team member acts as a mentor for about 14 to 16 students. If there are deep social or family problems that need addressing, these can be referred to the school's nurse or guidance counsellor. A change in the teachers' working conditions nationally means that they work office hours in schools, so are on the premises for much longer than in the past when they went home before the pupils. In the Elineberg school this means that students know they have ready access to an adult, throughout the school day, to discuss a problem. However, from the teachers' point of view it means they are on the school premises for at least 35 hours per week and often do not get time to prepare lessons, or mark papers, and end up doing such work at home.

The pupils meet their teachers in groups, on Monday morning, Tuesday morning and Thursday afternoon for 20-30 minutes each time. The first two sessions are to discuss the week's activities and the final session to monitor and review them. The size of the group varies and can be as low as ten. "It builds up the relationship as you can talk to him or her" as one student explained. The students choose their own mentor – they have to submit three names and are assigned to one. These teams cut across age levels and can stay together for up to six years. The students also have three hours in the week, which they can use at school in whatever way they choose, but they have to write up and evaluate the work. Students at age 16 can have up to 16 or 17 subjects and those in Elineberg appreciate the opportunity to decide which ones to give extra time to. Less motivated students get more attention from the teachers. The students also have their own council, which has an influence on the general direction of the school.

Team work has ended the traditional isolation of teachers working alone in their own classes. As one male teacher who has seen the transition commented "teaching was isolated before, but not today. We cannot close the classroom door to the world anymore". Ironically, some teachers now talk about a new kind of isolation – within their own particular team. If teams effectively run schools within schools, they can be cut off from their peers in other teams. In some cases, the establishment of teams across subject boundaries, as in the Elineberg school, means that they are cut off from other teachers of the same subject. This is reinforced by the arrangements whereby different teams take breaks at different times. As one teacher commented "there are so many positive things about this way of working that of course there must be some negative things as well. It means isolation within our subject and too little time to brainstorm with colleagues in the same subject". However, the relatively generous provision of "study days" in the Swedish system (up to 13 professional development days) compensates somewhat for this sense of isolation as it brings teachers of the same subjects together.

The other danger is that the teams become isolated from each other. In the case of the Elineberg school this is well-recognised and kept in check by the leadership team which engages in dialogue with the other teams about the goals for the school. It gets feedback from the teams and is conscious of the need for quality measures of assessment. The Elineberg school's way of organising itself has been studied and followed by many other schools, with varying degrees of success.

177|

Many Swedish schools now have teams but some of them are within subject areas and not across disciplines.

The Elineberg's arrangement is logistically challenging and certainly demanding on the staff. It is clear, however, from talking to the teachers in this school that few if any want to return to the traditional way of dividing up classes. More importantly, the reforms have been welcomed by the students who now feel a greater sense of "ownership" of the decisions taken by their schools, which affect them. Some still feel that the teachers define too much of their study time, and the school is currently considering how to respond to their demand to give them more time to plan their learning with their tutors.

Botvidsgymnasiet (Botvid Upper Secondary School)

Botvidsgymnasiet (Botvid Upper Secondary School) has 650 students in the Stockholm Botkyrka municipality, serving an area with many immigrants.

In 1999, there was a series of incidents at the school, which was portrayed in the media as "one of the most ill-disciplined in Sweden". A number of incidents had got out of hand, involving about 30 students who set off fire alarms by starting small fires in waste-paper baskets. The school occupies two floors of a multi-storey building from which 3 000 people had to be evacuated every time the alarm went off. Six security guards were then hired who checked students' identity cards before they were allowed into the building. Inevitably this attracted media attention and, suddenly, it was the most talked about school in Sweden.

Fighting fire with fire, however, did not work and expelling "trouble-makers" only sent the problem back to the local community. The municipal authority decided something had to be done and approached a principal who was just finishing his eighth year in a school with a similar intake, a large immigrant population, on the other side of Stockholm. The individualisation of salaries in Sweden allows flexibility to authorities to "head-hunt" and they were fortunate in approaching him at the right moment, as he was ready for a move. The school he was then working in had earned a coveted quality award and it was developing a sound academic reputation.

Following his appointment in 1999, he set about his new task with enthusiasm. His mission was to change the school's reputation from being the worst in Sweden to the best. Rejecting the media portrayal of himself as a super-head, he was not afraid to use the same media to portray more positive images of the school and Botvid *gymnasium* certainly needed them. Medias images were unfair to the vast majority of hard-working students, many of whom were attracted to the school for particular courses.

The first thing the new principal did was to open the door on the corridor leading to the school offices. The impact was felt immediately by the students who previously had to speak to somebody through a glass partition before they secured entry to an office. As one of the students remarked: "all of a sudden you didn't need to look at authority through a locked door. The school had suddenly become mine." This student-friendly approach was extended to abolishing most of the negative rules governing student behaviour. The word that features most frequently in discussions with the students about their relationship to the school head is "respect". They clearly respect the manner in which he treats them as young adults. They know him by his first name, they dine with him in the cafeteria, they confide in him when they have problems but there is always a respectful distance in their relationship with him.

The relationship between students, the school principal and, since his appointment, most of the teachers, is not patronising or based on false camaraderie. The principal refers to other schools where disruption becomes the norm as "fighting fire with fire, where surveillance cameras are installed so that all the pupils feel like villains of the piece or else the rules are drawn up in such a way that it conveys the message to students – we expect you to behave in a bad way".

The improvement could not have come about without the full co-operation of the teachers who were clearly looking for another way of relating to the young adults in their school. The principal presents his goals and visions for the school year, and an outline of plans to achieve them, to the staff at the beginning of the academic year. His overarching visions are:

- To change opinions on immigrants.
- To put the school on the educational map of Sweden and make it well known for the high quality of its work.
- To constantly seek to improve the organisation.

He is clear about his mission, why he is there and whom the school is supposed to serve. The many visitors to the school can see immediately why the media constantly seek him out. While quietly spoken, he has no inhibitions about speaking to the media. He allows them to personalise the school as long as the coverage helps his goal, which is improvement in the quality of what the school does for its students. The confidence comes from an innate belief in his own leadership skills when they are at the service of the students. "To be a school leader is to be the last guarantee that the students get the best education possible", he comments.

There is no doubt that the school has been transformed. But how much of this is due to the principal's unique brand of leadership, and can similar improvements be introduced elsewhere? He is of the firm view that any school can be transformed, given leadership and vision. His main principle is that you have to act in the manner in which you want others to act. A teacher is the leader of the pupils and the school leader is the leader of the teachers. "You have to act as a model and behave the way you want the teachers to behave towards the pupils."

He is demanding of himself and of his staff. "It is important to assume that the staff want to, and are able to, work with school improvement instead of supposing that they lack the knowledge and energy". While he tries to bring everybody along with his vision for the school, inevitably some will not relate to it or to the manner in which it drives changes at the school. However, one of his teachers paid him the ultimate tribute when she described him as "hard but not harsh".

The principal's vision has clearly been passed on to the students. Two hundred of whom took it upon themselves to protest to a Stockholm newspaper, when it ran yet another article they deemed to reflect unfairly on the changing circumstances of the school. The result was a series of positive articles, which highlighted, in particular, the plans for a new and more suitable school building. The school's intake is probably more racially and culturally mixed than any other school in the country, yet to the visitor, there is a clear absence of any tensions in the school. As one student commented "before I came here I had negative feelings but now I realise that they were unnecessary. You can take a walk in the cafeteria and see Muslims, Christians, Buddhists talking together...we all get along". Another commented "Tom uses the word respect a lot. There's a good teacher-student relationship here. They're still teachers but to us they are not superior". A third student commented "if there is conflict with a teacher, the principal gives us a chance to explain... we did not get that chance previously... teachers always had the last word".

Skare School and Children's Leisure Centre

This is an integrated school and children's leisure centre in the Skare catchment area of Karlstad. It has 450 pupils aged 6 to 12 years. The school is managed and run on the basis that it is a learning organisation in which all staff work in teams.

Schools in the municipality of Karlstad were re-organised in 2000 and divided into catchment areas, one of which is Skare which employs 25 teachers, seven pre-school teachers, 15 recreation instructors, three pupil assistants, three school cleaners, one janitor, one school assistant and four school meals staff. The integrated school and leisure centre has formed work teams comprising people of different pedagogical backgrounds.

However, it is necessary to go further back to appreciate how the learning organisation model came about. In 1994, the then principal set out a leadership declaration which stated that he wanted to achieve a professional preparedness for action based on competence – not on already established patterns of action. From this viewpoint, the most important task was to create different arenas for process-oriented learning among the staff. They began work in teams, at house meetings, in pedagogical forums and at study conferences.

An important part of the work was to stimulate and deepen the pedagogical debate at the schools, so that it was possible to combine both practice and theory. Many good teachers became much more secure in their professional role when they learned to put into words what took place in the classrooms. Silent knowledge became spoken knowledge, reflected upon, and discussed in a learning process among these professionals. They learned to develop their practical work by observing it, trying to understand it, and planning changes based on the shortcomings that were discovered.

This team work approach took root and faced a new challenge when it was decided to integrate childcare and primary schools. Previously, the pre-school teachers and the recreation teachers worked together in a separate building. Now, the activities are carried out by work teams, which are lead by pedagogical leaders. In most work teams, several professional categories such as: recreation instructors; pre-school teachers; pupil assistants; and teachers co-operate. The teams function relatively independently from one another. They form a sort of "school within the school", with great freedom to manage their own resources. The classes are mixed, and not divided along age-group lines. Classes could have six- to nine-year-olds learning together.

Some important points of departure at the school:

- To emphasise experiences and the importance of play and feelings for learning.
- To create processes in the pupils' ways of thinking which lead to reflections about their own learning, as well as their own ability to think and develop.
- To be pedagogues who challenge the pupils' ways of thinking and put forward relevant demands that are adapted to age and maturity.
- To be adults who are good role models.

The school sees as its assignment, the creation of a thirst for learning, as well as, providing a secure and stimulating environment that will favour the pupils' development. The underlying idea is that knowledge grows from interest, community spirit, context and a good environment. Knowledge is created in a learning process with its starting point in the knowledge and experiences the pupils bring with them, obtained both in and outside school.

This approach can be rewarding, and yet difficult. At one stage one of the teams asked for an outside expert to offer guidance in the best way to approach its many tasks. It recognised that it had reached a plateau and needed fresh insights if it were to develop. As one of the teachers remarked "It gave me a clearer insight into my own place on the team and that of the other members".

Working together in this way, lays bare and undermines any notions of a natural hierarchy in pedagogy. The three separate strands have a common first year course at university after which they specialise. The three groups are in the same union. While this brings them yet closer together, the system sends its own message by keeping them on different salary scales and by operating different working conditions, including length of holidays. A corollary of the integration would seem to be a movement to harmonise salaries and working conditions, but this is a long (and expensive) way off.

It is worth noting that when the pupils leave the integrated centre they go on to another school, that has decided against mixed-aged classes. The teachers in the latter school also work in teams but have decided that while mixing the classes might work for the younger age group, the differences in the older age group were too profound for mixed classes to work effectively. Nevertheless, the teachers in the integrated school laud integration and team-working as sharing responsibility and ending the sense of isolation they had felt previously. Some would like to go back to having separate classes for each age group, but none of them want to work alone again.

Innovation and Effectiveness

The most obvious conclusion, from the three case studies is that change and improvements are possible, even in situations where they might not appear so. There is no single management structure or leadership style that will suit all schools – one size does not fit all. But a number of lessons can be learned from the experiences of different types of leadership in Swedish schools:

- In some schools the head no longer manages individual teachers but groups or teams of teachers, who in turn operate schools within schools.
- Team work, which simply reinforces existing practice, will not change the culture of schools, and teams which are little more than one "big happy family" will not drive change from the bottom-up.
- If necessary, the teams can be re-structured and outside facilitators brought in to indicate how they can work more effectively.
- The task of the school leader is to challenge the teams to come up with answers to pedagogical questions.
- Students will take on more responsibility for their own learning if they are given properly structured opportunities to do so and shown how to work.
- Learning can be individualised to each student but it is important to look at the student as a whole, not just in terms of individual subjects, but taking into account their interests, where they are coming from, their environment, family, friends, etc.
- In one sense, every teacher is a school leader as she or he has to lead pupils in the learning experience.

In Swedish schools, there is often a conflict between administration and economy on the one hand, and the leadership of teaching and learning on the other. This, of course, is the result of modernisation and decentralisation. In a decentralised system there is need for clear lines of responsibility for planning, implementation, follow-up and evaluation. There is, at present, a tension between different views regarding the extent to which plans should govern activities – a conflict between the centre and the periphery, and between different views on evaluation (Linnell, 1996). The school leaders need time and energy to resolve these tensions and to look for solutions to pedagogical questions within their own schools.

The definition of pedagogical leadership in Sweden has changed, as have ideas of teaching in a different way. Put simply, the change proceeds from a teacher working by telling the students how they should understand the world around them, to the teacher organising the work process, which facilitates the students' understanding of the world around them. The change means that the teacher's work is displaced from being thought-prescriptive and knowledge-prescriptive, to being more thought-challenging and knowledge-challenging (Scherp, 1998). Teachers are verbal and literate people. They learn the official language of change quickly, but this does not necessarily mean that they make it their own and put it into practice. School leaders have to find ways to encourage them to internalise the goals and work out the solutions to their implementation.

The need for management training is accepted at national and municipal levels. Yet, there are instances of school leaders who have been in charge of schools for fifteen years without having received any (or limited) training. There is a view that management training should be an activity for all members of the school staff and should be given as part of initial teacher training. This view is guided by the reality that teachers have to lead students to manage their own studies. They also have to work as part of a team and understand how that teamwork is essential to the running and management of the school. Democracy, of course, is deeply ingrained into the Swedish national psyche and notions of authority and leadership have negative connotations for some. Yet, it is necessary that teachers have a clear understanding of what is going on in their schools.

Three further points are worth making. One is that an unexpected consequence of the changes is that parental influence at the national level seems to have been weakened. It is not that parents are no longer interested in their children's educational progress (the reverse is true), but the dismantling of the national system has been followed by the lowering of representation of parents at national level. In the upper secondary schools, the parents have no representatives in the decision-making bodies. In the primary and secondary schools it is possible to establish boards with a parental majority, but this provision is seldom put into action.

The second point is that, under the 1985 Education Act, all children and young people are entitled to, and are expected to, have access to equal educational opportunities. This is still very much the guiding principle governing Swedish schools but, if anything, inequalities seem to have grown since 1991. That is the real challenge for school leaders in a decentralised system – how to promote equality of opportunity.

The final point is that decentralisation and deregulation allow for greater freedom and flexibility for municipalities, schools, teachers and students in working out their own pedagogical solutions to problems within the framework of national goals. But it takes courage and clear-sightedness on the part of politicians, local school directors/superintendents and school leaders to use these opportunities successfully.

Bibliography

EKHOLM, M. AND LINDVALL, K. (1997),
"The Recruiting of School Leaders – Movements in Time: Research on School and Children", Research Report No. 97:12, Social Science, University of Karlstad, Karlstad.

FALK, T. AND SANDSTRÖM, B. (1995),
"School Leaders'Experiences of a National and a Municipal Assignment: A Balancing Act on a Slack Rope", A working report within the National Agency for Education's project, Collaboration between the state's school leader training programme and the municipal school leader training programme.

LINDBERG, E. (1998),
Management in Sweden Upper Secondary Schools, Luleå Technical University, Department of Industrial Economics and Social Science, 22.

LINNELL, U. (1996),
"Policy and Practice of Education Management Development in Sweden", International Conference on Education Management Development, Wilderness, Western Cape, South Africa.

SCHERP, H.A. (1998),
"Challenging or Challenged Leadership: School Management, The School Organisation and Change of Teaching Patterns within the Upper Secondary School", Acta Universiltatis Gothoburgensis, Gothenberg.

UNITED KINGDOM (ENGLAND)

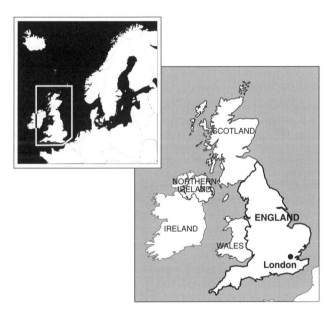

Land area in square kilometers: 245 000

Total population (1998): 59 237 000

Per capita GDP (1999 prices): 22 300 USD

Percentage of GDP on education (1997): 4.2%

Amount spent per student (1997):
 – 3 206 USD (Primary)
 – 4 609 USD (Secondary)

Teacher salary range (1998):
 – 22 393-50 656 (Primary)
 – 22 661-52 023 (Secondary)

Note: Data above are for the United Kingdom, but this report relates only to England.
Sources: *Labour Force Statistics: 1978-1998*, OECD, Paris, 1999; *Main Economic Indicators*, OECD, Paris, April 2000; *Education at a Glance – OECD Indicators 2000*, OECD, Paris, 2000.

Country context

The United Kingdom which has a population of around 60 million is a leading trading power and financial centre. Services, particularly banking, insurance, and business services, account by far for the largest proportion of GDP while industry continues to decline in importance. Agriculture is intensive, highly mechanised, and efficient by European standards, producing about 60% of food needs with only 1% of the labour force. The United Kingdom has large coal, natural gas, and oil reserves; primary energy production accounts for 10% of GDP, one of the highest shares of any industrial nation.

Over the past two decades successive governments have greatly reduced public ownership and contained the growth of social welfare programmes. However, 17% of the population is estimated to be below the poverty line. Unemployment was at 6% in 1999, but some areas, particularly in the North of England had higher rates while London experienced shortages of skilled workers, particularly in high-tech areas. Economic growth slowed in 1998 and 1999, however in 2000 growth exceeded potential, approaching 3%. This recovery was based mainly on domestic demand.

The Blair government, which made "education, education, education" its three priorities, has continued with and developed many of the education policies it had inherited. During the 1980s, the then Conservative government had become increasingly frustrated as its own educational policies were modified or delayed by local authorities which were frequently not under its political control and often had fundamental differences with them over policy direction. The mid-eighties had also been a period of conflict with teacher unions, resulting in a series of "work-to-rule" and strike actions by teachers, which caused great dissatisfaction to parents and was making the government's educational reforms generally unpopular.

Against this background of unrest and in the face of a lot of opposition, the Conservative government pushed through the most sweeping reforms that the education system had seen in over a hundred years of public provision for schooling. These reforms aimed at creating a new balance of power within the system, with a much stronger role for central government, a more clearly defined set of management functions at the school level, and restrictions on the role of the Local Education Authorities (LEAs). The reforms were promoted as offering a radical restructuring of management roles and functions in the school system. A more efficiently and effectively managed education service was promised, with a strengthening of the links between schools and parents, and a greater responsiveness to the needs and preferences of the school's community.

Challenges Facing School Management

The major developments in school management structures and processes in England and Wales start from the Education Reform Act of 1988. Prior to this act, the LEAs, a branch of local government, were responsible for the provision and regulation of schools within their areas. Although the powers of the LEA were exercised in partnership with central government (which controlled overall spending levels) and school governors (appointed for each school to oversee the day-to-day management), they were considerable. LEAs determined funding and staffing levels for individual schools, set catchment areas from which the school could take students, and often had a major influence on curriculum policies.

The 1988 Act was a very detailed and complex piece of legislation. Four of its main provisions directly impacted on the work of school management: the national curriculum; the operation of school budgets; competition between schools; and the privatisation of services traditionally provided by the LEAs.

The act established a national curriculum model covering years 1 to 11 of compulsory schooling. The implementation of the national curriculum created a common pattern of educational experience for all, whereas previously the curriculum varied between schools. The prescribed curriculum brought with it a series of standardised national tests at ages 7, 11 and 14. There was general consensus in the educational community that a national curriculum was desirable. Although there have been subsequent modifications, the national curriculum remains a substantial reform that is largely intact.

The 1988 Act also changed the arrangements for funding schools. Prior to this, school budgets were set by the LEA which also directly controlled staffing levels within the school. The act delegated budgets to schools, relating these to the numbers and ages of students enrolled. Although LEAs continued to set the "formula" used to calculate specific allocations for students of particular ages, they were no longer able to fix arbitrary budgets for individual schools or to control staffing levels. They were required to delegate the greater part of the education budget to schools, retaining a smaller percentage to fund central LEA functions and services than they had previously retained – a percentage further reduced over subsequent years. The control of the budget was delegated to school governors, but inevitably the principal's influence over decisions increased markedly. With the control of the budget went several related and important areas – for example the number and level (*i.e.* salary grade) of staff employed by the school. Schools (or their governors) became "employers" of their teachers, not places where the LEA's teachers were deployed. They became free to hire their own staff, with little or no LEA involvement. The appointment of head-teachers became the responsibility of governors, though the LEA retained the right to offer an opinion, but not determine the outcome.

187|

The relationship between schools and LEAs was altered quite fundamentally. The LEA could continue to offer services, such as supply teachers, advice, and in-service training which had to be offered on a "buy-back" basis. The LEA could only maintain these services if schools agreed to buy into them, using the additional funds they had acquired from the LEA's slice of the budget. Some LEAs offered complicated "service agreements" to schools, hoping to attract back the lost funding by persuading schools to pay for LEA services. Other LEAs moved rapidly to a market relationship, simply offering "products" like training courses or specialist advice to schools. Most LEAs found that it was difficult to maintain the scale of their activities, as schools began to spend the money on other things or with different providers.

In the new financial climate, many schools began to consider how they might increase income. Basically, as funding was now attached to student numbers, more students meant more money for the school. Even modest increases in student numbers could make a substantial difference to resource levels, allowing the employment of an additional teacher or the purchase of books or equipment. This stimulated competition between schools for the available students. "Successful" schools, no longer restrained by LEA admissions policies, were able to expand to fill excess capacity and thus increase income. This meant that "less successful" schools would lose students and suffer reductions in income. The early nineties witnessed a period of growth and decline, depending on the school and its circumstances.

Additional impetus to this new competitive culture was given by the new status that schools could apply for – Grant Maintained (GM) status. GM schools effectively opted out of LEA control altogether. Instead of being funded through the LEA, they were funded through an agency set up by the government. This offered a more direct route to funds and to influence, and severed connections between the schools and their LEAs. In addition to receiving the student related funding level of other schools in their area, GM schools also received a payment in lieu of LEA services, so that they received directly whatever percentage of the total education budget had been retained to fund the work of the LEA. In the early years additional incentives were available which made GM status even more attractive. This widened the gap between schools, creating further movements of students. Some schools suffered dramatically, seeing reductions in student numbers and consequently in staffing. It became more and more difficult for such schools to "compete". It tended to be children of middle class parents or those with the highest ability and home support levels who moved away. This left some schools with a smaller and skewed population, with a disproportionate level of educational and behavioural difficulties. Schools began to regard one another as competitors and it became more difficult to promote collaboration. One obvious response to this "marketplace" mentality was the growth of a marketing function within school management arrangements.

At the same time, there was some feeling that GM status bestowed an unfair competitive advantage. In the early years the rewards were high, both in terms of funding levels and in terms of access to capital grants, though these tapered off somewhat over time. There was also a north-south divide in patterns of opting out, with large numbers of secondary schools leaving LEAs in the south of England but much lower numbers in the north. Recently the funding discrepancy has been addressed through the Labour government's "Fair Funding" initiative. This abolished GM status putting all schools back on to the same financial footing. However, the degree of freedom now enjoyed by all schools is closer to the GM model than to the old LEA-school relationship.

Local financial management has placed the spending power in the hands of the schools. The consequence of this has been the displacement of LEA controlled services by a number of alternative providers. Some, such as the provision of school meals, have been successfully transferred to private contractors. The range of staff development and training activities available has diversified – much of it offered by "consultants" or "agencies" outside the education system. The supply of replacement teachers for absence has also become an important private agency function. Large numbers of those currently working within the private sector to provide services to schools, are former LEA employees and the majority have, at some stage, been teachers.

All these trends have continued since the 1988 Act, so that the context in which schools are managed in the year 2000 is very different from that of a dozen years earlier. Not all schools were able to respond to the new context at the same pace. The early nineties saw schools spreading out quite rapidly in terms of their management structures and practices. Over the decade, the vast majority of schools has adjusted to the new roles and responsibilities. The powers enjoyed at school level by governors and head-teachers are now widely exercised, with schools more in charge of their own destinies. The past ten years have seen further central policy initiatives as governments, too, have begun to exploit the more direct influence over the school system that the act provided.

Main Policy Approaches

Apart from the legislation, several other initiatives were taken that impact on school management and school managers such as: the introduction of school performance tables comparing the results children achieve in 11-year-old tests and in public exams at 16 and 18; a national system of school inspection; the setting of targets; performance management; and Beacon and specialist schools. The first two in particular have had a dramatic effect on schools and the manner in which they are managed.

Performance tables show student achievements school by school. They are published and freely accessible within the school's community and, especially, to parents. Initially, the reporting of student performance focused on the results of secondary phase public examinations, at 16 and 18, as well as information on school attendance. Two statistics seem to have been adopted by the public as shorthand indicators of school quality. These are the number (percentage) of students gaining at least five higher level (grades A*-C) passes in the GCSE examinations at 16, and the average number of Advanced level points per student at 18.

There is a multitude of factors that contribute to these statistics: whether or not the school is selective; average ability of students on entering the school; the socio-economic status of students; the educational level of parents and so on. But, teachers and head-teachers operate in communities where in general only the raw data of league tables are published. It is hard to explain that the school is actually performing quite well, given its circumstances, if its raw results compare poorly with its neighbours'. Equally, though some of the schools at the top may actually be adding relatively little value, given the ability levels of students and favourable parental circumstances, they will still tend to be regarded as "successful schools". Performance tables are important annual barometers of the school with an influence on its popularity, and through the student-related funding mechanism, on its capacity to maintain or possibly increase its income. They can also affect the morale of stakeholders.

Subsequently, the government began publishing the results obtained in the National Curriculum Key Stage tests taken at eleven. This means that primary schools also are finding that parents are beginning to scrutinise performance differences between local schools.

The second development concerns the introduction of a national system of school inspection under the auspices of the Office for Standards in Education (OFSTED). Few policies have caused as much controversy as the OFSTED inspection regime. The system provided for a pattern of school inspections that guaranteed that every school would be inspected within each four-year cycle. Inspections are carried out by teams of inspectors who have been trained for the role, using procedures and criteria set out in a Framework for Inspection. It involves a review of the quality of teaching and learning in each subject of the curriculum and of the management arrangements. It includes evidence from parents and students, and results in a formal report following the inspection visit. It also involves classroom observation of all teachers and each lesson observed is graded according to the published criteria.

The system is remarkably open – the manual, with its sample forms and lists of criteria, is on public sale. Teachers and parents see how their school will be inspected and how their performance will be assessed. The inspection report is also a public document – schools are required to circulate a summary of the main points to all parents, and to inform parents how they can gain access to the whole report from the school. Reports are posted on the OFSTED website (*www.ofsted.gov.uk*). Once the report has been presented to the school, the school's governors have forty days to respond to its recommendations with an action plan, which is also available to interested parties.

The very transparency of this system caused disquiet in schools – issues that had traditionally been regarded as "professional" and confidential were being openly placed into the public domain. The scale of the inspection process was seen as intrusive and disruptive. The "privatisation" of this process, whereby OFSTED listed schools to be inspected and, invited appropriately qualified groups to tender for schools, also attracted criticism. LEAs were required to "bid" for schools in their own areas and were not always successful. Smaller LEAs could not, under the straitened financial circumstances created by the 1988 Act, afford to retain inspectors in every national curriculum subject, and so could not always maintain an inspection team. Private inspection groups became a major feature of the process. Despite criticisms, the Conservative and subsequent Labour governments were resolute and few concessions were made as inspection was promoted as a significant measure for school improvement.

The Labour government has also introduced a performance management scheme for teachers which represents a major challenge to school managers. A performance threshold has been proposed which, once it has been achieved, will give teachers access to new levels of pay. This means agreeing objectives with the line manager and reviewing progress regularly. Performance management also applies to heads and deputy heads, with governing bodies responsible for reviewing the performance of heads with the assistance of a trained external adviser, and heads responsible for reviewing the performance of deputies. The government is funding the scheme and providing training and support for its implementation. Performance management in schools is still in its early stages and its primary purpose is to improve school performance focussing on the activities of teachers and managers, both as individuals and as members of teams, and to ensure that those who are meeting performance targets are appropriately rewarded.

Labour's White Paper – *Excellence in Schools* – in 1997 picked up the theme of target setting and has developed it over the past few years. Attainment targets are set for students at different stages of their schooling and are related to the government's national targets for 11- and 16-year-olds which it hopes to secure by 2002. National targets provide a framework and context for more detailed work. The Governing Body of every school is required by law to set school-level targets by 31 December each year, for performance by pupils at the end of the following academic year (*i.e.* five terms later). These targets cannot then be changed, either by the Governing body itself or externally. Each LEA prepares its Education Development Plan, informed by individual school targets, which is then submitted to the Secretary of State. Target setting is placed at the heart of the recipe for effectiveness because it ensures that development plans relate to improvements in student achievement.

The Labour Government has also developed the notion of Beacon Schools which are defined by the Department for Education and Employment as those that have been identified as amongst the best performing in the country – they represent examples of successful practice which are to be brought to the attention of the rest of the education service with a view to sharing that practice with others.

The 75 schools selected for DfEE funding during the pilot phase from amongst 150 applicants (themselves identified through OFSTED inspection evidence) began operating as Beacon Schools in September 1998. The group had been identified as having specific strengths from which other schools could learn. Beacon school status indicated areas of expertise in particular schools that could be tapped into by the wider school community and provided the "Beacons" themselves with additional funding to finance various methods of disseminating practice.

Beacon Schools will not only feature good classroom practice. The particular activities to be offered by a Beacon School conform to an agreed programme in defined areas of expertise, for which, at present, the schools receive additional funding averaging around £32 000 a year. By September 2000 there were 550 Beacon Schools around the country. The plan is to have 1 000 such schools by 2002. They will tend to have a management approach: that emphasises self-evaluation; that identifies weaknesses as well as strengths and then tackles these; and that establishes a collaborative culture in which teachers work in partnership with colleagues inside and outside the school. It is not excellence as such, but the capacity to share practices and experiences with other schools, that underpins Beacon status.

An independent evaluation of the pilot phase has shown that even in its first year the initiative started to have a major impact. The evaluation has shown that Beacon schools can be a lever for change, acting as a catalyst for debate, challenging other schools to review their own practices. It has demonstrated the existence of a felt need amongst school staff to learn from each other; it has served to reinstate the value of the principle of collaboration and partnership between schools and to re-establish local networks; and it has potential for school improvement through professional development. It has shown that both Beacon schools and their partner schools are benefiting from participation in Beacon activity – Beacon schools cite staff development opportunities and a constant impetus to improve their own practice as their main benefits; partner schools value the opportunity to draw on ideas of practising classroom teachers and to implement what they have learned. The evaluation also suggested that the Beacon schools initiative has the potential to be one of the key links in the process of establishing a culture of self-reflection and systematic self-evaluation for school improvement.

Specialist schools are secondary schools which, in addition to teaching the National Curriculum, give special emphasis to one of the following areas: technology, science and mathematics; modern foreign languages; sport; or the arts. Any maintained secondary school in England can apply for designation. The programme is competitive and schools must raise £50 000 of private sector sponsorship and prepare four-year development plans with a range of realistic but challenging targets for provision, results, and subject take-up. Designated schools receive £100 000 capital grant and around £120 per pupil per year extra revenue funding. The grant is renewable for periods of three years, subject to acceptable progress against targets and new development plans.

This programme began in 1994 but the government has greatly increased its size, with a target now of 800 specialist schools (about 25%) by September 2003, and a strong new community dimension. All specialist schools must now spend about one third of their additional funding helping other schools and making provision for the wider community. The government sees specialist schools as central to the modernisation of the comprehensive system and an integral part of the overall school improvement agenda. Research by the London School of Economics (examining the impact of the specialist schools programme) suggests that the programme has delivered improvements in examination results over and above those in other schools during the same period as well as "a wide range of other positive effects".

Framework

Schools, as we have seen, operate within a tight framework, now bounded by the School Standards and Framework Act of 1998 and by various policy initiatives such as target setting, performance management, publication of performance tables, and the OFSTED inspection system. These define and limit the principal's role very considerably and nowhere is this more clearly seen than in the operation of the national curriculum. Whereas previously curriculum patterns varied between schools the national curriculum has remained largely uniform and the principal's role has become one of administrating the implementation of a centrally determined curriculum, rather than developing and managing a curriculum model within the school.

Case Studies

Francis Combe School

The school in Garston, Watford, has 830 students, aged 11-18 as well as 30 adult learners from the local community. The majority of students come from lower

193|

socio-economic backgrounds, with a high proportion from one-parent families. A very high proportion of the students are on the Special Needs Register and 83 of them have formal Statements of Special Educational Needs. A high proportion of students move in or out of the school, with a relatively high percentage in Year 7 who will not be there in Year 11. Many of the "casual" entrants during the school year are disaffected, and consequently require special attention.

Despite these difficulties, Francis Combe has grown (by about 300 students) over the past five years, and has begun to develop strong links with its community. This is evident in the presence of adult learners, the School Council and the school representation in many community groups outside the school. It is currently developing a Performing Arts Centre which will have strong community involvement, and there are plans to locate a Family Service Centre (involving all the Social Service agencies) in the school. The school's capacity to offer quality education in difficult circumstances was recently acknowledged through a (second) Schools' Curriculum Award.

There is a wealth of innovative management practice in the school. The school has developed a modularised curriculum (based on seven-week cycles) which gives opportunities to focus student attention and renew student commitment at regular intervals. The scheme includes each student setting targets, and recording these in an Individual Action Plan (IAP) for each module or cycle. Although this system has developed considerably following the government's target-setting initiative, the school scheme pre-dates this. Data about student achievement and predicted "targets" are reviewed regularly, and are used in decision making about future teaching and curriculum development.

The current principal was appointed in 1993 to the school which at that time was somewhat insular and lacking, perhaps, in a shared vision. She integrated the "best of the old" into the changing school and placed the curriculum leaders at the centre. An entirely new school management and communication structure was implemented in 1998. There are three deputy head-teachers, a Senior Executive Group (SEG) and a Senior Advisory Group. Teacher attendance is very good. School development planning is of a high quality and a model for other schools. The use of systematic, formal and regular review of key areas of performance is both unusual and important in maintaining the culture of continuous scrutiny and improvement. The school is benefiting from strong leadership and a clear sense of direction.

The curriculum is divided into seven areas: communication (English and Modern Foreign Languages), mathematics, expressive arts, humanities, learning support, science and vocational studies. Each curriculum area has a member of the SEG assigned to it. There is also a curriculum area leader appointed.

The school council meets once in each 7 week module. External activities include visits to the District Council and Magistrates Court. The school council has lively discussions on local citizenship, sports equipment, new block, and teacher of the year award. Positive and appreciative attitudes to the council were expressed. The student council has an important role in interviewing teachers for posts. Fortunately, to date, the students' view has coincided with that of the management. Prospective teachers find the student council interview to be more daunting than the formal interview board discussion.

Francis Combe School has strongly developed procedures for reception of casual entrants. Records from previous schools are located as far as possible. Casual Entrance Assessments are held in weeks one and four of the seven week module. The assessment includes literacy, numeracy and general. An individual education plan is prepared. Parents are met and a tour of the school is arranged.

There are particular caring procedures for the student's day one at Francis Combe. These are designed to allow for a personal pastoral care plan to be devised. In addition, a temporary timetable for week one is operated in association with a "form buddy". The individual education plans in operation at Francis Combe are very detailed and include: learning needs; priority targets; strategies to meet targets; progress reporting. Follow through and monitoring of pupils' progress are excellent.

The school has developed a social inclusion policy which caters for: those students at risk of permanent exclusion; those permanently excluded from another school; students with a physical disability or health concern; and school refusers. It offers: full access to the national curriculum; access to the careers service; access to an educational psychologist; and re-integration into mainstream as a priority.

The social inclusion unit which has its own manager and dedicated classroom offers a calm and stimulating environment with its own entrance. Subject teachers visit the unit to deliver the national curriculum. This adds to the unit's credibility with general staff. Students have the opportunity to experience a vocational curriculum including food technology, business studies and art. Mixing with peers is a privilege that must be earned. The unit's work is displayed around the school.

In summary, this case study shows how a principal has succeeded in transforming a school over a short period. The OFSTED (Inspection) report enabled the head-teacher to further develop and encourage habits of co-operation and teamwork among teaching staff. When she took over, the current principal head felt there was a need to raise staff morale. She communicated a sense among staff that the school was undergoing redevelopment. She regarded herself as fortunate in having the senior vice-principal's experience at her disposal. The principal's personal qualities are much appreciated by teachers in general. Staff now have a real participation role in decision-making; there is strong emphasis on planning to ensure a degree of consensus among staff. According to the OFSTED report of 1997, "the school is strong and wisely led".

Sharnbrook Upper School and Community College

This co-educational comprehensive school with 1 530 students and over 100 teachers is regarded as one of the most successful in Bedfordshire. It is a designated Media Arts College, under the government's specialist schools scheme and is a Beacon School. It is the lead school in Bedfordshire Local Education Authority's Upper School Improvement Project, which is co-ordinated by the school's principal. Its Beacon School areas of expertise are: school improvement; development of leadership capacity; staff and governor development; initial teacher education; research into professional practice; classroom teaching; cognitive acceleration and thinking skills; school-to-school partnerships; and collaborative development and improvement activities.

The current principal was appointed in 1987. Management is clearly structured through the senior team, extended senior team and heads of year team, followed by the curriculum area teams each with their own area leaders. The senior management team comprises the principal and two vice principals. Their responsibilities are discrete and cover values and direction, internal processes and student issues. The extended senior team comprises four senior teachers who deal with curriculum, professional development, estates and finance and administration. There are heads for years 9, 10, 11 and the sixth form. In the curriculum area there are heads for English, mathematics, humanities, business education and technology, expressive arts, physical education and science.

The breakdown of area of responsibility is well thought out and there is great clarity in the division of labour. Sharnbrook teachers teach across the entire ability range. Each curriculum area has its own grouping policy. There is a ten-day timetable in operation. There are about 14 staff meetings each academic year. Sharnbrook has a staff support group for stress counselling and bereavement. There are co-ordinators for off-site and on-site learning.

"Building Excellence" is a collective term used to describe a wide range of activities undertaken by members of the Staff and Governing Body. It is a forum for exchanging good ideas and "What Next" brainstorming. Its main work is in non-curricular activities and includes fundraising, bids for development funds and income generating enterprises. The group is able to draw on the wide range of knowledge and expertise in the area of project management and implementation. It was particularly helpful in preparing the bid for Media Arts College status and in "futures" planning for ICT. The group works at establishing better links with the community of Parishes. It meets local groups and councils to inform them of the facilities available at Sharnbrook. It is seeking to secure National Lottery funding for development of sports facilities on the campus.

One of the OFSTED Inspection report's recommendations was for an improvement of provision for arts and music in Year 9. In September 1996 the amount of teaching time for expressive arts was increased and was doubled for music. Smaller groups were created for expressive arts, providing more contact and more hands-on experience. Liaison with feeder schools was developed greatly. As a result of the school's designation as a specialist Arts College, facilities, resources and staffing have seen major expansion. The new purpose-built music centre, is witness to the developmental approach of the head-teacher and governors. Prior to the development of the new expressive arts programme at Sharnbrook, science had been taking over to the detriment of arts. The school now has: a swing band, a concert band, an orchestra, a string group, a flute choir, a sax group, a brass group, a percussion ensemble and a choir. There are 12 visiting instrumental teachers. There is a full concert programme at Christmas and in the spring term.

Sharnbrook uses a school improvement programme developed in the University of Cambridge which seeks to build internal capacity through the establishment of research and development teams to carry forward particular initiatives. A feature of the Improving the Quality of Education for All (IQEA) teams is that they are deliberately selected to represent staff at all levels of the school hierarchy, and are not therefore dominated by senior management. There are six research groups at Sharnbrook looking at various areas of the curriculum including:

- *Teaching for Thinking* – identifies and adapts accelerated learning techniques.

- *Teaching with Style* – is looking at ways of maximising learning by consideration of the style needs of different learners. Learning styles are classified as visual, auditory or practical.

- *Learning through Digital Technology* – looks at how digital technology is best harnessed for powerful teaching and learning. It looks at ways of evaluating the effectiveness of strategies for integrating technology into the curriculum. It analyses use of computer facilities.

- *Interactive Whole-Class Teaching* – is undertaking a series of observations of colleagues by students, collecting examples of different approaches and their outcomes.

- *Learning through Co-operative Group Work* – looks at how this model of learning can be used to maximise student learning, and analyses of what makes group work an effective learning environment.

- *Teaching for Responsibility* – is enabling students to take greater responsibility for their own learning. Time management and planning skills are critical for students wishing to optimise their performance. The group seeks to enable students to become more independent in managing their coursework.

In summary, Sharnbrook is a successful school under many criteria. It has a high number of applicants for intake. It has favourable levels of academic achievement. There is high teacher satisfaction with the management team. The teaching staff trust the principal and have every confidence in his judgement. He emphasises the importance of the staff perception of himself as principal. He respects their views and is caring and supportive of staff development. The school has well thought out and clearly enunciated policies on several matters: consultation and decision-making; planning; marking; spelling; homework; library usage; display (of work); school development; equal opportunities; multicultural education; gender; special education needs; staff development; and pupil discipline. The school constantly works at defining, identifying, validating and generating good practice and its most recent OFSTED inspection report states:

> "Sharnbrook is an outstandingly good school. It serves its community well and fulfils its aim to provide quality education for all its pupils. The Head provides excellent leadership and has attracted staff of high calibre. Staffing is a strength of the school. In particular, the coherence and imaginative arrangements for their induction and professional development is providing an education of high quality for students."

Deacon's School

Deacon's is an 11-18 co-educational school serving the city of Peterborough. It has 1 039 students on roll, with about 200 in the sixth form. A significant proportion of students come from ethnic minorities. The school is proud of its multi-cultural dimension. It has high levels of achievement in relation to its catchment area and gains excellent "A" level results. The curriculum at Deacon's is innovative and exciting. The management structure is based around the core business of raising standards through the planned development of teaching and learning.

The school has responded to the policies and opportunities of the 1990s. In 1993, it won inclusion in the Technology Schools Initiative, and was subsequently one of the first schools to be designated a specialist school – being awarded the Technology College status. Throughout the 1990s, it has been extensively involved in the range of initiatives focused on the Initial Training of Teachers (ITT), and the Continuing Professional Development of staff. It has Beacon School status and the cited areas of expertise are the use of Advanced Skills Teachers and its Appraisal System.

The current principal was appointed in 1992 and he has a teaching staff of 65. The Senior Management Team comprises the head-teacher and four vice principals. Thus, there are five school leaders. As a foundation school, Deacon's has total control of the school site and building. The school operates a 30-period week over five days from 08.55 to 15.30. Student attendance is good. The main difference in Deacon's management is due to the influence of the governing body and of the senior management team. The principal's objectives in hiring teaching staff are worth noting – they are: to appoint people with knowledge/experience/skills. This is done at first interview stage. Then he looks for what he terms the core qualities: leadership (of pupils); communication; positive attitudes to teamwork; and positive attitudes to change. These last two are key criteria in the appointment of teachers. As part of his strategy to build up a staff capacity for change, he wants people who would participate in the life of the school. One teacher had this to say about the principal: "He has created a success culture and he refused to accept negativity, he brought with him values and integrity".

Deacons's School was one of the first in the country to achieve accreditation of Advanced Skills Teachers (AST), a grade introduced by the government to improve the spread of good practice within and between schools. In this particular school the objectives of the ASTs are:

- To raise standards of achievement at Deacon's School as measured by examination results and other performance indicators.

- To share and increase best practice in Deacon's School, and AST partner schools, with the focus on improving quality of teaching and learning.

- To increase staff awareness of research into effective teaching and learning strategies.

- To develop collaborative partnerships with Peterborough LEA to raise standards locally;

- To further develop Initial Teacher Training partnership activities with higher education institutions.

- To demonstrate to all teaching staff the benefits of working in a technology-rich curriculum.

Another feature found in the school is "Feedback", an annual survey conducted to ascertain what is right and what is wrong within the school from the staff viewpoint. All teaching and non-teaching staff take part in the survey. It is a much used management tool and the outcomes are acted upon where possible.

Sections deal with the various aspects of the work of the school. Questions deal with: working for Deacon's School; curriculum managers/team leaders; key stage managers/support; senior management overall; "your job"; and change in Deacon's. The final section is a three-part, free form question inquiring what staff would like Deacon's "to stop doing", "continue doing" and "start doing" that would make Deacon's School an excellent employer. Examples of "stop" replies are: stop developing only the best people; stop watering the stones (*e.g.* wasting a disproportionate amount of time on a few individuals who are NOT with us). Examples of "continue" replies are: continue staff development; continue sharing good practice; continue consistency in staff discipline. Examples of "start" replies are: start making "older" teachers feel that they are valued; start challenging negativity for the sake of the majority. The results are collated and circulated to all staff. The final section is published separately and is read with interest by the management teams. No management decisions are made without reference to the feedback survey.

The school also has an appraisal system whose aim is to recognise the good work of staff, to develop staff professionally, and to achieve improvement at individual and whole school levels. Appraisal is working well and to the advantage of Deacon's School's management and staff. The advantages for all are readily recognised and it can be said that the appraisal system is good for Deacon's.

In summary, the management strategy at Deacon's School has successfully transformed the resistance from traditional school culture, coupled with organisational inertia, to a programme attractive to all staff. Much of the success of the new management practice at Deacon's is due to the skilful, challenging and effective presentation of change. The principal sees himself as being concerned, not just with maintenance of the school, but also with continuing change and development. Teachers at the school mentioned several areas in which new ideas had been carried into action. The senior management team members are highly analytical, they reflect on their school and are able to point to lessons learned and tasks accomplished. Deacon's is a school which has achieved considerable success through co-operation, dynamic leadership and the ready ownership by staff of new systems and change.

Innovation and Effectiveness

The three case studies have not been drawn from the top of the school performance tables, but from different positions which reflect a cross-section of the range of circumstances in which schools in England and Wales find themselves. Nevertheless, each offers opportunities to view innovative and successful management practice, practice that has been developed in response to the landscape formed by educational policies and that has been shaped and sustained over a number of years.

Each of the three schools is striving to improve, and doing so successfully. They are raising the achievement levels of the pupils, which is evident in their test and exam results. The schools are also widening the professional experiences of staff. Particularly noteworthy is the way that the leadership base within each of the schools has been enlarged. Staff feel empowered and now have a real stake in the school. Management expectations are high and the creation of teams allows for a sharing of those high expectations. So too, especially in the case of Deacon's School, does the use of an appraisal system whose aim is to achieve improvement at individual and at school level. In all three cases, the teaching staff can truly say that the school is "all our future". Consensus is the password.

The three schools fit within the wider national context about what schools should be about, coupled with a local vision. Obtaining change in professional practices is difficult. Moving from talking and thinking about change to effecting it is more difficult. The development of a core management group in each school to lead the changes was the key to movement and, although slow at first, the three schools have been transformed. Communication with staff in each of the schools is excellent. The interest shown and the success in achieving the new statuses offered to schools by the Department for Education and Employment, is a pointer to the forward looking, open minded desire for professional advancement of the governors and management in the schools. The needs of the pupils are always placed first.

Bibliography

DfEE (1998),
    Teaching: High Status, High Standards, London.

DfEE (1999*a*),
    Code of Practice – School Admissions, London.

DfEE (1999*b*),
    Code of Practice – School Admission Appeals, London.

JESSON, D. and TAYLOR, C. (1999),
    Value Added in Specialist Schools, Technology Colleges Trust, London.

OECD (1995),
    Schools under Scrutiny, Paris.

OECD (1997*a*),
    Parents as Partners in Schooling, Paris.

OECD (1997*b*),
    Education at a Glance – OECD Indicators, Paris.

OECD (1998*a*),
    Staying Ahead – In-service Training and Teacher Professional Development, Paris.

OECD (1998*b*),
    Education at a Glance – OECD Indicators, Paris.

OECD (1999),
    Overcoming Exclusion through Adult Learning, Paris.

OECD (2000*a*),
    Motivating Students for Lifelong Learning, Paris.

OECD (2000*b*),
    Education at a Glance – OECD Indicators, Paris.

OECD (2000*c*),
    Knowledge Management in the Learning Society, Paris.

OFSTED (1999*a*),
    Annual Report of Her Majesty's Chief Inspector of Schools, 1997-98, London.

OFSTED (1999*b*),
    Inspecting Schools – The Framework, London.

OFSTED (1999*c*),
    Lessons Learned from Special Measures, London.

OFSTED (1999*d*),
    Handbook for Inspecting Secondary Schools with Guidance on Self-evaluation, London.

OFSTED (2000*a*),
   Annual Report of Her Majesty' s Chief Inspector of Schools, 1998-99, London.
OFSTED (2000*b*),
   Improving City Schools, London.
TEACHER TRAINING AGENCY (1999),
   Gaining the National Professional Qualification for Headship, London.

UNITED STATES

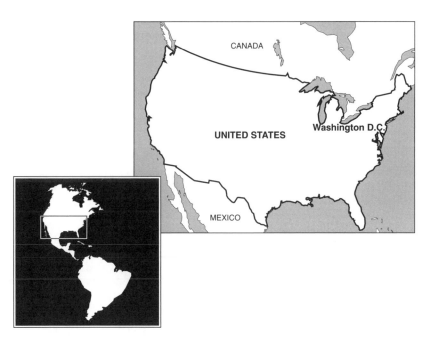

Land area in square kilometers: 9 372 000
Total population (1998): 269 092 000
Per capita GDP (1999 prices): 33 900 USD
Percentage of GDP on education (1997): 5.2%
Amount spent per student (1997):
  – 5 718 USD (Primary)
  – 7 230 USD (Secondary)
Teacher salary range (1998):
  – 25 165-42 185 USD (Primary)
  – 24 869-43 457 USD (Secondary)

Sources: *Labour Force Statistics: 1978-1998*, OECD, Paris, 1999; *Main Economic Indicators*, OECD, Paris, April 2000; *Education at a Glance – OECD Indicators 2000*, OECD, Paris, 2000.

Country context

The federal republic of the United States of America has a population of 270 million of predominantly European heritage. It has the world's strongest economy producing about 25% of the global GDP. This is accomplished by only 5% of world population, occupying but 7% of the earth's arable land. The 1990s have seen the longest peace-time economic expansion in US history creating 18 million new jobs. Unemployment has been the lowest in 41 years reaching 4.3% in 1999 with the rate for African-Americans declining to 7.8% and Hispanic unemployment reaching 6.6%. Recovery of the construction and manufacturing sectors, as well as continued growth in service employment, has led the way.

Seventy-five per cent of Americans are urban dwellers and in spite of the booming economy, 30% of workers earn poverty or near-poverty wages. Low-wage workers are now the lowest-paid in the industrialised world with more than 20% of children in the United States living in poverty. The number of US citizens who work more than one job has increased 92% between 1973 and 1997 with 43% of workers putting in more than 50 hours per week. Young entry-level workers without a college education saw their real wages fall by 20% between 1979 and 1997. On the other hand, the CEOs (Chief Executive Officers) of major corporations now earn 419 times more than the average salary of their employees. The richest 1% of the population now earns as much wealth as the bottom 95%.

In 1983, the National Commission on Excellence in Education (NCEE), in its influential report, A *Nation at Risk*, set the political tone for the closing years of the 20th century by strongly criticising American schools and setting an agenda for education reform. The eminent American educator John I. Goodlad, in his book *What Schools are For*, also defined the nature of public schooling in the United States: "The fabric of our society blends 'the soft and tender' and 'the hard and tough' with one tending to dominate the other in successive cycles. With regard to schools, I once conjectured that each cycle had a lifespan of approximately 22 years, during which either the soft and tender or the hard and tough rose and then faded from dominance as the other began its ascendancy" (Goodlad, 1994).

According to the United States Constitution, the responsibility for public education is divested to the states. Each of the fifty states has its own department of education, which delegates the actual operation of schools, from kindergarten to grade 12, to a number of local public school districts. One approach to school reform has meant that virtually every state has set standards of accountability for curriculum content and academic performance for students at each grade level and for each subject area. These results are typically made public, with comparison data across districts, so that communities can assess their district's performance in relation to other districts.

Country context (*cont.*)

A second approach to school improvement is known as "renewal". This is more of a "bottom-up" process with the people in and around schools improving their practice and developing the collaborative mechanisms necessary to improve the quality of their schools relatively free of the linearity of specified ends, means and outcomes. It addresses such fundamental issues as social justice, racism, sexism, and economic inequality to equip citizens for a productive life in a democratic society.

The corporate "top-down" language of school reform is complemented by a sense of "bottom-up" renewal, which continues to exist among many educational theorists and practitioners. All agree, however, that American schools need to improve in an age of "test-score Olympics" where other nations' maths and science standardised test results (particularly in the East) are seen to be consistently superior to those of the United States. Just as the launch of Sputnik galvanised the American public to improve scientific outcomes, the test-score deficit is seen to represent a threat to maintaining international economic dominance in the new millennium.

Challenges Facing School Management

Public opinion, fuelled by electronic and print media commentary, has translated into practice policies that are designed to ensure school performance and local accountability. The fact that this quest for improvement comes at a time of fiscal conservatism devoted to reducing public spending and taxation, has created a crisis in educational resource management. The continuing withdrawal of more affluent students from public to private schools and the advent of charter schools (and the voucher system in some states) have further complicated and threatened the role of the school administrator.

District and school management practice may be strongly influenced by state and district accountability policies designed to compel an improvement in school performance. Incentive systems may attach consequences for low performance and rewards for high performance towards a set of standards. Such systems may include intervention or redesign directions for low-performing or non-improving schools, standardised assessments for students, and rewards for schools or teachers in high performance or significantly – improving schools (see Cincinnati case study). The threat of such "top-down" intervention policies being adopted has caused many schools and school districts to stress standard-based instruction to improve student test scores.

The role of the principal has been described as complex and demanding, depending upon the education and management approach in the district. There are currently about 100 000 principals in the United States, with about 80% working in public school systems. Principals are most often paid slightly more than teachers, while being held accountable for overall school performance. They have usually been practising teachers who have received additional administrative and supervisory training through university-based programmes, which may include an internship with a practising principal or experience as a vice-principal. There is a growing perception that the traditional preparation system is inadequate in an era of local fiscal accountability and increasing demand for improvement in student performance.

In 1996, the Council of Chief State School Officers developed a set of six standards for administrative preparation called the Interstate School Leaders Licensure Consortium (ISLLC). The ISLLC standards have been adopted by several states or modified to reflect state policies and anticipated outcomes. The availability of quality candidates to fulfil these standards continues to be a concern, both today and in the recruitment of future school leaders.

The standards state that "A school administrator is an educational leader who promotes the success of all students by:

- Facilitating the development, articulation, implementation and stewardship of a vision of learning that is shared and supported by the school community.

- Advocating, nurturing, and sustaining a school culture and instructional programme conducive to student learning and staff professional growth.

- Ensuring management of the organisation, operations and resources for a safe, efficient and effective learning environment.

- Collaborating with families and community members, responding to diverse community interests and needs, and mobilising community resources.

- Acting with integrity, fairness and in an ethical manner.

- Understanding, responding to, and influencing the larger political, social, economic, legal and cultural context" (Background Report).

Main Policy Approaches

Both teacher unions, the National Education Association (NEA) and the American Federation of Teachers (AFT), have sought to partner with school districts to improve educational performance. Beginning in 1985, through its Mastery in Learning Project, the NEA found that, while individual schools and faculties might improve their performance, they seldom had any impact on the performance of neighbouring schools within the district. Such school-based changes were also most often dependent upon a climate of support from the school district or external resources (*e.g.* foundations or government grants).

This led the NEA to seek change at a more systemic and sustainable level – the district itself. In 1989, it introduced the concept of the Learning Laboratories Initiative. The initiative was designed to identify one district per state where all the key stakeholder groups would commit to "innovation, learning, and improvement in pursuit of the highest quality of education for all students". A key feature of this commitment was shared leadership between school management, local boards, and the local education association. Thirty "learning labs" were established in 30 different states for a period of five years (NEA).

The American Federation of Teachers has also addressed the concern for school improvement by adopting its Redesigning Low-Performing Schools policy at the AFT Convention in July 1998. The first essential step in improving low-performing schools is to establish a redesign intervention process shaped by policies, which:

- Are grounded in high academic standards.
- Enforce high standards of behaviour.
- Use criteria for the identification of low-performing schools that are clear and understood by all stakeholders.
- Address the particular needs of the individual school.
- Are backed by solid research.
- Involve staff and provide them with the professional development, time, and resources they will need to be effective (AFT, 1999).

The state and national focus on accountability has also meant a stronger emphasis on the quality of professional development and the quality and content of an instructional programme likely to improve student performance. Teacher quality is an issue, as a number of states are modifying teacher licensing procedures and raising entrance requirements for admission into the teaching profession.

The Carnegie Corporation's 1986 Task Force on Teaching as a Profession resulted in the establishment of a professional standards movement – the National Board for Professional Teaching Standards (NBPTS). This standards system has identified the knowledge, skills and abilities of expert teachers with an assessment process to certify them. The NBPTS has achieved high levels of acceptance from both the National Education Association and the American Federation of Teachers and has influenced state policies. In 1999, 4 800 teachers were certified with another 6 800 applying to participate. Many states and school districts provide salary bonuses and other incentives for National Board certified teachers.

Another important teacher-led development has been the New Unionism movement. A group of local union leaders has formed the Teacher Union Reform Network (TURN). Twenty-four reform-minded locals (including Cincinnati and

Seattle) embody TURN's goal of refocusing union efforts to improve student achievement through strong collaborative working relationships with district and school management. Innovations supported by TURN include: peer review programmes (see Cincinnati case study); support for National Board Certification; the development of knowledge and skill-based pay; and performance systems to support teacher career development and standards for the demonstration of teacher knowledge and skills.

A further interesting movement is the Coalition for Community Schools, a national Washington, D.C. based organisation, whose mission is "to mobilise the resources and capacity of multiple sectors and institutions to create a united movement for community schools". Its goals are to: "share information about successful community school policies, programmes, and practices; build broader public understanding and support for community schools; inform public and private-sector policies to strengthen community schools; and develop sustainable sources of funding for them" (Blank, 2000).

In a community school, youth, families and community residents work as equal partners with schools and other community institutions to develop programmes and services in five areas: quality education; youth development; family support; family and community engagement and; community development.

Community schools build strong learning partnerships, and share accountability for high academic standards. Each community school identifies its own individual needs and assets while embracing diversity in a process of community betterment (see Rural Wisconsin case study).

School-based management (SBM) is another policy to promote improvement by decentralising control from central district offices to individual school sites. Administrators, teachers, parents and other community members are to gain more authority over budget, personnel and curriculum in individual schools. In order to achieve performance improvement through SBM, control of four resources needs to be decentralised throughout the organisation:

- Power to make decisions that influence school practices, policies and directions.

- Knowledge that enables staff to understand and contribute to school performance, including technical knowledge to provide the service, interpersonal skills, and managerial knowledge and expertise.

- Information about the school's performance including revenues, expenditures, student achievement, progress towards meeting its goals and how parents and other citizens perceive its services.

- Rewards that are based on school performance and the contributions of individuals. (Wohlstetter and Mohrman, 1993).

Research indicates that school-based management "can help foster an improved school culture and higher-quality decisions". It is a potentially valuable tool for engaging more talents and enthusiasm among stakeholders than traditional, top-down governance systems. There is a concern, however, that principals receive improved pre-service and in-service training to be better school-based managers (see Seattle case study).

Framework

The United States Department of Education has traditionally provided funding to states and school districts to encourage improvement in high-poverty and low-achieving schools (*e.g.* Title I). In 1998, Congress introduced the Comprehensive School Reform Demonstration (CSRD) programme (also known as Obey-Porter) to raise student achievement by helping public schools across the country implement successful, comprehensive school reforms (US Department of Education, 2000).

The focus of CSRD is on school-wide plans, which promote the use of reliable research and effective practices to improve basic academics and parental involvement. Each school participating in the programme receives at least $50 000 per year, renewable for up to three years. By the spring of 2000, approximately 1 800 elementary and secondary schools in urban and rural areas were using $210 million in CSRD funds to support their school-wide initiatives. Schools typically use well-researched and documented models developed by "external partners" from universities or other technical assistance providers. A team of trained experts provides on-site assistance to teachers and other staff in using effective strategies for teaching and learning.

Schools also have the option of developing their own models, and a small percentage has chosen this option. In several states, CSRD is leveraging additional resources to support school reform efforts. These range from state, to federal Title I intervention funds, to private foundation resources.

A relatively new movement in the United States is the creation of charter schools – non-sectarian, tuition-free public schools that are founded through a performance contract with either a state agency or a local school board. The school's charter gives autonomy over its operation and frees the school from regulations that other public schools must follow. The charter sets out how student performance will be measured, and what levels of achievement the school will attain. If the school fails to attract students, achieve performance objectives, or violates conditions of the contract (by breaking remaining laws or regulations) it can be closed. By the year 2000, 39 states had passed charter school legislation, and 1 700 charter schools enrolled 10% of the overall public school enrolments (US Department of Education, 2000).

In 1994, the United States Congress established the Public Charter School Programme (PCSP) as part of Title X of the Elementary and Secondary Education Act. Since then, the United States Department of Education has played a role in the development of the charter school movement. As part of the Charter School Expansion Act of 1998, Congress authorised "dissemination grants for charter schools with three years of experience and demonstrated success". This provides each state with between $50 000 and $700 000 to support partnerships between high-quality charter schools and non-chartered public schools (US Department of Education, 2000).

The importance of community involvement in schools was stressed in the 1983 report A Nation at Risk. "At the heart of the learning society are education opportunities extending far beyond the traditional institutions of learning, our schools and colleges. They extend into the homes and workplaces; into libraries; art galleries; museums; and science centres; indeed, into every place where the individual can develop and mature in work and life. But without lifelong learning, one's skills will become rapidly dated" (NCEE, 1983).

The state of Wisconsin has a long history of public schools as neighbourhood hubs for learning and sharing. It was the first state in the nation (1911) to promote citizen use of school facilities and the unique partnership that exists between a school district and the community it serves (Potts et al., 1992).

In 1990, Wisconsin's Commission on Schools for the 21st Century called for "restructuring our public schools to achieve a new set of goals which reflect the importance of having an educated and responsible citizenry for a democratic society capable of competing in a world class economy. A renewed partnership among schools, parents and the community will be required" (Wisconsin Department of Public Instruction).

Case Studies

Cincinnati Public Schools

Cincinnati, the third largest city in Ohio, has about 47 000 students consisting of approximately 70% African Americans, 27% Caucasians and 3% others. The district has experienced a continuing decline in enrolment, particularly among Caucasians who make up 60% of the population. 20% of school-age children in Cincinnati attend private schools (versus 11% in the United States) with a growing number of charter schools being established by African American parents. The result is a powerful incentive for the Cincinnati Public Schools (CPS) and the Cincinnati Teachers Federation (CTF) to work together to improve the quality of education. This sense of partnership has produced a number of initiatives.

An urgent necessity in the Cincinnati public schools has been to raise student achievement and reduce dropout rates. Beginning in 1997-98, every school was given targets for improving academic standards and other indicators of success. Each school must develop a comprehensive plan for achieving these targets. A review of the performance of the previous year requires revisions to improve performance. A performance review is based on student achievement scores on the Ohio Proficiency Test (or Off-Grade Proficiency Test for primary schools).

Schools showing a high degree of success are rewarded through the School Incentive Award as negotiated and ratified in the collective agreement. Schools in the next category, School Achievement, are deemed to be performing satisfactorily. Schools not achieving a high degree of success and/or improvement are placed into the School Assistance and Redesign Plan (SARP). The Superintendent establishes a district level School Redesign Team consisting of lead teachers, school building leaders and senior district leaders to implement the SARP process (CPS, 1998). A detailed description of the SARP process is included in Part One of this volume.

Parham Elementary is an example of an inner-city school placed under Redesign and closed in June 1999. It reopened the next September with a new teaching staff and instructional format. Teams of four teachers were employed for every 60 students. The school day was extended from 8:00 a.m. to 3:00 p.m. with no recess period. Previously a kindergarten to grade six school, grades seven and eight were added to the school's enrolment. A new comprehensive phonics-based, teacher-centred reform model known as "Direct Instruction" (previously called DISTAR) was adopted to improve basic reading, writing and mathematics skills.

Each teacher selected for the redesigned school was required to sign a "letter of commitment" and attend a summer course (on their own time) to prepare for the school opening in September. Teachers were committed to the following ideals:

- Children taught to mastery.
- "Raising the bar" of excellence in achievement.
- Challenge and motivation – not pity.
- Ongoing rapport with parents and students (e.g. teachers agreed to visit homes to meet parents and students before school opening).

The principal at Parham is a strong instructional leader whose energy and determination motivate the staff and students to "raise the bar" in their quest for excellence. Children in primary classrooms practice a form of recitation in demonstrating their literacy and numeracy skills. Kindergarten children recite the alphabet and number sequences while another group had memorised the names of all the Presidents. The learning environment is very teacher-directed and regimented with an emphasis on discipline and repetition. The results reported are encouraging with

213

some kindergarten children reading at a grade two level while other fourth-graders are "ready to tackle algebra".

The principal wants to make Parham the "Number One Neighbourhood School in Cincinnati". She and her teachers strive to develop the "whole child". While Parham parents may have a limited educational background and financial means, the school is committed to enabling their children to achieve academic success, win scholarships and go on to college.

In 1985, the Cincinnati Federation of Teachers (CFT) and the Cincinnati Public Schools (CPS) reached an agreement for a "Peer Appraisal Programme". Four teachers, appointed by CFT, joined four administrators, appointed by the Superintendent, to form the "Peer Review Panel". It selected six elementary and four secondary "consulting teachers" to serve during the 1985-86 school year. The Panel revised and expanded the programme (currently up to 20 consulting teachers) after its first year and decided to change its name to the Peer Assistance and Evaluation Programme (PAEP).

The "role of the school principal" is also defined. They are required to conduct annual observations on all teachers not included in the Peer Assistance and Evaluation Programme (PAEP). They conduct routine appraisals during the third year of a teacher's service in the CPS, or those changing schools or subjects. They liase with consulting teachers regarding their observations of any teachers receiving PAEP appraisal. After two formal observations of experienced teachers and interns, the principal may refer those with teaching deficiencies to the Intervention component of PAEP (CFT/CPS, 1999).

Another reform introduced jointly by the Cincinnati Federation of Teachers and the Cincinnati Public Schools has been the Career in Teaching Programme. Implemented in 1990, the programme offers ongoing professional development incentives to keep talented teachers in the classroom, and opportunities for highly proficient teachers to play leadership roles within the profession. Teachers progress through Intern, Resident, Career Teacher and Lead Teacher levels. Financial rewards are provided at each step based on a combination of assessment, advanced education and experience.

The new lead teacher roles complement Cincinnati's administrative reforms, whereby more than 50% of central administrative positions have been eliminated since 1991. The programmes' goal is for lead teacher positions to equal 10% of the teaching force.

The Cincinnati Public Schools (CPS) and the Cincinnati Federation of Teachers (CFT) have also got together in a unique learning partnership to establish the Mayerson Academy. The city's business community donated four million dollars when the Academy was founded in 1992. A state-of-the-art training facility, the Academy, was opened adjacent to the CPS central offices and is managed by a Board of

Directors which includes the Superintendent, representatives of the school board and CFT, and six members of the business community (Mayerson Academy, 1999-2000).

CPS contracts with the academy for professional development services according to the expressed needs of local school personnel. The academy operates six days per week from 7:00 a.m. to 9:00 p.m. in "a very cost effective manner". To support the CPS mandate, to shift decision-making from the central office to the local school, a series of "core courses" are provided (*e.g.* co-operative discipline; developmentally appropriate practice; instructional alignment; managing diverse classrooms K-8; school improvement; standards driven curriculum; standards into practice: 7-8 maths; and team-based classrooms). The future emphasis of the academy will be to deliver team-based training and support, directly on-site at the local school and targeted to local needs.

The academy maintains a half-time position to work with new principals, inspire existing principals, and entice new candidates into the field. The academy's chief executive officer believes that the principals' role should be redefined to that of reflective practitioners who constantly renew their knowledge of research and development in the field to share with others as inspirational leaders and "promoters and developers of teachers and teaching". He sees new principals being recruited "directly" from the ranks of gifted classroom teachers, retiring senior managers from business and industry, and senior officers from the military.

In conclusion, the Cincinnati Public Schools project is engaged in some of the most innovative human resource management experiments in the country. Faced with a significant decline in enrolment and budget restraint, the school district and union leadership have learned to work together. Despite financial hardships, a relationship of collaborative self-interest continues to be forged: to develop and adopt new innovative strategies; to improve student achievement; enhance public accountability; optimise instructional performance; and encourage leadership development. The challenge of the future will be to maintain this sense of union-management trust and human resource solidarity, while renewing community confidence in the quality of public education.

Rural Wisconsin

The focus for this case study is a partnership of several rural school districts in a geographically isolated, and economically depressed area, of north western Wisconsin about 200 miles north of Madison, the state capital. Employment for residents centres on farming, logging, tourism, small business enterprises and limited manufacturing. The unemployment levels are the highest in the state, with family income 32% below the state average. 66% of students are receiving free or subsidised lunches. The area includes the Lac Courte Oreille (LCO) tribal school with 100% American Indian students on an Ojibwe reserve (NPP, 2000a and b).

215|

In 1993, a dynamic community education director in the Flambeau School District utilised a school reform grant from the Institute for Responsive Education, to bring together a group of fifteen school leaders committed to educational improvement. The result was a non-profit consortium – New Paradigm Partners Inc. (NPP). The original partnership of five public school districts, a tribal school and a private college has continued to grow.

In addition to local and state resources, it has received funding from: the Annenberg Rural Challenge; the W.K. Kellogg Foundation; MacDonald Charities Fund; and the Soros Foundation. NPP was created in the belief that "a powerful synergistic network of learning partners would give new life to our schools and communities and make a dramatic impact on student learning" (NPP).

NPP's work is grounded in principles of community education, which promote parent and community involvement in education, the formation of community partnerships to address community needs, and the expansion of lifelong learning opportunities.

Of particular concern is the future of small rural schools and communities. A depressed rural economy may either not motivate students to achieve, or result in the best students having to leave the community in search of employment. The goal of NPP is to establish an inclusive, entrepreneurial culture, which is supportive of innovation, creative collaboration and leadership.

Early in June 2000, the NPP partners met to review the year's accomplishments, and plan for the future. This meeting of school district superintendents and administrators provided the following progress reports about a new K-12 curriculum that has been integrated into the schools with a focus on local history, culture, entrepreneurship and "hands on" interdisciplinary approaches to learning. Multi-age, project-based learning activities include the following:

- *Journalism*: Youth Press is a community-based media project where 250 students work with media professionals within five regional "news-bureaus". Students produce articles on a regular basis for local print media and publish *Pass It On*, a state-wide journal with a readership of 15 000. They create videos, public TV programmes and produce *Rebel Radio*, a monthly two-hour Saturday morning radio show broadcast on local FM stations. An electronic variety magazine, M.ZINE, now features short stories, editorials, poetry, illustrations, photography and student reflections – on the Internet. Activities of Youth Press have gained national renown and students travel throughout the US speaking at conferences and workshops (NPP, 1998).

- *Student-run businesses*: Entrepreneurial enterprises operated by students of all ages include: a wood-drying and manufacturing business; a community newspaper; two greenhouse operations; several video production, graphic

arts, web-design and technology consulting enterprises; two canoe trip out-
fitting ventures; and a card and balloon business (*Milwaukee Journal*, 1994).

- *Intergenerational learning*: Students, through Circle of Light projects, have
interviewed elders and transcribed historical tales later disseminated
through print media articles, videos, educational CDs and a web site. With
help from a professional song-writer, students write songs based on the stories and perform them with the elders at community events, including the
American Folklife Festival in Washington, D.C. At the Lac Courte Oreille
Ojibwe School, tribal elders assist in the classrooms providing individualised attention, nurturing, self-esteem building, and cultural enrichment
while encouraging student-learning across the ages.

- *Environmental Restoration*: Students are involved in detailed environmental
research and all phases of project planning and implementation. Through a
variety of student funding initiatives, projects have included: trout stream
and other water quality improvements; reforestation; park developments;
prairie restorations; and wildlife habitat improvements.

New Paradigm Partners Inc. has also provided school reform, community education, and leadership training workshops. Curriculum development and teaching
methods classes have been offered for graduate or undergraduate credit. For
example, Mt. Senario College recently established a new leadership programme,
as a minor at the college, in which students develop leadership skills in the process of planning and implementing community and school projects. A regional
Leadership Development Committee (LEARN), with representation from numerous agencies and schools, is giving shape to a series of new, highly collaborative
leadership opportunities for principals, teachers, students, parents, and other
community members.

An expectation of all training is that participants apply their learning to some
tangible school or community improvement initiative. Careful collaborative planning is emphasised as each participant networks with others to plan and implement projects. Mentorships are facilitated when appropriate, and mini-grants
have been made available using funds from a variety of sources.

The case study also included site visits to two school districts, Weyerhaeuser
and Birchwood. Weyerhaeuser school has an enrolment of 247 students, with
25 teachers, from kindergarten to 12th grade. Over the years, Weyerhaeuser
School has become famous for its student-led enterprises:

- The Blue Hills Manufacturing Partnership LLC (BHMP) provides Weyerhaeuser (an old logging community with virtually no industry) with a student-
run entrepreneurial venture in preparation for future education and employment. With help from the state's Co-operative Educational Service Agency
(CESA), and the federal School to Work Opportunities Act, students formed a

217|

Limited Liability Company (LLC) which is registered with the state and federal governments. Students have legal stock in the company, which they can: purchase from graduating seniors; earn by working for the corporation; or earn through academic achievement.

- Because there was no facility to dry green lumber in the area, BHMP built a solar-powered custom lumber drying operation. The enterprise also serves as an incubator for spin-off businesses such as successful snowshoe and snowshoe furniture manufacturing and woodcraft ventures now located at the school.

The second visit was to Birchwood, a K-12 school with 355 students serving an area of 200 square miles with vast socio-economic disparities among property owners and residents. 70% of property owners are comparatively wealthy summer dwellers. The majority of the remaining 30% are retirees. Only 10% of residents have children in the school and these residents have a low level of family income in the region. They have traditionally survived at an impoverished subsistence level, with limited interest in education and support for student achievement. Consequently, Birchwood students remained near the bottom on state academic test scores.

In 1994, Birchwood began a community education programme, which brought together a leadership team of staff and community members to conduct a school/community needs assessment, and to assist in communications, morale building, visioning and goal setting. The result was a school/community partnership to promote lifelong learning and educational opportunities for Birchwood students and staff.

A major source of pride has been the Birchwood News. As no newspaper previously existed in the community, students, teachers, and community members worked together to publish a community newspaper. Students write stories, do page layout on computers, sell and develop advertising and print the paper on an offset printing press. They gain skills, course credits and valuable work experience while fulfilling a community need. In 1995, the project was featured in USA Today, as one of seven schools selected nationally for its Community Solutions through Education award.

Another innovation, to bridge socio-economic differences and improve support for education, has been the Senior Tax Exchange Programme (STEP) intergenerational volunteer programme. Elder residents, who volunteer their time to assist the school as classroom tutors, mentors, and role models, earn a decrease in their property taxes. It should be noted that Wisconsin has one of the highest tax rates in the country.

Birchwood has become a "lighthouse" school in which the community has developed a sense of ownership. Learning activities for family members of all ages take place during the day, in the evening and during the summer through the Families and Schools Together (FAST) programme.

The community education process has had other positive outcomes for Birchwood. The inclusionary nature of the programme has meant that all taxpayers, including summer residents, now have a sense of ownership in the school and support for public education. Persons of all socio-economic levels are meeting and sharing. Academic test scores continue to rise. The school completion rate, once among the lowest in the state, is now above the state average. Where once there was a call to close the school, and bus the kids to neighbouring Rice Lake, there is now a recognition of the importance of the school in retaining the town's identity, social, cultural, and economic well-being.

The community education process, as envisioned by the NPP consortium, has also retained the confidence and support of school leaders. To quote the Birchwood School District Superintendent, "Our community views New Paradigm Partners as an agent of change within the school district. Involvement in the consortium has broadened our scope, and helped to create community spirit, integrating all ages, and people of all experiences" (NPP, 1998).

Seattle Public Schools

Seattle is a 130-year old school district which currently has a student population of about 50 000, of which 59% are visible minorities, including 24% Asian and 23% African-American students. 21% of the student population is bilingual (predominantly Spanish) and 88 languages are spoken in the homes of the district. Several factors contributed to the current state of management innovation including the following:

- During the 1980s, there was a growing dissatisfaction with the quality of public education and a perception that the school district "was broke and needed to be fixed". The situation came to a head in the 1989 Mayoral election which turned out to be a referendum on school reform. The successful candidate, in response to the sense of "yearning and despair" among voters, promised to work to improve public education. (This was ironic, as schools are not part of the city council mandate.)

- In 1991, the state's Governor (a former Seattle Councillor) ordered a review of public education in Seattle. The resulting report was a "blistering" critique of the city's public school system.

- As a result, in the early 90s, a new slate of school board members was elected promising to work for radical school reform.

- In 1995, a group of key industrialists, known as the Seattle Alliance (which later became the Alliance for Education), expressed serious concerns about leadership and directions in the public school system. They helped to develop a strategic plan and began to recruit strong candidates for the Superintendent's position. That year, John Stanford, an African-American former 2-star Army General and County Executive in Georgia, was appointed Superintendent of Seattle Public Schools. His strong managerial background and sense of hope and commitment for the quality of schools were deciding factors in his appointment.

Stanford acknowledged that the system was broken and that tinkering with change was not enough. He demanded a mandate for deep, systemic transformational changes to restore faith in public education. One of his first acts was to hire a young financial service executive to be his Chief Financial Officer. The officer later replaced Mr. Stanford (who died in 1998).

Their core vision became "community schools" where both schools and their communities are deeply connected. The basic premise is to maximise peoples' freedom, power and authority. Second was to maximise accountability and focus on performance. Instead of traditional top-down direction, they created a freedom and greater flexibility agenda devoted to student outcomes.

This freedom agenda includes the following factors:

- *Freedom of Choice* – Any student can choose any school, and schools are competing for enrolment. As the district has excess capacity (especially in north Seattle) students become free-agents in a student-driven system.

- *Freedom of Funding* – Each school becomes a private enterprise in a market-based system where they compete for enrolment and resources.

- *Freedom of Staffing* – In a new union contract teachers can now be aligned according to the interests and needs of individual schools and individual teachers rather than by seniority.

- *Freedom of Programme* – This allows schools to adopt different programmes to suit the different needs of the school enrolment. As a result, schools may become more entrepreneurial with their own sense of identity and marketing strengths (*e.g.* theme or boutique schools). To date, the freedom agenda has found more favour in elementary than secondary schools.

The district has developed and adopted a decentralised financial management strategy. Resources are allocated to schools based on a "weighted student enrolment formula", in which students with greater learning resource needs generate a larger allocation of funds to the school site. Principals act as chief executive officers for their schools, and have broad authority to allocate resources to school-determined priorities. The district has developed a web-based budget and management system to enable schools to successfully carry out the formula budgeting policy.

Decentralisation of financial and management decisions produced a need for stronger professional development of principals. A community-based non-profit organisation, the Alliance for Education, provided significant support for Seattle Public Schools programmes; including professional development for principals and teachers. In 1996, the Principal Leadership Institute (PLI), was established by the Seattle Public Schools and the Alliance for Education to provide principals with the skills to be strong instructional leaders and chief executive officers of their schools. The programme provides training for all principals in the district as well as programmes that develop and mentor new and aspiring principals for leadership positions.

The district enjoys strong financial and political support from the Seattle community. The community routinely supports the district through positive votes on tax levies for capital construction and school programmes. In this regard, Schools First is a citizens' lobby group whose membership includes representatives from parent and teacher associations (PTA), Chamber of Commerce, Alliance for Education and other members of the community. The Alliance for Education encourages educational reform through significant financial support for the district. For example, in 1998 the Alliance contributed $8 million to support a variety of district programmes and initiatives. In March of 2000, the district also received a commitment from the Bill and Melinda Gates Foundation of $25.9 million to provide resources for every school in the district for planning, technical assistance, staff training and the purchase of technology resources to enhance learning. The donation will also provide selected schools with resources to implement comprehensive school reform models (Alliance for Education, 1999).

Madison (MMS) is a middle school (grades 6-8) in the south end of Seattle. Twenty-six teachers serve a student population of 900 including: 44% Caucasian; 31% Asian; 12% Latino; 1% African American; and 3% American Indian. English-as-a-second-language instruction (ESL) is provided to 14% of students while 9% receive special education. In the 1970s, students were bussed to the north end as part of desegregation provisions. Today, the system's master plan is to reconnect families to their local neighbourhood school.

The school principal explained that 50% of her students live below the poverty line. In the "weighted budget formula", funding dollars are based on the enrolment and degree of student need. As the number of poor and special needs students decline, the school receives less financial support and staff allocations. The fact that the school can bank any surplus dollars from one budget year helps to ease any enrolment-driven funding decline in a subsequent year.

Madison's "bible" is the Staff Handbook, which consists of a thick policy manual with specifics of "everything we do in the school" (*e.g.* field trips, discipline, student intervention team, etc.). Each person on the staff is responsible for some

221

policy or procedure in the handbook. Other highlights of the Madison programme include:

- *Academic Achievement Plan* – The focus of the plan is to improve academic achievement for all students through specific strategies to increase test scores and performance results. School-wide incentives increase readiness-to-learn capabilities. Curriculum standards and essential learning align with school delivery systems. The school budget and master plan are aligned to support academic achievement. Special education students are served through an inclusive design providing individual assistance, while maximising participation in the regular standards-based curriculum. Academic performance is assessed throughout the year by each teacher. Standardised test scores now approach state averages (MMS, 2000).

- *Challenge Curriculum* – This is a multi-level "thinking skills" curriculum designed to keep every learner "engaged and excited" according to individual learning needs, multiple intelligence theory, and "Best Practices" research. While respecting diversity, Challenge ensures the twin values of equity and excellence for all students. Challenge builds self-esteem while "raising the bar" for every student (MMS *Challenge Curriculum*).

- *Budgetary Planning* – The school has used its budgetary decision-making to link educational objectives to school-based resource allocation decisions.

- *Parent/Community Involvement* – Madison has an involved and enthusiastic Parent, Teacher and Student Association (PTSA). As school partners, parents work in collaboration with staff, students and the community in all aspects of the school's programme. Nordstrom (a department store chain) has been an active and visible partner since 1988, investing resources and sponsoring numerous activities. Southwest Youth and Family Services provide a network for counselling and referral services. During 1998-99, 221 parent/community volunteers contributed a total of 2 239 hours to the school (MMS, 1999).

In general, the Seattle Public School District has demonstrated a number of management innovations. It has been a leader in decentralised resource allocation giving individual schools more control over fiscal and management decisions. Its priorities for the 1999-2000 school year included improving academic performance for all students by implementing academic standards in all schools. Expanding student enrolment, teacher recruitment, and completing the neighbourhood choice option, continue to be key challenges. Finding a better way to produce school leaders and site managers is also a priority. Entrepreneurial, instructional leaders, comfortable with decentralised resource allocation and freedom of choice, are critically needed to achieve Seattle's mission "to build a world-class, student-focused, learning system".

Innovation and Effectiveness

This chapter has attempted to provide an overview of "what works" in a nationally designated sampling of exemplary policies and programmes related to school management and educational improvement. The fact that the United States has a federal system, with fifty different state jurisdictions divided into thousands of local school districts, makes the choice of innovations particularly daunting. Complementarity exists between the relative success of some top-down reform and bottom-up renewal policies and programmes. The decentralised nature of many school districts gives principals significant discretion and power in management decisions (*e.g.* budget, personnel, curricular, etc.).

Selecting three case studies was a difficult task. They were chosen largely by district/programme, with districts given discretion as to what schools to visit, based on their school management expertise in such areas as human resources policy (Cincinnati), community development (NPP) and decentralised budgeting (Seattle). In general, the situation in the United States is as follows:

- Everyone seems committed to improving the quality of education in the nation's schools.

- Every state has some system of standardised testing or assessment by which to identify and compare academic outcomes.

- Most states and school districts recognise the importance of parental and community partnerships in improving schools.

- Most states utilise federal educational policies and incentive funding to promote school improvement in impoverished areas (*e.g.* CSRD).

- The majority of states has approved a legal framework for the establishment of charter schools.

- Many school districts have adopted site-based management policies.

- Most school districts have teacher and principal appraisal procedures in place.

- All states require pre-service training for school administrators, while some school districts also provide in-service training for administrative personnel.

- Many school districts are having difficulty recruiting competent, qualified teachers and administrators.

- A future direction is for teacher unions to work with school district management to promote school improvement (*e.g.* TURN).

- School districts are making increasing use of alternate sources of support (*e.g.* business and industry, foundations, federal programmes, etc.).

- Many school districts subscribe to the concept of "community schools" as part of their school reform/renewal plan.

223|

- Most states and school districts are reviewing and revising curricular content to reflect new economic and employment realities.

The National Commission on Excellence in Education's A *Nation at Risk: The Imperative for Educational Reform* (1983) strongly criticised the quality of American education, using military language to "exhort schools to prepare students for service to the nation's economy". But this is no longer an industrial-age top-down, hierarchical marketplace. The "job for life" no longer exists as both parents and their children struggle to find and retain employment and a sense of identity in a "new globalised economy".

The new US economy is not really about the old sectors of manufacturing and resource harvesting. These have been replaced by electronics, robotics, software, the Internet, genomics and personal service "niches". There is a dramatic change in the production and distribution of goods and services, the organisation of companies and workplaces and indeed the over-all economy. Do American schools, as they were known in the industrial age, have a part to play in this paradigm shift? "What are schools for" in the new millennium? (Crane, 2000).

Some would say the United States must adopt a corporate business-like model to redesign, restructure, and reform schools based on rigid instruments of assessment to coerce new more rigorous academic standards. Others would say "communities of learning" must be created at the local level which: involve all stakeholders; are committed to excellence; and are self-renewing. Both agree that literacy, numeracy and co-operative problem-solving are among a universal set of essential skills. How are school leaders to be developed to deliver these outcomes in a turbulent, increasingly complex, ever-changing society? US policymakers seem to be seeking the best of both the top-down and bottom-up approaches. It is hoped that the research, development and practical experience to be found in the policies and case studies described above, will help to find the way. More effort is needed to define what a school manager should be as well as how to prepare and sustain such leadership.

Bibliography

ALLIANCE FOR EDUCATION (1999),
   Expanding the World of Learning, Annual Report.

AMERICAN FEDERATION OF TEACHERS (1999),
   Redesigning Low Performance Schools: It's Union Work.

BLANK, M.J. (2000),
   Coalition for Community Schools: A Call to All, The Education Digest, Ann Arbor, MI, February.

CINCINNATI FEDERATION OF TEACHERS, AND CINCINNATI PUBLIC SCHOOLS (1999),
   Raising Professional Standards in Teaching.

CINCINNATI PUBLIC SCHOOLS (1998),
   School Assistance and Redesign Plan.

CRANE, D. (2000),
   "Only Fittest, Fastest Survive in New Economy", *The Toronto Star*, June 7.

GOODLAD, J.I. (1994),
   What Schools Are for (rev. ed.), Phi Delta Kappa Education Foundation, Bloomington, IND.

MADISON MIDDLE SCHOOL (1999),
   Challenge Curriculum.

MADISON MIDDLE SCHOOL (1999),
   Annual Report.

MADISON MIDDLE SCHOOL (2000),
   Academic Achievement Plan.

MAYERSON ACADEMY (1999-2000),
   Registration Guide.

MILWAUKEE JOURNAL (1994),
   Branching Out: Students Run Own Business, October.

NATIONAL COMMISSION ON EXCELLENCE IN EDUCATION, NCEE (1983),
   A Nation at Risk: The Imperative for Education Reform, US Government Printing Office, Washington DC.

NATIONAL EDUCATION ASSOCIATION (1997),
   Leadership and School Change – Lessons from the Labs.

NEW PARADIGM PARTNERS (1998),
   Networking Small Communities Through Learning, Summer.

NEW PARADIGM PARTNERS (2000),
   Networking Small Communities Through Learning, June.

225|

NEW PARADIGM PARTNERS INC. (2000),
Final Evaluation Report to the Annenberg Rural Challenge, June.

OFFICE OF EDUCATIONAL RESEARCH AND IMPROVEMENT (1998),
The Charter School Roadmap, US Department of Education.

OFFICE OF EDUCATIONAL RESEARCH AND IMPROVEMENT (2000),
The State of Charter Schools, US Department of Education.

PINELLAS COUNTRY SCHOOLS AND NATIONAL EDUCATION ASSOCIATION,
Quality Challenge – An Integrated Approach to School Improvement.

POTTS, S.J., STEWART, J., DOLD, S. and GRINDE, J. (1992),
Community Education – A Resource and Planning Resource and Planning Guide, Wisconsin Dept. of Public Instruction, Milwaukee, WI.

SEATTLE PUBLIC SCHOOLS (2000),
Delivering on the Dream – Weighted Student Formula, January.

USA Today (2000),
Education is Top Issue, June 7.

US DEPARTMENT OF EDUCATION (2000),
The State of Charter Schools, Office of Research and Improvement.

WISCONSIN DEPARTMENT OF PUBLIC INSTRUCTION,
Community Education in Wisconsin.

WOHLSTETTER, P. and MOHRMAN, S. (1993),
"School-Based Management: Strategies for Success", CPRE Finance Briefs, Feb. 02, Comprehensive School Reform Demonstration Program, Office of Elementary and Secondary Education, US Department of Education, Madison, WI.

OECD PUBLICATIONS, 2, rue André-Pascal, 75775 PARIS CEDEX 16
PRINTED IN FRANCE
(96 2001 04 1 P) ISBN 92-64-18646-8 – No. 51839 2001